T0054502

TO

....

FROM

....

DATE

....

Daily Devotions

TO CONQUER
ANXIETY &
DEPRESSION

365 Days of
COMFORTING INSPIRATION
for Women

BARBOUR
PUBLISHING

WHERE SHOULD YOU TURN WHEN YOU'RE STRUGGLING WITH ANXIETY AND DEPRESSION?...

To God and His Word!

"Take charge! Take heart! Don't be anxious or get discouraged. GOD, my God, is with you in this."
1 CHRONICLES 28:20 MSG

Each of the meditations and prayer starters in this reassuring daily devotional will remind you that you're never alone in your struggles. With each turn of the page, you'll encounter a memorable scripture, a truth-filled reading, and a prayer that promise to encourage, inspire, and strengthen your faith.

As you read every heartfelt word, trust in and lean on the one who "is with you in this" (1 Chronicles 28:20 MSG)...the one who's with you in *all things*. With the heavenly Creator by your side, you'll be well on your way to conquering your anxiety and depression.

Day 1
ANXIETY CHECK!

Do not be anxious about anything, but in every situation, by prayer and petition, with thanksgiving, present your requests to God.
PHILIPPIANS 4:6 NIV

Twenty-first-century women are always checking things. A bank balance. Email. Voice mail. The grocery list. And, of course, that never-ending to-do list. We routinely get our oil, tires, and brake fluid checked. And we wouldn't think of leaving home for the day without checking our appearance in the mirror. We even double-check our purses, making sure we have the essentials—lipstick, mascara, and our cell phone.

Yes, checking is a part of living, isn't it? We do it without even realizing it. Checking to make sure we've locked the door, turned off the stove, and unplugged the flat iron just comes naturally. So why do we forget some of the bigger checks in life? Take anxiety, for instance.

When was the last time you did an anxiety check? Days? Weeks? Months? . . . Chances are you're due for another. After all, we're instructed to not be anxious about anything. Instead, we're to present our requests to God with thanksgiving in our hearts. We're to turn to Him in prayer so that He can take our burdens. Once they've lifted, it's bye-bye anxiety!

Father, I get anxious sometimes. And I don't always remember to turn to You with my anxiety. In fact, I forget to check for anxiety at all. Today I hand my anxieties to You. Thank You for allowing me to present my requests to You.

Day 2
HE REMAINS

*For He Himself has said, "I will never desert
you, nor will I ever abandon you."*
HEBREWS 13:5 NASB

Life is full of disappointments, broken promises, failed relationships, and loneliness. It may seem like you are the only person you can really trust. But the Lord will never desert you or forsake you. He promises to be with you through this life and the next. When all else feels hopeless, know that He remains steadfast.

For those who have trusted people in the past but have been let down, this may be a hard concept to accept. But this is no idle promise based on the feeling of a moment. When Christ hung on the cross, He was forsaken by God. The sin that was laid on Him was so horrific and abhorrent that the Father, who was one with Jesus, could not look at Him. In the most heart-wrenching act in history, the holy Father turned His face away from His once blameless Son. Because Christ was willing to be forsaken and utterly alone, you never will be. God won't ever have to turn away from you—you now bear the pure innocence of Christ. Christ took your sins upon Himself so you would never have to experience what it's like to be completely alone and forsaken by God.

*Lord, I can't possibly be grateful enough for what You have
done for me. I humbly praise You that You have promised never
to desert or forsake me. Thank You for always being there.*

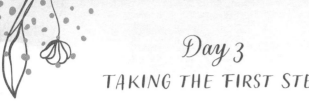

Day 3
TAKING THE FIRST STEP

"My grace is all you need. My power works best in weakness."
2 CORINTHIANS 12:9 NLT

A grief response to loss feels a lot like depression. Having been widowed twice, Elisabeth Elliot knew that feeling well. A poem that helped her is called "Do the Next Thing." We may feel like we can't go to work or carry out our responsibilities, but we should do them anyhow. There is power in obeying. Before God parted the Jordan River, the priests had to step into the water (Joshua 3). God gives strength when we take the first step. He has promised to exchange His power for our weakness.

As a missionary, Elisabeth Elliot served the tribal people of Ecuador, including those who martyred her first husband. Her work as a speaker and author of more than twenty books is timeless (elisabethelliot.org). Schooling herself in the poetry of Amy Carmichael, Elisabeth often quoted Amy's poem "In Acceptance Lieth Peace." We may seek solace in denial, busyness, withdrawal, or defeatist attitudes (martyrdom), but God's peace comes from accepting the "breaking sorrow, which God tomorrow will to His [child] explain."

Often when we feel depressed, we want to hibernate and brood, but that does nothing to change our condition. Telling God we accept His will and timing pacifies internal chaos. Then, choosing to move—to do something useful—will improve our mood.

*Gracious Father, I know You are wise and loving and good
even when I don't feel that could possibly be true. Although
I cannot see You with my limited understanding, I want
to trust You and do the right things. Help me, Lord.*

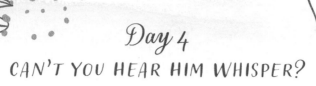

Day 4

CAN'T YOU HEAR HIM WHISPER?

He says, "Be still, and know that I am God."
PSALM 46:10 NIV

Our society is so fast paced that there is little time to take care of our mental and physical health, let alone our spiritual health. We are beings created for eternity, and we are made in the image of a supernatural God, and yet paying attention to our spiritual journey gets put off and off and off.

Until something terrible happens. Like a financial crisis. Or infidelity in our marriage. Or bad news at the doctor's office. Or a death in the family. Then we do far more than pause. We go into a full-body panic mode, drenched in fear, racing around, grasping at anything and everything, desperate for answers. For peace.

But had we been in close fellowship with the Lord all along, we wouldn't be so frantic, our spirits so riddled with terror. What we need to do is to be still and know that He is God. Know that He is still in control, even though we think the bad news is in control. It's not. God is.

Life would be more peaceful, more focused, more infused with joy, if we were already in the midst of communion with God when troubles come.

Can't you hear Him whisper to you, "Be still, and know that I am God"?

*Lord, help me to want to spend time with You every day
of my life—in fair weather as well as stormy. Amen.*

Day 5
POWERFUL ONE

He who forms the mountains, who creates the wind,
and who reveals his thoughts to mankind, who turns
dawn to darkness, and treads on the heights of the
earth—the LORD God Almighty is his name.
AMOS 4:13 NIV

Ever pondered the power of our Lord God Almighty? Meditating on God's power can soothe our biggest worries and calm our deepest fears.

The Word of God speaks often of His power—we know He created our universe in less than a week. But if that's too much to comprehend, consider the enormity of a single mountain or ocean. Those vast, mighty things came into being simply by God's voice—and they're only a tiny fraction of everything He made. What power!

The Lord opens the morning curtains to reveal the dawn and pulls the sky shades back at night to bring darkness. He plots the course of the wind, arranges for rainfall, and causes grass, crops, and trees to grow. He feeds the gigantic whales of the ocean and every tiny little bird. If our Lord has enough knowledge and power to handle these jobs, surely He can (and will!) look after us.

Problems that seem insurmountable to us are simply a breath to Him. Let's not be anxious today—God holds each one of us in the palm of His hand.

Lord God, You are my provider. Thank You for holding such
power—and for choosing me to be Your child. Please give
me a greater understanding of who You are, helping me to
remember that You, the Lord God Almighty, love me.

Day 6
SUBMIT AND TRUST

"But blessed is the one who trusts in the LORD, whose confidence is in him. They will be like a tree planted by the water that sends out its roots by the stream. It does not fear when heat comes; its leaves are always green. It has no worries in a year of drought and never fails to bear fruit."
JEREMIAH 17:7–8 NIV

Have you ever been asked to place your trust in the hands of a surgeon? That moment, just before the anesthesia kicks in, is one of complete surrender. What else can you do but trust that the doctor has things fully in hand and will perform his finest work as he operates on you? You drift off to sleep, anxieties lifted, cares behind you. He does his best work when you're completely submitted to the process. The same is true when it comes to trusting God. We have to relax. Submit. Lay ourselves at His feet, trusting that He will do His very best work. We can't look to ourselves or others for answers. They come from Him alone.

So many times I've put my trust in others, Lord, only to be let down. How grateful I am to know that You will remain faithful, no matter what. I can trust You, Father. . .and I choose to do so, no matter how difficult life's circumstances might get. Amen.

Day 7
UNFAILING LOVE

LORD, do not rebuke me in your anger or discipline me in your wrath. Have mercy on me, LORD, for I am faint; heal me, LORD, for my bones are in agony. My soul is in deep anguish. How long, LORD, how long? Turn, LORD, and deliver me; save me because of your unfailing love.

PSALM 6:1–4 NIV

David was deeply anguished. Thoughts of his sinful state likely kept him up at night. His troubles weighed heavily on his soul. His words here in Psalm 6 reveal his absolute dread of God's anger and discipline. In fact, David begs for God's mercy.

And after airing his negative thoughts and feelings, David then acknowledges that God is fully capable of delivering him from his torment. Because God is a God of "unfailing love," David knows, without a doubt, that all will be well if it is God's will for his life. And that's that!

Like David, do thoughts of your sinful past interfere with a good night's sleep? Do your troubles weigh heavily on your spirit? Today is the day to approach the heavenly Father in bold confidence. Let Him know that you trust Him with the outcome...you trust Him to see you through to better days ahead. He will hear you, and He will act. Praise Him!

*Heavenly Father, I trust You for my comfort...
for deliverance from my troubles. Thank You for saving me!*

Day 8

A GOD—CENTERED LIFE

Except the Lord builds the house, they labor in vain who build it;
except the Lord keeps the city, the watchman wakes but in vain.
It is vain for you to rise up early, to take rest late, to eat the bread
of [anxious] toil—for He gives [blessings] to His beloved in sleep.
PSALM 127:1–2 AMPC

God wants to be involved in every aspect of your life—your home, work, play, family, church, neighborhood, and country. When He is, you get closer to what He intends, not just for you but for the people around you.

At the same time, God wants you not to work yourself to the bone. Nor to be anxious about the results of your endeavors. Instead, you are to leave all outcomes of your efforts to Him.

The Lord knows that a life lived without Him at the center is a life not worth living. So be sure to put God in the center of your processes as you build your life with Him by your side. As you do so, you will find yourself blessed with peace and so much more, including a good night's rest.

Lord, too often I get so wrapped up in my work, family, and
church that I forget to include You in the process. Remind
me each day to look to You for all things, to do my best in
all endeavors, and to leave all the results to You.

Day 9
THUNDER ROARS

"But everyone who calls on the name of the Lord will be saved."
JOEL 2:32 NLT

Do you ever tremble with fear? Whether it be from dangers without or emotional distress within, fear can paralyze people. It is as though a hand grips us by the throat and we are pinned in place with nowhere to go. Yet the Lord our God has said do not be afraid—He will save us.

The book of Psalms reveals a man who quivers and hides in caves to escape his enemies. Time and again David calls out to the Lord, because he has been taught God will calm his fears. The circumstances do not always change, the thunder may still roar, but just like David we can know our lives are secure in the hand of the almighty Creator of the universe. He *will* save us. It's a promise.

Today, make a list of those things which cause you to quake in your boots. Read the list out loud to the Lord and ask Him to provide the necessary bravery to overcome each one. Ask Him to see you through the deep waters and to hold you tightly over the mountaintops. For when you call on His name, He hears and answers. Listen closely and remember He saves.

Father, I'm scared. Please hold me close and calm my anxious heart. Tune my ears to hear Your Word and know what to do. Amen.

Day 10

LOVE IN THE DARK

I recall this to my mind, therefore I wait. The LORD's acts
of mercy indeed do not end, for His compassions do not fail.
They are new every morning; great is Your faithfulness.
LAMENTATIONS 3:21–23 NASB

This is a familiar and beautiful passage. The Lord will always show you loving-kindness. He will never cease to have compassion on you. He is forever faithful. And yet, if you are going through a time when God's love seems farther away than it's ever been, you may think these sentiments are only for those who are experiencing good things in their lives.

Though these verses are familiar, they are almost always taken out of context. These verses are a small island of hope in an otherwise desolate chapter. The author of these verses is suffering deeply. He is greatly afflicted and nearly without hope. But even in the deepest pit of despair he has the experience to back up his claims that God's love has never ceased from his life. When you go through a dark period in your life, be encouraged by the testimony of this fellow child of God. God is not a fair-weather God who abandons you when the going gets rough. His love will find you and carry you through the darkest and most soul-wrenching of trials. You can have the same faith and unwavering confidence in His compassion that you have in the fact that the sun will rise in the morning. There is hope even in the darkest place.

Lord, may I experience Your compassion in amazing ways so
that I too can have faith in Your love in the midst of trials.

Day 11
PRESENT HELP

For I, the LORD your God, hold your right hand; it is I who say to you, "Fear not, I am the one who helps you."
ISAIAH 41:13 ESV

We shake hands to greet each other; it's a sign of welcome. We reach for the hand of a child when we're walking in a crowd or near a street; it helps protect and comfort the child. In times of great emotion or anticipation, we grab the hand of a nearby friend or family member; it says, "I am with you." By a hospital bed, we clasp the hand of a sick loved one; our hand tells them we are present, suffering with them. With every gripping of another's hand, we are bearing witness to God.

He holds your hand. He welcomes you into His kingdom. He protects you. He comforts you. He is with you in your most anxious moments and in your darkest hours. With the clasp of His hand comes courage for any situation. He tells you not to fear, for He is your ever-present help in times of trouble. He has a hold of you.

Almighty God, I am grateful that You hold my hand. Forgive me for the times I have forgotten this and let fear reign in my life. Help me to remember I am never alone. Grant me the courage that comes from knowing You as my helper.

Day 12
WHEN?

All day long I put my hope in you.
Psalm 25:5 nlt

When you whack your alarm for the fifth time and rise in a haze of groggy bitterness, that's when.

After your second cup of coffee and your twenty-second mistake of the day, that's when.

At the busiest hour, when you just can't take it, that's when.

In the dusty stillness, when the loneliness settles like a heavy blanket, that's when.

When you're walking away, and you want to just keep walking and never come back, that's when.

When you snuggle up at home, in your favorite spot and with your favorite people, that's when.

When things don't go as you planned them, that's when.

When things go better than you could have ever imagined, that's when.

When the chapter seems too hard to get through, that's when.

When the happy ending finally appears, that's when.

When you're on top of the world, that's when.

When you're in the very bottom corner of the pit of despair, that's when.

When all seems horribly, cruelly lost, that's when.

From the moment you open your eyes until darkness comes, that's when.

When can you trust God?

All day long, that's when.

Lord, I put every minute in Your hands. Amen.

Day 13
VICTORIOUS!

"For the LORD your God is going with you! He will fight for
you against your enemies, and he will give you victory!"
DEUTERONOMY 20:4 NLT

Victory! It's a word we know well from our high school days when cheerleaders hollered, "V-I-C-T-O-R-Y!" in rousing chorus. Every team wants to win. Every business owner wants to succeed. Every married couple wants to thrive. We all want the same thing: victory. But victory over what? An invisible enemy? Financial woes? People who are out to get you? Drugs? Alcohol? Depression? What are you hoping to declare victory over today? Instead of looking at that thing, focus instead on the one who promises victory. If your eyes are on Him, not the problem, your chances of success are increased dramatically. Don't you love the promise in today's scripture, that He will go with you? Not only that, He will fight for you! You might be heading into some scary places, but He's right there, offering comfort and guidance and assuring your success. With your hand in His, victory is surely on its way!

I don't like to fight, Father. That's one reason I'm so grateful that
You fight my battles for me. All I have to do is show up, face my
enemies with my faith secure, and then watch You move on my
behalf. How can I ever thank You for all You've done? Amen.

Day 14
SEARCH ME

*Search me, God, and know my heart; test me and know
my anxious thoughts. See if there is any offensive way
in me, and lead me in the way everlasting.*
PSALM 139:23–24 NIV

When our cars aren't working properly, we take them to the experts—
the mechanics. When we feel something isn't quite right in our bodies,
we see our doctors. When we want to know if our finances are in
order, we ask an accountant.

And sometimes, when we ask for help from the experts, we come
to them in fear and embarrassment. We come that way because we
know that what we've been doing on our end to take care of things
ourselves has been less than perfect. But we still come, because we
need the help. We need the expert wisdom. We need guidance.

When our spiritual fitness is in question, shouldn't we then go to
the expert? We must go to God, ask Him to test out our systems and
tell us what's gone wrong. Instead of just worrying about our troubles,
we should bring them to Him and ask Him to sift through them, to
tell us what's at the heart of our problems.

Today, ask God to look at your heart, and then be ready to listen
to what He tells you. It will no doubt be a painful process, but it is
the only way to life everlasting.

*Lord, I'm anxious about many things.
Show me what truly matters. Amen.*

Day 15

FAITH, THE EMOTIONAL BALANCER

*No man is justified by the law in the sight of God,
it is evident: for, The just shall live by faith.*
GALATIANS 3:11 KJV

Our moods often dictate our actions. For instance, we schedule lunch with a friend for Saturday afternoon, but on Saturday morning we regret having made plans. Or we strategize what to accomplish on our day off but suffer from mental anemia and physical fatigue when the day arrives. So we fail to do what we had intended to do in a more enthusiastic moment.

Emotions mislead us. One day shines with promise as we bounce out of bed in song, while the next day dims in despair and we'd prefer to hide under the bedcovers. One moment we forgive, the next we harbor resentment.

The emotional roller coaster thrusts us into mood changes and affects what we do, what we say, and the attitudes that define us.

It has been said that faith is the bird that feels the light and sings to greet the dawn while it is still dark. The Bible instructs us to live by faith—not by feelings. Faith assures us that daylight will dawn in our darkest moments, affirming God's presence so that even when we fail to pray and positive feelings fade, our moods surrender to song.

*Heavenly Father, I desire for my faith, not my emotions,
to dictate my life. I pray for balance in my hide-under-the-
cover days, so that I might surrender to You in song. Amen.*

Day 16

A LOVELY CAUSE FOR CELEBRATION

*Take a good look at me, GOD, my God; I want to look life
in the eye, so no enemy can get the best of me or laugh
when I fall on my face. I've thrown myself headlong into
your arms—I'm celebrating your rescue. I'm singing at
the top of my lungs, I'm so full of answered prayers.*
PSALM 13:3–6 MSG

When you become a Christian and accept Jesus Christ as Lord and leader of your life, it's cause for serious celebration. Out with the old and in with the new; you're a beautifully transformed creation of almighty God!

The old you may have been fearful, insecure, doubtful, depressed, and dismayed. But when you accepted the gift of salvation, you surely felt a significant shift within your spirit. With the power of Jesus Christ in you, you're rescued from the burdens that weigh down the soul. And a growing relationship with the heavenly Father brings about feelings of courage, confidence, belief, joy, and contentment. . .just the things you need to fulfill the wonderful purpose God has for you!

If you've chosen to be a Christ follower, make the choice to celebrate—starting today! Thank Him for the gift of salvation. Sing at the top of your lungs! Praise the Lord for your lovely, transformed life!

*Father God, thank You for the lovely transformation
You've begun in my life. Because of You, I am
a new creation, and I am so grateful!*

Day 17

TAKE A TIME—OUT

*And they went and woke him, saying, "Save us, Lord;
we are perishing." And he said to them, "Why are you
afraid, O you of little faith?" Then he rose and rebuked
the winds and the sea, and there was a great calm.*
MATTHEW 8:25–26 ESV

During Jesus' ministry, He healed many people and performed miracles.
Yet today's verses make it clear that putting faith, hope, and trust in
Jesus most likely won't make life any easier. But having a relationship
with Him can help provide healing, peace, inspiration, wisdom, and
direction in an often chaotic and callous world.

The disciples sitting in the boat with Jesus had calamity all around
them. A storm had surged at sea, and they were anxious about what to
do. Like children who awaken their parents during a middle-of-the-
night thunderstorm, the disciples woke up Jesus because they believed
He had the authority and power to calm the water. And they were
right. When Jesus rebuked the winds and the sea, those elements of
nature obeyed. Like misbehaving children on the verge of receiving
a time-out, the winds and waves ceased.

Take some time out today to be with God. Share with Him the areas
in your life that need healing and peace. Then follow His guidance,
assured He *will* calm your storms within and without.

*Lord, help me carve time out of my day to be
with You. I long for Your miraculous touch.*

Day 18

BE STILL, MY SOUL

Be still in the presence of the LORD,
and wait patiently for him to act.
PSALM 37:7 NLT

When life doesn't go the way we planned, it's easy to become upset, discontented, even distrustful. As women, we're pulled in so many directions. Inevitably, parents get older and need care. Husbands require much of our time and energy. Children may have birth defects or illnesses or behavioral problems.

And anxious thoughts beset us. Our dreams and plans are put on hold. We may wish we could be somewhere else. It can all add up to a restless soul, as we chafe at the unfairness of life.

But God asks us to quiet our spirits before Him, to submit to His will for us. As people of God, we wait expectantly for Him to work all things for our good and His glory (Romans 8:28). Let's follow the advice of the hymn writer Katharina von Schlegel, who wrote the great "Be Still, My Soul":

> *Be still, my soul: the Lord is on thy side;*
> *Bear patiently the cross of grief or pain;*
> *Leave to thy God to order and provide;*
> *In every change He faithful will remain.*

> *Father, may I quiet my soul before You today.*
> *Help me to see Your loving hand in every difficulty I face,*
> *knowing that You are accomplishing Your purposes in me.*

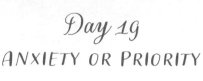

Day 19
ANXIETY OR PRIORITY

Martha, Martha, you are anxious and troubled about many things; there is need of only one or but a few things. Mary has chosen the good portion [that which is to her advantage], which shall not be taken away from her.
LUKE 10:41–42 AMPC

Three siblings—Mary, Martha, and Lazarus—lived together in Martha's house in Bethany. When Jesus entered the village, Martha invited Him into her home then began preparing supper for the crowd. As she did so, she noticed her sister, Mary, had sat down at Jesus' feet, listening to the words that fell from His mouth. "But Martha [overly occupied and too busy] was distracted with much serving" (Luke 10:40 AMPC). So, she asked Jesus to tell her sister, Mary, to get up and help her.

Yet instead of telling Mary to help her sister, Martha, Jesus told her, "Martha, Martha, you are worried and upset about many things, but one thing is necessary. Mary has made the right choice, and it will not be taken away from her" (Luke 10:41–42 HCSB). In other words, Martha had opted for being anxious about many things instead of focusing on one main thing: making Jesus, His presence, and His teachings her highest priority.

Today, choose to focus on making Jesus your highest priority instead of living a worldly life rife with high anxiety.

Jesus, I choose to make You my priority in this life. As I sit at Your feet, Lord, speak to me. I'm listening.

Day 20
SHINE ON!

For God, who said, "Let light shine out of darkness,"
made his light shine in our hearts to give us the light of the
knowledge of God's glory displayed in the face of Christ.
2 CORINTHIANS 4:6 NIV

Did you ever sit outside, enjoying the sunlight, and find yourself feeling more peaceful and serene? Light has that effect on us all. That's why in the winter months, when there is a decrease in the sunlight's power and duration, a small percentage of people become agitated and depressed.

Yet the light of God is even *more* powerful than that of the sun. Just as He created, sustains, and brings you physical light, God has created, sustains, and can bring you spiritual light, if only you'd open your eyes to it. This "light" is the knowledge of God, which He has given us all through His Word. And with it comes the peace that this knowledge brings.

As you bask in God's awesome light, remember that it's not to be hidden under a blanket or hoarded from the crowd but to be shared with others and spread to all you encounter. So put God's light in a prominent place, perhaps upon a pedestal, for all to see. And you'll be doing your part to illuminate all.

Dear Lord, let Your divine light shine upon and
through me. Allow it to bring me Your peace. Help me
to share Your light with those around me. For through
Your light, Lord, I find the illumination I need.

Day 21
GOD'S LOVE

For I am convinced that neither death, nor life, nor angels, nor principalities, nor things present, nor things to come, nor powers, nor height, nor depth, nor any other created thing will be able to separate us from the love of God that is in Christ Jesus our Lord.
ROMANS 8:38–39 NASB

In this life we often feel we need to work for love. Love can grow stale or be lost altogether or given to another. The promise of love can be used as a weapon against us. But in this passage, an eternal, genuine love is promised to you. This promise can be trusted because the love of God has been secured through the sacrifice and death of Christ. This is no promise made on a whim or as a manipulation but one made in blood by the perfect Lamb.

No natural or supernatural power can separate you from God's love. Nothing that is currently happening in your life will separate you from God's love. No matter how scary or uncertain the future seems, it will not separate you from God's love. No height of success or depth of depression and despair will separate you from God's love. Nothing that this life and those in it can throw at you and nothing that you do will separate you from God's love. Not even death, which separates us from everything else we know, will separate you from God's love.

Therefore, go forward in peace and boldness, knowing that you are eternally secure and eternally loved.

Lord, I can't comprehend this kind of everlasting love, but I thank You that I can rest in the promise that You will always love me.

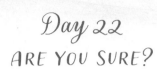

Day 22

ARE YOU SURE?

*No unbelief or distrust made him waver (doubtingly question)
concerning the promise of God, but he grew strong and was
empowered by faith as he gave praise and glory to God.*
ROMANS 4:20 AMPC

Doubt and uncertainty can upend us if we let them. When we are
unsure of something, our steps falter, our words stutter, and our hearts
rattle in our chests. Fear can set in. We must guard against this anxious spirit and trust the word God has spoken. To protect against an
onslaught of concern, we must learn to lean on Him and allow the
Holy Spirit to flow within us.

Paul wrote about doubting God's promises and said that feeling
can only be combated by rejoicing. He who was chained, in prison,
shipwrecked, and often in danger speaks of singing praises and being
full of joy! But how, in our world, are we able to overcome our moods
and rejoice? It is difficult, most certainly, and has to be a conscious
choice. Steeping your heart in the Word of God, knowing verses that
will comfort you, is a great beginning.

A doubting spirit is not of God, for He is not the author of confusion. Theologian Matthew Henry stated, "God honours faith; and
great faith honours God." To truly give Him the glory, we must trust.
Of this we are sure.

*Lord, help us in our unbelief. Our very human nature
causes us to look to the right and to the left. Help us to
keep our focus on You and to trust implicitly. Amen.*

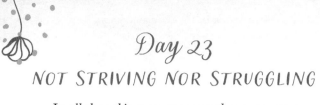

Day 23

NOT STRIVING NOR STRUGGLING

In all these things we are more than conquerors
through Him who loved us.
ROMANS 8:37 NKJV

Hudson Taylor was one of history's most successful missionaries, but it didn't start out that way. He longed to reach the Chinese and establish the China Inland Mission (CIM), but when he reached China, Hudson experienced language difficulties, homesickness, and personality conflicts with the other missionaries, and he was in financial crisis.

The final straw came when Hudson injured himself while trying to dye his hair black. A friend comforted Hudson in his depression, telling him to try "abiding, not striving nor struggling." Because Christ is "the only power for service; the only ground for unchanging joy." That was the spiritual surge Hudson needed, and by the time he died, the CIM had eight hundred missionaries.

How much sweeter would our own Christian lives be if we took the same advice and applied it to everything we do?

Stop striving in marriage. Stop trying to create perfect children. Stop trying to control every situation, and abide in Christ. Let the love of God flow through you, and trust Him to shine.

The Christian life will be filled with obstacles and struggles, but the Holy Spirit has given us the power to overcome. When we abide in Christ, those struggles become the fertilizer that brings about the fruit of the Spirit.

Lord, You promised that we are more than conquerors
through You. Help me to embrace the truth and
live in confidence of those promises. Amen.

Day 24

OVERWHELMED BY LIFE

"The waves of death swirled about me; the torrents of destruction
overwhelmed me. . . . In my distress I called to the LORD. . . . From
his temple he heard my voice; my cry came to his ears."
2 SAMUEL 22:5, 7 NIV

Some days the "dailyness" of life seems like a never-ending grind. We get up, eat, work, rest—and do it again the next day. Then when tragedy strikes, we're swept up in grief. What once seemed doable now seems a huge challenge. Depression sinks its claws deep into our spirit. Fatigue sets in, and we are overwhelmed: Life is hard. We may be tempted to question, "Is this all there is?"

Here's the good news: There's more. God never meant for us to simply exist. He created us for a specific purpose. He longs for us to make a difference and show others His love and grace. What's more, He never asked us to do life alone. When the waves of death swirl around us and the pounding rain of destruction threatens to overwhelm us, we can cry out to our heavenly Father, knowing that He will not let us drown. He will hear our voice, and He will send help.

So, next time you feel that you can't put one foot in front of the other, ask God to send you His strength and energy. He will help you to live out your purpose in this chaotic world.

Lord, thank You for strengthening me when the "dailyness"
of life, and its various trials, threatens to overwhelm me.

Day 25
A VOICE FROM THE SHORE

At dawn Jesus was standing on the beach. . . . He called out, "Fellows, have you caught any fish?" "No," they replied. Then he said, "Throw out your net on the right-hand side of the boat, and you'll get some!" So they did, and they couldn't haul in the net because there were so many fish in it.
JOHN 21:4–6 NLT

You may, at times, find things aren't going your way. You're surrounded by darkness, at a loss, hands empty, in despair, adrift. As dawn breaks, you hear a voice from the shore, questioning you: "What do you need? What are you looking for?"

You answer the questions as best you can, putting into words the lack you feel. Then the same voice gives you direction, advice, and you obey. As soon as you take action, you find so much of what you'd been searching for that you have trouble taking it all in. And that's when you realize that voice, that prompting, was from Jesus!

When you find yourself in a sea of despair, know that Jesus is ready to call out from the shore and help you. Trust that His directions will lead to your bounty. And after you've made your haul, celebrate with the master fisher of men!

I'm feeling adrift, Lord. Call to me from the shore. Give me the direction I so desperately need!

Day 26
SUFFICIENT GRACE

"Therefore you shall do my statutes and keep my rules and perform them, and then you will dwell in the land securely. The land will yield its fruit, and you will eat your fill and dwell in it securely. And if you say, 'What shall we eat in the seventh year, if we may not sow or gather in our crop?' I will command my blessing on you in the sixth year, so that it will produce a crop sufficient for three years."
LEVITICUS 25:18–21 ESV

A Sabbath year and a year of Jubilee required a lot of faith from the Israelites. While they already knew how to obey God, today's commandments (in Leviticus 25:18–21 above) meant trusting God at His word to provide the right amount of crop. For God didn't want them to sow anything, which seemed audacious. Yet He promised He would provide more than enough for His chosen people.

These words are a reminder that God's grace is sufficient enough for all of your needs. You love, serve, and obey a God who cares about your deepest needs and desires. When you worry about the things of this earth, you sink into despair and rage. Yet when you look up at God and recount His goodness, you can rest assured that everything—including you and His plans for your life—is under His control.

Heavenly Daddy, please show me You are truly in control of my life. I want to witness more and more of Your sufficient grace.

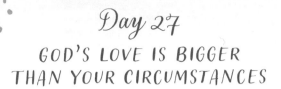

Day 27
GOD'S LOVE IS BIGGER
THAN YOUR CIRCUMSTANCES

*Who shall separate us from the love of Christ? Shall trouble or
hardship or persecution or famine or nakedness or danger or
sword? As it is written: "For your sake we face death all day long;
we are considered as sheep to be slaughtered." No, in all these
things we are more than conquerors through him who loved us.
For I am convinced that neither death nor life, neither angels nor
demons, neither the present nor the future, nor any powers, neither
height nor depth, nor anything else in all creation, will be able to
separate us from the love of God that is in Christ Jesus our Lord.*
ROMANS 8:35–39 NIV

If these things cannot separate us from God's love, then they aren't an
indication of the absence of God's love either. But have you noticed
that we still doubt God's love based on what happens in our lives? If
we get what we want, we believe God has accepted us and loves us.
If we do not receive what we long for, we believe He has abandoned
or rejected us. What desperate tragedies of the heart befall us when
we measure God's love by our circumstances! We pierce ourselves
through when we believe that God only receives and loves us when
life goes our way. We must remember that this is not heaven; the final
story will be told later. Until then, life sometimes is hard. But still,
nothing can separate us from Christ's love. Nothing.

*Lord, help me to remember how much You
love me, no matter what I face. Amen.*

Day 28
HEART CHECK

Why are you cast down, O my inner self? And why should you moan over me and be disquieted within me? Hope in God and wait expectantly for Him, for I shall yet praise Him, Who is the help of my countenance, and my God.
PSALM 42:11 AMPC

A woman can be going through her day, minding her own business, and suddenly find herself frowning, discontent. At such times, she would do best to stop whatever she's doing and perform a heart check by asking her inner self, "What's up? What's the matter? Why so down?" She may come up with a specific instance when someone slighted her. Or maybe it's the anniversary of a tragedy in her life. Or maybe it's the holidays, and her mind is filled with voices of those no longer among the living. Or maybe she's just plain blue, for no reason at all.

Whatever the cause of her being down, the remedy is certain: She is to tell her inner woman to hope in God. To wait for Him. Because no matter how she feels today, or may feel tomorrow, she will in all certainty "yet praise Him"! There's no doubt about it. So, after allowing herself one quick moan, she can turn her phaser to "expectation of praise" and squeeze the trigger. Before she knows it, praises will be bubbling up from her heart and come streaming through her lips, turning her frown upside down.

Help me to remember to check my heart each day, Lord, making sure I'm tuned out of hopelessness and tuned in to great expectations in You.

Day 29
GREAT GRUMBLING

Then all the congregation raised a loud cry, and the people wept that night. And all the people of Israel grumbled against Moses and Aaron. The whole congregation said to them, "Would that we had died in the land of Egypt! Or would that we had died in this wilderness!"

NUMBERS 14:1–2 ESV

God had done great and awesome things through Moses and Aaron to benefit those they were called to lead. Unfortunately, many still wanted to go back to Egypt, where God had freed them from slavery. But, after spying, leaders Joshua and Caleb assured the people the promised land was a good place for them. Numbers 14:7–9 (ESV) says:

> *"The land, which we passed through to spy it out, is an exceedingly good land. If the LORD delights in us, he will bring us into this land and give it to us, a land that flows with milk and honey. Only do not rebel against the LORD. And do not fear the people of the land, for they are bread for us. Their protection is removed from them, and the LORD is with us; do not fear them."*

If you find yourself grumbling at God when He is really trying to bless you, push the PAUSE button on your anger and pray with hope.

God, instead of looking down with despair, I want to look up at You with hope. Fill me with Your divine wisdom and perspective. Help me to walk uprightly in You.

Day 30

YOURS FOR THE TAKING

*Why, my soul, are you downcast? Why so disturbed
within me? Put your hope in God, for I will
yet praise him, my Savior and my God.*
PSALM 42:5 NIV

If you've ever been depressed, you're not alone. Depression can be caused by circumstances, biology, environment, or a combination of all of those things. Research indicates that as many as 25 percent of Americans suffer from depression at some point in their lives.

We are blessed with scriptural accounts of godly people like David and Jeremiah who struggled with depression. These stories let us know that it's a normal human reaction to feel overcome by the difficulties of life.

While feeling this way is normal, it doesn't have to be the norm. As Christians, we have hope. Hope that our circumstances will not always be the way they are right now. Hope that no matter how dismal the world situation seems to be, God wins in the end. Hope that eternity is just on the other side.

Hope is like a little green shoot poking up through hard, cracked ground. When you're depressed, do what David and Jeremiah did— pour out your heart to God. Seek help from a trusted friend or godly counselor.

Look for hope. It's all around you, and it's yours for the taking.

*Father, even when I am depressed, You are still God. Help me to
find a ray of hope in the midst of dark circumstances. Amen.*

Day 31
A CLAY JAR

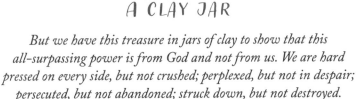

But we have this treasure in jars of clay to show that this all-surpassing power is from God and not from us. We are hard pressed on every side, but not crushed; perplexed, but not in despair; persecuted, but not abandoned; struck down, but not destroyed.
2 CORINTHIANS 4:7–9 NIV

God has given you the honor of carrying the hope and truth of Christ within you. It's wonderful to carry this treasure, but at times it hurts to be a jar of clay. Made of a breakable substance, you feel the knocks and kicks of everyday life with regularity. You may be overwhelmed or underappreciated, or lonely and longing. You may feel sad or confused, devalued or distressed. Welcome to the life of a jar of clay.

But take heart! You are not alone. In fact, you are in good company. The world is full of jars of all ages and nationalities, keeping the faith.

Through your troubles, you can rest in the promise that God is powerful and He will not toss you aside or forsake you. He holds you in His hand and loves you. His protection surrounding you, you can trust Him to care for and comfort you. He is aware of all your needs. The treasure of Christ in you, and your faith in Him, is your great reward.

God, I know You understand my struggles and frailty.
Please allow me to persevere through this day with Your power.

Day 32

CALMER OF SOULS AND STORMS

*They all saw Him and were agitated (troubled and filled with
fear and dread). But immediately He talked with them and
said, Take heart! I AM! Stop being alarmed and afraid.*
MARK 6:50 AMPC

After feeding five thousand men with five loaves and two fish, Jesus
told His disciples to get into a boat and sail ahead of Him to Bethsaida.
Meanwhile, Jesus sent the crowd of people away then went off by
Himself to pray. When evening came, a storm rose up on the sea.

With the wind against them, the disciples had trouble rowing.
Jesus, seeing their futile efforts, walked on the turbulent sea toward
them then acted as if He were going to pass them by. The frightened
disciples thought they were seeing a ghost! To ease their fear, Jesus
spoke, knowing His followers would recognize His voice. He identified
Himself and encouraged them to stop being afraid. Once He got into
their boat, the wind ceased.

Remember who Jesus is and the amazing things He has done for
you. Never think He's overlooking you. Take courage that you will
recognize His voice, His presence, and His power when He is near.
Be assured He's looking out for you. He will never pass you by. He
has words to calm your spirit. He's ready to get into your boat and
still your storms. Simply allow Him into your vessel.

*Lord, come to me now. Speak to me.
Calm my inner and outer storms.*

Day 33
HE WILL LIFT US UP

*The LORD upholds all who fall, and raises
up all who are bowed down.*
PSALM 145:14 NKJV

Once we grow beyond the toddler stage, most people don't fall very often. Unless we go skiing. My first time on skis I learned several things, including how hard it is to get up after a fall with those ungainly things attached to my feet.

Day one on the slopes I probably set a world record for being the slowest person to come down the mountain. After countless tumbles and struggles to right myself, I just sat for a while, soaking up the beauty of snow-covered mountains. I figured it was a gorgeous place to die, or at least wait for the ski patrol to rescue me.

But I was with a friend who wouldn't let me give up. Each time I fell, she pulled me up again and encouraged me to keep trying. One of the incredible things about the experience was that I was eager to go out again the next morning, and I finally learned to ski without falling.

In our daily lives, the Lord is the one who picks us up when we fall. Our falls may not be the kind that lead to broken bones, but we plunge into sin or slip on some stupid temptation or collapse into a pit of depression. Through everything that comes our way, He teaches us to depend on Him to lift us up and encourage us to go on. Always.

*Precious Lord, I cannot fall so low You won't rescue me. I rejoice
in Your faithfulness, my Redeemer. You rescue me. Amen.*

Day 34
HE'S FOR US

You keep track of all my sorrows. You have collected all my tears in your bottle. You have recorded each one in your book. . . . This I know: God is on my side! I praise God for what he has promised; yes, I praise the LORD for what he has promised. I trust in God, so why should I be afraid? What can mere mortals do to me?
PSALM 56:8–11 NLT

When you're in the middle of a rough season, does it ever feel as if no one else, including God, notices what you're going through?

In Psalm 56, David recounted when he was in a tough spot. From morning till night, the Philistines lurked and threatened and trampled him. Yes, David was greatly troubled, *but* he knew one thing: God was for him. God had not overlooked what was happening; in fact, He was keeping track of *every* sorrow and collecting *every* tear. In his trouble, David trusted God all the more, because only that trust—only God Himself—could rescue him from despair. No wonder the shepherd-boy-turned-king advised, "O my people, trust in him at all times. Pour out your heart to him, for God is our refuge" (Psalm 62:8 NLT).

Sister in Christ, God is on your side! Turn to Him when rough times pull you down. He'll pull you back up.

> *God, You see everything that's going on, and You care. I can put my trust in You always. Amen.*

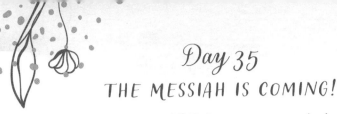

Day 35
THE MESSIAH IS COMING!

For unto us a child is born, unto us a son is given:
and the government shall be upon his shoulder: and his
name shall be called Wonderful, Counsellor, The mighty
God, The everlasting Father, The Prince of Peace.
ISAIAH 9:6 KJV

Troubled times lay ahead. An Assyrian invasion and a Babylonian captivity would leave gloom in their wake. But Isaiah also prophesied dawn on the horizon: "That time of darkness and despair will not go on forever. . . . There will be a time in the future when Galilee of the Gentiles. . .will be filled with glory. The people who walk in darkness will see a great light" (Isaiah 9:1–2 NLT). What was that light? A child would be born, bringing with Him the brightest ray of hope ever! God's people could look beyond the hardship to the coming Messiah.

These days, we might fear that troubled times lie ahead. Our world is aching, and there's already abundant gloom. But Isaiah's words promise dawn on the horizon. The Messiah is coming back! He's coming back to put things right for good and for certain: "His government and its peace will never end. He will rule with fairness and justice. . .for all eternity. The passionate commitment of the LORD of Heaven's Armies will make this happen!" (Isaiah 9:7 NLT). Look beyond any hardship to the returning King.

Jesus, You are the Light of the world and of my life! Amen.

Day 36
SENSE OF GRATITUDE

Pray diligently. Stay alert, with your eyes wide open in gratitude.
COLOSSIANS 4:2 MSG

Gratitude is defined as the *feeling* of being grateful or thankful. Many times in our human bodies, our feelings don't match up with the truth. We may have all our needs met and a loving family, and still we struggle with a depression we don't understand.

When you have trouble with your feelings, immediately run to the truth of God's Word and recount what you know to be true. Write down truths from God and keep them in your regular line of vision:

- I am free and clean in the blood of Christ.
- He has rescued me from darkness and has brought me into His kingdom.
- I am a precious child of the Father.
- God sings over me.
- He delights in me.
- I am a friend of Christ.
- Nothing can separate me from God's love (certainly not my feelings!).
- God knows me intimately.
- God sees me as beautiful and I am wonderfully made.
- God is for me, not against me.

This is truth from His Word! And when you focus on truth, your confusing thoughts start to become clear. . .and amazingly enough, your feelings begin to turn back on!

God, please remind me of what is true. I want to feel a sense of gratitude for You, for others, and for all the blessings in my life. Amen.

Day 37
HOLD ON!

Let us not become weary in doing good, for at the proper time we will reap a harvest if we do not give up.
GALATIANS 6:9 NIV

Have you ever felt that God abandoned you? Have the difficulties in your life pressed you to physical and mental exhaustion? Do you feel your labor is in vain and no one appreciates the sacrifices you have made?

When Elijah fled for his life in fear of Jezebel's wrath, depression and discouragement tormented him. Exhausted, he prayed for God to take his life, and then he fell asleep. When he awoke, God sent an angel with provisions to strengthen his weakened body. Only then was he able to hear God's revelation that provided the direction and assistance he needed.

God hears our pleas even when He seems silent. The problem is that we cannot hear Him because of physical and mental exhaustion. Rest is key to our restoration.

Just when the prophet thought he could go on no longer, God provided the strength, peace, and encouragement to continue. He does the same for us today. When we come to the end of our rope, God ties a knot. And like He did for Elijah, God will do great things in and through us, if we will just hold on.

*Dear Lord, help me when I can no longer help myself.
Banish my discouragement and give me the rest and
restoration I need so that I might hear Your voice. Amen.*

Day 38
THE RESCUER

"But I will rescue you on that day, declares the LORD;
you will not be given into the hands of those you fear."
JEREMIAH 39:17 NIV

As the voice of God, Jeremiah endured many hardships while living in a land besieged by Babylonians. Thrown into a pit and left to die, Jeremiah had his life saved by a brave man named Ebed-Melek. God repaid the courage of this man with the promise of protection from those he feared, those who would take him prisoner.

Just as God promised to protect Ebed-Melek, He promised to protect Joshua. In Deuteronomy 3:22 (NIV), God reminds him, "Do not be afraid of them; the LORD your God himself will fight for you."

Fear is something against which everyone struggles. And there will be many situations in which each of us will have to face our fear. Yet all we need to do is remember God's words telling His people to rest assured, to not be afraid.

The Lord your God *will* rescue you on your hardest days. He *will not* deliver you into the hands of your darkest fears but *will* bring you into the light and protection of His presence.

Dear Lord, the words You gave me through Your Son,
Jesus Christ, tell me that You will deliver me from evil.
I pray You will take away my fears and in my darkest
day will rescue me from the depths of despair.

Day 39
WORDS TO LIVE BY

When the soldiers crucified Jesus, they took his clothes,
dividing them into four shares, one for each of them, with
the undergarment remaining. This garment was seamless,
woven in one piece from top to bottom. "Let's not tear it,"
they said to one another. "Let's decide by lot who will get
it." This happened that the scripture might be fulfilled.
JOHN 19:23–24 NIV

How did Jesus' followers react as they watched His crucifixion? Some were probably brokenhearted at the sight of the Savior's suffering. Still others probably panicked, thinking all their hopes were dying on that cross. But the ones who were paying attention would have seen that everything was going as expected.

God foreknew every detail of that dreadful day—down to the soldiers divvying up Jesus' clothes. Centuries earlier, David had written, "They pierce my hands and my feet. . . . They divide my clothes among them and cast lots for my garment" (Psalm 22:16, 18 NIV).

In trying times, we may be so focused on the trouble that we miss God's messages. No, the details of our particular troubles aren't predicted in the Bible, but God has given us details about who He is in *any* trouble—He is omniscient, trustworthy, all-powerful, compassionate—and those details see us through the trouble. Rest in His Word. All is going according to His plan.

God, make Your messages clear to me as I read
the Bible. Encourage me with Your words.

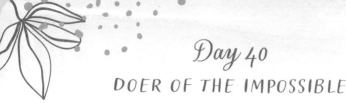

Day 40

DOER OF THE IMPOSSIBLE

"It is easier for a camel to go through the eye of a needle than for a rich person to enter the Kingdom of God!"... "Humanly speaking, it is impossible. But with God everything is possible."
MATTHEW 19:24, 26 NLT

Your God is a doer of the impossible.

At Mount Horeb, God's people were thirsty. So Moses cried out to God. And God told him to hit the rock with his staff. Moses did, and water flowed out (Exodus 17:1–6).

When an enemy army came out to fight the Israelites, Moses stood on the top of a hill. When he lifted "the staff of God" (Exodus 17:9 NLT) in his hands, the Israelites prevailed. When he lowered it, the enemy prevailed.

Woman of the Way, the Word reminds you that your God can do anything. No matter what your circumstances, there is no need for alarm, fright, despair, or hopelessness. For the one who can part the seas, calm the storms, and make a whale vomit can pull you out of harm's way, lift you from the pit, and shut the mouths of lions. All you need to do is trust, hope, pray, and believe. Your God will do the rest.

Thank You, Lord, for giving me the hope and strength I need to trust in You—the doer of the impossible. Amen.

Day 41

JOYFUL PROMISES

Looking at his disciples, he said: "Blessed are you who
are poor, for yours is the kingdom of God. Blessed are you
who hunger now, for you will be satisfied. Blessed are you
who weep now, for you will laugh. Blessed are you when
people hate you, when they exclude you and insult you and
reject your name as evil, because of the Son of Man."
LUKE 6:20–22 NIV

If ever there were uplifting words to take to heart, it is those above.

Jesus was addressing a large gathering of poor, sick, and otherwise downtrodden people. This crowd was in desperate need of encouragement and help. Notice that Jesus addresses the crowd in the second person, using the word "you" instead of a more impersonal third person of "whoever." He is speaking to each and every individual in that crowd that day, peppering His words with promises of hope. What a wonderful message to a despondent crowd!

Are you feeling downtrodden or fearful? Read Jesus' words again. The promise of better times is clear. For He follows the verses above with "Rejoice in that day and leap for joy, because great is your reward in heaven" (Luke 6:23 NIV).

Woman of God, rejoice! Leap for joy! God's promises are always fulfilled. Your reward in heaven is guaranteed!

Dear God, thank You! I take heart in knowing
that I am blessed and that my reward awaits me
in Your kingdom! I rejoice and leap for joy!

Day 42
BIBLE BOOKENDS

"Look, I am coming soon. . . . I am the Alpha and the Omega, the First and the Last, the Beginning and the End."
REVELATION 22:12–13 NLT

God often used literary structure in His Word to call attention to something important. For example, the Bible has "bookends," showing that history (His-story) will go full circle and accomplish His purposes. These bookends are the first two and the last two chapters of the Bible.

In Genesis 1–2 the world had perfect environment, no sin or death, and God conversing with His people. Revelation 21–22 portrays a new heaven and earth, again without sin or death and with unhindered fellowship between God and His people. The 1,185 chapters in between contain rebellion against God, people in conflict, evil and violence, tears, pain, and death. However, those chapters also display God's redemptive plan through Jesus, who atoned for our sins, conquered death, and will destroy the works of the devil. He lived a sinless life, experienced the death we deserve, and rose again.

At this time in history, we are in the "between" chapters. Corruption and evil abound. Society grows increasingly godless and amoral. Families are fragmented; relationships are disposable. But Revelation 21–22 will come. Everyone who has accepted the redemption Jesus provided will live with Him forever, because He said, "Let anyone who is thirsty come. Let anyone who desires drink freely from the water of life" (Revelation 22:17 NLT).

Until You come again or I go to You, Lord, help me to abide in You and depend on Your Word so I will not live in depression or fear, despite conditions in the world. Amen.

Day 43

TO LOVE LIKE HIM

"A new command I give you: Love one another. As I have loved you, so you must love one another. By this everyone will know that you are my disciples, if you love one another."
JOHN 13:34–35 NIV

"Let go of that which does not serve you" is a popular mantra used in yoga and meditation. It can help you identify anxious behaviors, but many times it's used as permission to write off difficult people in your life. That mantra doesn't fit with Jesus' command to His followers— aside from toxic or abusive relationships, which must be considered prayerfully and with godly counsel.

Jesus does not say, "Love the Christians who make you feel your best"; you are to love all your brothers and sisters in the way *He already loves you*. Present and strong before you ever loved Him back (see Romans 5:8), His love is steadfast, unchanging, persevering, nurturing, encouraging, and forgiving, even in your worst moments.

Jesus knows the difficult people in your life, in your church. And because He loves them and you, He will help you live out His love toward them. Dwell on His Word and His abundant mercy; as you witness His steadfast love and seek to obey His commands, He will grow your heart's capacity beyond what you thought possible, His love through you encircling those who before felt beyond your reach.

Holy Savior, I trust Your love's perfect power to change and strengthen me!

Day 44
HEALER OF AFFLICTIONS

What can I say for you? With what can I compare you,
Daughter Jerusalem? To what can I liken you,
that I may comfort you, Virgin Daughter Zion?
Your wound is as deep as the sea. Who can heal you?
LAMENTATIONS 2:13 NIV

Everyone experiences tough times, days when things seem bleak and there appears to be no way to escape despair. In those times, many may seek to commiserate with friends or family and take some solace in the fact that others are worse off. While this is small consolation, it *is* consolation nonetheless. Yet as well-meaning as those friends or family members are, their advice does not solve your problems.

The accounts related in the book of Lamentations make it clear the people of Jerusalem were going through tough times. However, their struggle would not last forever. God alone was the solution to their problems. God alone was able to heal their afflictions.

God alone can help you too. Allow Him to uplift you right now with these words: "I will restore you to health and heal your wounds" (Jeremiah 30:17 NIV).

Dear Lord, sometimes I feel overwhelmed by hardship and can
see no way out. Please open my eyes to see You and my ears to hear
You. I trust that You will heal me and restore peace in my life.
I have faith, Lord, that no matter how bad things look, I truly
am blessed, and I am grateful for Your presence in my life.

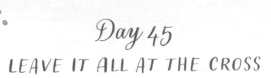

Day 45

LEAVE IT ALL AT THE CROSS

As for me, may I never boast about anything except the cross of our
Lord Jesus Christ. Because of that cross, my interest in this world
has been crucified, and the world's interest in me has also died.
GALATIANS 6:14 NLT

So often we allow the troubles and cares of life to weigh us down. We get depressed or give way to fear. During political seasons we get worked up and allow ourselves to feel despair over the condition of our county, state, or nation.

God wants us to care about the goings-on around us, but they shouldn't be a driving force in our lives. Instead, we're to drop our cares in a place where He exchanges our anguish with hope. That place is the cross.

When Jesus died on the cross, He accomplished all that needed to be accomplished. His death, burial, and resurrection didn't just ensure our place in heaven; it gave us a way to live in victory and peace, unencumbered by the troubles each day might bring.

What's holding you back today? Have you left it at the cross? Release it to the Lord and watch Him free you up to live a full, abundant life.

Father, today I come to the cross, not just to lay
my burdens at Your feet, but to thank You for being
my burden bearer. How can I ever repay You?
From the bottom of my heart, I bring You praise. Amen.

Day 46

THE HOLY SPIRIT, OUR GREAT GIFT

*Therefore I make known to you that no one speaking by
the Spirit of God says, "Jesus is accursed"; and no one
can say, "Jesus is Lord," except by the Holy Spirit.*
1 CORINTHIANS 12:3 NASB

For twenty-nine years a desperate woman waded through the motions
of life, wondering whether the Creator really cared for her at all. Her
loneliness and despair seemed to confirm to her that He didn't. And
then came the day when the gospel message finally penetrated her
soul with its extraordinary light and she began to call Him Lord.

I was that woman. When I heard today's scripture, the truth flew
straight and sure as an arrow to the deepest part of my being.

It's no accident that despair caused me to succumb to messages
of doubt concerning God's nature and character. The evil one is, after
all, the author of confusion and lies. However, as I tested the spirits
the truth became clear. "By this you know the Spirit of God: every
spirit that confesses that Jesus Christ has come in the flesh is from
God; and every spirit that does not confess Jesus is not from God;
this is the spirit of the antichrist, which you have heard is coming,
and now it is already in the world" (1 John 4:2–3 NASB).

*Lord, I know if I'm listening to a message that makes me
depressed and defeated, that's from Satan. I know the
one that says I'm worth dying for is from Christ.*

Day 47
LEAN ON ME

*Elisha replied, "Listen to this message from the LORD!
. . . By this time tomorrow in the markets of Samaria,
six quarts of choice flour will cost only one piece of silver."*
2 KINGS 7:1 NLT

The people in Samaria were going through a *terrible* time. The Syrians had besieged the city, which resulted in a famine. Prices skyrocketed: a donkey's head cost eighty pieces of silver; dove's dung cost five pieces of silver. Things were so desperate that mothers were eating children (2 Kings 6:28–29). Good, godly leadership was needed, but Israel's king gave up on God: "All this misery is from the LORD! Why should I wait for the LORD any longer?" (2 Kings 6:33 NLT). And his captain—a man "on whose hand the king leaned" (2 Kings 7:2 ESV)—doubted God despite Elisha's prophecy of relief. "That couldn't happen even if the LORD opened the windows of heaven!" he said (2 Kings 7:2 NLT).

But relief *did* come; God saw to that (2 Kings 7:3–20). Where the leaders lost hope in God, Elisha saw his rock, his rescuer, the God on whom the people could lean and never be let down. In the most terrible times imaginable, God is still God. His promises are still His promises. Lean on that truth today.

*Lord, thankfully, I have not seen such terrible times.
But in any amount of trouble, Lord, relief is found in You!*

Day 48
DON'T FORGET

*Praise the LORD, my soul; all my inmost being, praise his holy
name. Praise the LORD, my soul, and forget not all his benefits.*
PSALM 103:1–2 NIV

The phrase "praise the Lord" is found scores of times in the psalms,
whether things were good—*or bad*. How is praise possible when our
world is in turmoil? How is praise possible when all that meets our
eyes is negative? We must choose to keep God's blessings in mind,
to think on all God does. That's what David did. He told his soul to
praise and to forget not. . . .

Forget not that God forgives every sin—even the ones we have a
hard time letting go of ourselves. Forget not that God heals us, body
and soul. Forget not that God redeems lives from the deep, dank, dark
pit. Forget not that God then crowns us with love, with compassion
that we don't deserve but that we need desperately. Forget not that
God satisfies our desires with good things—yes, the *best* things—so
that we are renewed like eagles soaring high above it all. (See Psalm
103:3–5.)

In light of God's benefits, nothing on earth can douse our praise if
we don't allow it. And nothing on earth can take God's benefits away.

*God, whatever happens around me or to me,
Your benefits are for sure. Praise the Lord, my
soul—and there is so much to praise You for!*

Day 49
CALL ON GOD

In the day of my trouble I will call upon You,
for You will answer me.
PSALM 86:7 NKJV

Who do you call when you are in trouble? If your car breaks down, perhaps it's roadside assistance, but if your air conditioner breaks, it may be your HVAC company. What about when real trouble strikes? Do you hit speed dial and talk for an hour to your sister or best friend? Is it a parent you call, or perhaps a mentor from church? None of these are bad phone calls to make in times of need, as long as you remember that first and foremost you are to take your troubles to God.

God is there for you night and day. His Word tells you He never sleeps. When you are depressed or lonely, He's there. When you don't know what to do, He's there. There's no trouble you could encounter that would cause God to turn His back on you. He's ready and waiting for you, His daughter, to call out to Him.

Think about the best earthly father you know. Would that daddy desert his children in a time of need? Would he ever be too busy to come running? How much more does your heavenly Father long to attend to the needs of His own?

God, I know that You are always ready to help. May You
be the first one I turn to with my troubles. Amen.

Day 50
A HIDING PLACE

GOD is good, a hiding place in tough times.
He recognizes and welcomes anyone looking for
help, no matter how desperate the trouble.
NAHUM 1:7 MSG

Think about some of the most troublesome things in your life. What do you stress over and worry about the most?

Your health?

Your finances?

Your relationships?

Your career?

Your family?

Or something else? . . .

No matter what troubles you may encounter in this life—big or small—remember that in all of it, God is good. He is compassionate and kind. And in the uttermost darkness, God is your light. He protects His children—and that's a promise you can count on! With Him in your life, you can overcome any hardship. The Bible says to "give all your worries and cares to God, for he cares about you" (1 Peter 5:7 NLT) and "Don't be discouraged, for I am your God. I will strengthen you and help you. I will uphold you with my victorious right hand" (Isaiah 41:10 NLT).

Isn't it wonderful? God recognizes what you're going through—*and* what's more, He's standing by, ready to offer His help. In fact, He *welcomes* you and all your troubles. So hand over your worries and cares to Him today—and then be sure to thank Him for His unending goodness!

God, You are so, so good. Thank You for rescuing me
from my troubles. I give You all the glory. Amen.

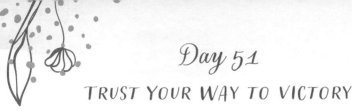

Day 51

TRUST YOUR WAY TO VICTORY

With God we will gain the victory,
and he will trample down our enemies.
PSALM 60:12 NIV

Few things in life are guaranteed. As you venture through it, you may encounter many different situations, some more difficult than others. Adversity is inevitable. But in the verses of Psalm 60, you learn that with God in your corner, you'll eventually be victorious.

Earlier in this chapter, David speaks of the many obstacles he faced, fighting his many enemies. However, in the final verse of Psalm 60, he reminds you that with God, you will always come out on top.

During recent times, there may have been many days that you faced fear or doubt as the struggles of everyday life challenged you and caused you to suffer anxiety. It's during those difficult days that you want to remember God is in your corner and that no matter what or who your enemy might be, He will always bring you through victorious.

The words of Proverbs 30:5 (KJV) offer this assurance: "Every word of God is pure: he is a shield unto them that put their trust in him." *Trust.* That's the key word. Trust in God. Always. And you will be victorious.

Dear God, how easy it is, in the thick of my daily battles,
to forget that I am not alone. Remind me that You are
with me always, to defeat my enemies and keep me
safe. Help me put my trust and faith in You.

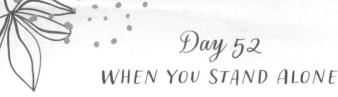

Day 52
WHEN YOU STAND ALONE

"You will be hated by all for my name's sake.
But not a hair of your head will perish."
LUKE 21:17–18 ESV

One of the most heartening practices in the courtroom is the tradition of having the defense lawyer stand beside his client as the verdict is handed down. The defendant, whether innocent or guilty, does not stand alone to hear his or her fate. He or she is supported by the person who knows the most about the case, the motives, the angles, the minute details.

In His earthly life, Jesus often spoke to people's fears of the future. He knew that humans were apt to worry about what's coming and be anxious about how to handle it. When His disciples questioned Him, Jesus supplied the answers. His listeners didn't always understand the descriptions He gave them because they weren't used to looking at life through the lens of a heavenly kingdom. But Jesus tried to prepare them for the fall of Jerusalem and the destruction of the temple, for wars and future conflict.

It's encouraging to realize we'll never stand alone in the defense of our faith. Although it may appear as if there's no one else in the well of the courtroom with us, our spiritual eyes can recognize the empowering presence of Jesus standing beside us.

Dear Lord, I am trusting in You for the strength and confidence
I need when my time comes to stand up with and for You. Amen.

Day 53
FAULTLESS

*To him who is able to keep you from stumbling and to present you
before his glorious presence without fault and with great joy.*
JUDE 1:24 NIV

Who is at fault? Who is to blame? When something goes wrong at work, at home, or at church, someone is held accountable. People want to know who is responsible, who made a mistake. The ones pointing fingers of accusation don't always care about the truth as much as they care about making sure they aren't blamed for the transgression.

Ever since God confronted Adam and Eve in the garden of Eden, we have been pointing fingers at someone else instead of taking responsibility for our own actions. Shame and fear make us want to deny we have done any wrong even when we have done so accidentally or by mistake. We value what God and other people think of us. When we are at odds with God or others over a transgression, we often become depressed.

Jesus loves us so much despite our shortcomings. He is the one who can keep us from falling—who can present us faultless before the Father. Because of this, we can have our joy restored no matter what. Whether we have done wrong and denied it or have been falsely accused, we can come into His presence to be restored and lifted up. Let us keep our eyes on Him instead of on our need to justify ourselves to God or others.

*Thank You, Jesus, for Your cleansing love and for
the joy we can find in Your presence. Amen.*

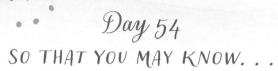

Day 54
SO THAT YOU MAY KNOW. . .

I write these things to you who believe in the name of the Son of God so that you may know that you have eternal life. This is the confidence we have in approaching God: that if we ask anything according to his will, he hears us. And if we know that he hears us—whatever we ask—we know that we have what we asked of him.
1 JOHN 5:13–15 NIV

When you know Jesus. . .when you've trusted Him as leader of your life. . .you gain a fantastic gift—the gift of confident assurance. As a child of God, you can trust and truly "know" that. . .

You are forgiven.

You have eternal life.

You can have freedom from fear and anxiety.

God hears your prayers.

When you pray according to God's will, He will give you what you've asked of Him.

And so much more!

Every day of your life, you can trust in His precious promises. What makes this beautiful assurance even better? . . . It comes with an abundance of joy!

What about you, friend? Are you living joyfully through Jesus? Have you fully trusted in the saving power of Jesus today? Are you becoming more and more unshakable every day?

Heavenly Father, thank You for the confident assurance I have because of Your precious promises. I trust You, Lord, as leader of my life—today and for all my days to come! Amen.

Day 55
FOLLOW ME

Then Jesus said to Simon, "Don't be afraid; from now on you will fish for people." So they pulled their boats up on shore, left everything and followed him.
LUKE 5:10–11 NIV

Nothing was going right for Simon Peter and his fishing crew. They had fished all night, trying different locations, but every time they had let down their nets, they came up empty. They were at the point of despair. Exhausted, they had basically given up and headed back to shore.

As they were washing their nets, Jesus came up to the fishermen, directing them to row out a short way and cast their nets again. This would be like a coworker coming up to you after you had tried everything you could think of, telling you to try one more time. Surely, you would be slightly put off, certain you had exhausted all possibilities.

And yet, something must have told Simon Peter to listen to this Man. So he did as he was told and caught so many fish that his nets began to rip at the seams! Suddenly the impossible proved possible. He knew immediately he should leave everything and follow Jesus.

And so it is with you too. Follow where Jesus directs, and your despair will morph into delight.

Dear God, I know I can do great things if I follow You. Please inspire me to rely on Your direction always.

Day 56
CONTINUALLY SAVED

After our parents left Egypt, they took your wonders for granted, forgot your great and wonderful love. They were barely beyond the Red Sea when they defied the High God—the very place he saved them!—the place he revealed his amazing power! He rebuked the Red Sea so that it dried up on the spot—he paraded them right through!—no one so much as got wet feet!
PSALM 106:7–9 MSG

Have there been times in life when, amid a crisis, you prayed for God to help you? And then when He did something amazing to lift you up out of trouble, you soon forgot all about it?

That's what happened to the Israelites. Time after time, God delivered them from some oppressing force by performing a miracle. But then, as time went by, His people forgot about it. Instead of taking comfort, courage, and confidence from all those past life-saving experiences, the Israelites focused on the next obstacle, the next problem that was before them. Sound familiar?

Today, look back over your own life. Consider how many times God saved you from despair and difficulty. Make a list of all He has done for you. And take comfort, courage, and confidence He will do so again, no matter what lies before, beside, or behind you.

Thank You, Lord, for continually saving me. Help me take comfort, courage, and confidence from all You have done for me. In Jesus' name, I pray and trust. Amen.

Day 57

ATTITUDE MAKES THE DIFFERENCE

*I will sing to the LORD all my life; I will
sing praise to my God as long as I live.*
PSALM 104:33 NIV

Have you ever noticed a difference among elderly individuals? Some seem depressed. They go through their days focusing on their ailments and woes. Others are bright and happy with cheerful spirits and never a word of complaint. Are the chipper seniors healthier? Have they been spared arthritis, diabetes, heart issues, and digestion troubles? Not at all! The difference lies in a little thing that makes a big difference—the attitude they choose to take!

If you determine to sing to the Lord all the days of your life, as the psalmist did, then you will have a hard time listing off all your troubles to everyone who will listen. It's pretty tough to sing praises to Jesus while whining about what aches.

Happiness is a choice. If you have the joy of the Lord planted deep within your soul, you will be able to shine for Him, regardless of your circumstances. Commit today to praise Him all the days of your life. It will make all the difference in the world!

*Heavenly Father, You are so good. You are my provider
and my companion. Whether I have plenty or am
in need, whether I am among others or on my own,
You are my God, and I will praise You. Amen.*

Day 58

ARMLOADS OF BLESSINGS

*Bring rains to our drought-stricken lives so those who
planted their crops in despair will shout "Yes!" at the
harvest, so those who went off with heavy hearts will
come home laughing, with armloads of blessing.*
PSALM 126:4–6 MSG

There are so many moments that can't be explained in this life. Why is
it so hard to make ends meet? Why can't those who love one another
stay together? Why do terrible things happen to amazing people?

The answer is that God created His children to live a joyful and
fulfilling life, but this world became a broken one ever since Adam
and Eve ate the forbidden fruit in the garden.

Although you may not be able to figure out why certain things
happen in your life or the lives of those you love, you can be sure God
will use those trials for your ultimate good. To further His will. To
mold you into the daughter He created you to be.

God will eventually turn your despair into delight and your tears
into laughter. For He's poised to fill your arms with blessings.

*Father, I realize I may not get all the answers in my lifetime.
But I know that You will use everything I go through
for my spiritual growth and that in the end I will have
armloads of blessings. In the meantime, give me faith and
endurance to keep going even when the going gets hard.*

Day 59
HE ALONE

With the aged [you say] is wisdom, and with length of days comes understanding. But [only] with [God] are [perfect] wisdom and might; He [alone] has [true] counsel and understanding.
JOB 12:12–13 AMPC

When Job fell into hard times, he had various people giving him their opinions as to why he'd lost his family, servants, animals, wealth, and health. His so-called friends described Job—a man who "was blameless and upright, one who feared God and turned away from evil" (Job 1:1 ESV)—as a sinner! Yet, in this confusing time, Job was able to relate a major truth to his friends and himself: God alone was wise and powerful. He alone had the advice and understanding that humankind could rely on.

Distress can sometimes cloud the fact of who God is and has been since before time began. Despair can make one temporarily forget that it is God who holds all the answers and has all the wisdom one could ever need.

When you come upon a hard time or you need to make a difficult decision, you may want to go to friends and family for advice. But God wants to be your first choice. He wants to have the final say. Because to Him alone belong wisdom, power, and understanding.

Lord, You hold the ultimate truth and wisdom in Your hand. Instead of looking to others for advice and understanding, I will look to You, the one who holds all power, strength, and wisdom. Amen.

Day 60

FEEL THE LOVE

*[I can feel] his left hand under my head
and his right hand embraces me!*
SONG OF SOLOMON 2:6 AMPC

Can you recall a time when you felt scared and lost and perhaps all alone? It's when you are the weakest that the Lord's strength comes through to you. It's then that God sustains you, that He places His left hand under your head, supporting you and lifting you up from the depths of your despair. It's then that He places His right hand around you, embracing you and energizing you.

God's loving support, His care and attention, His strength and power, will keep you from falling, even when you feel the weakest. A life-sustaining embrace from the Lord is all you need to emerge from the depths of your despair. When you feel as if you cannot even rise from your bed, all you have to do is reach out to God. He who knows you, both spiritually and physically, will uphold and strengthen you.

Today, reach out for God's presence; feel His love. Allow Him to guide you, protect you, and calm you until all danger has passed. Know that He loves you, holds you, and firmly secures you. Empowered, you can and will rise stronger and do what He calls you to do.

*Dear God, I thank You for Your loving and sustaining embrace
and for Your holy hand under my head, supporting and
empowering me, giving me the strength to do all You call me to do.*

Day 61

A GREAT LIGHT

The people walking in darkness have seen a great light;
on those living in the land of deep darkness a light has dawned.
ISAIAH 9:2 NIV

Isaiah was a well-known and respected prophet in Judah in the eighth century BC. The people of his time were walking in darkness and despair. Isaiah's prophecies covered the reigns of many kings and leaders of the land, but nothing he'd written or spoken compared to his words in today's verse. He delivered the hopeful message the Israelites needed to hear. Just when they needed some bright news, Isaiah predicts the greatest gift of all—the coming of the world's Savior, Jesus Christ.

As John wrote in his gospel, "In him was life, and that life was the light of all mankind. The light shines in the darkness, and the darkness has not overcome it" (John 1:4–5 NIV).

Have you ever felt as if you were walking in darkness? On those difficult days, remember the words of Isaiah and John. Remember "the true light that gives light to everyone" (John 1:9 NIV), the light that was born in the little town of Bethlehem over 2,000 years ago. He alone will illuminate your darkest days.

Dear God, what a joyful prophecy for those living in darkness years ago. Remind me that I have that light within my heart as I journey through difficult days. I have the light of hope! Amen.

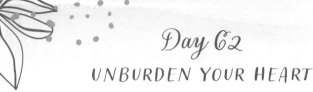

Day 62

UNBURDEN YOUR HEART

Casting the whole of your care [all your anxieties, all your worries, all your concerns, once and for all] on Him, for He cares for you affectionately and cares about you watchfully.
1 Peter 5:7 AMPC

Because He cares for you. Not because you have to. Not because it's the "right" thing to do. Not because it's what you're supposed to do. No. Read it again. . . . *Because He cares for you.* That's right, He cares for you!

Our Father isn't standing there with His hand on His hip, saying, "All right, spit it out. I don't have all day," or worse. . .holding His hands to His ears, saying, "Enough! You have way too many problems."

Because He cares for you. How humbling and emotionally overwhelming it is to realize that our Lord and God, Jesus Christ, actually wants us to unburden our hearts to Him. Not just because He knows that's what's best for us but simply because He cares. To know He isn't just informing us of one more requirement we have to meet. No. He asks each one of us to cast all our cares and anxieties on Him because He cares for us.

Father, I am overjoyed at Your concern for me. Thank You! Please teach me to cast my cares into Your arms. . .and leave them there.

Day 63
SAFETY NET

*Do you not know? Have you not heard? The LORD is
the everlasting God, the Creator of the ends of the earth.
He will not grow tired or weary, and his understanding
no one can fathom. He gives strength to the weary and
increases the power of the weak. Even youths grow tired
and weary, and young men stumble and fall.*
ISAIAH 40:28–30 NIV

Everyone gets tired; everyone stumbles. Little children and adults
alike grow weary, trip and fall. No one is immune. But there is always
someone there to pick them up, dust them off, and ensure they are
all right.

Just as a child is lifted by his parents, your almighty God, Father,
and Creator lifts you when you are struggling, when you can't seem
to find your feet. It is His loving arms that will gently raise you up
when you feel weak. He is the one who will guide you back to safety.

God never grows tired. Day and night, He watches over you. Because
of His relentless love for you, you are never out of His sight. When
you're weak, in despair, and helpless, He gets you back on your feet and
steadies you. He, your eternal safety net, will always be there to catch
you when you fall.

*Dear God, I may stumble and I may fall, but I know You are
always there to catch me and get me on my feet again. Thank You!*

Day 64
SPIRITUALLY ROOTED

*Praise be to the LORD, for he showed me the wonders of
his love when I was in a city under siege. In my alarm
I said, "I am cut off from your sight!" Yet you heard
my cry for mercy when I called to you for help.*
PSALM 31:21–22 NIV

As human beings, we're accustomed to judge reality based on what our
five senses tell us. When circumstances seem frightening or hopeless,
we often feel we've somehow lost God's presence in our lives. We may
blame ourselves—or we may blame God. Either way, that feeling of
abandonment doesn't reflect reality, for we are never cut off from God.

The Lord is always with us, no matter what our physical senses
or our emotional perceptions tell us. We may feel depressed, scared,
frustrated, or angry. We might not be able to see where God is present in our lives. But God is always listening, always watching, always
loving us, and always ready to help.

*Lord, when my eyes and ears can't see You in the circumstances
of my life, when my heart feels lonely and afraid, give me
the spiritual confidence that You are always present, even
when I can't see or hear You. Remind me that Your reality
can't always be seen with physical senses or experienced
at an emotional level. Keep me spiritually rooted in
You, no matter what happens in my external life.*

Day 65

THAT SINKING FEELING

"Come," Jesus said. So Peter went over the side of the boat and walked on the water toward Jesus. But when he saw the strong wind and the waves, he was terrified and began to sink. "Save me, Lord!" he shouted. Jesus immediately reached out and grabbed him.

MATTHEW 14:29–31 NLT

How do you ward off the sinking feeling of fear? You focus your eyes and mind on Jesus.

It can take a lot of courage to ask God to command you to step out of your comfort zone. To lift your leg over the side of a familiar vessel and suddenly stand on an unfamiliar, undulating terrain. But there you are!

And then you take your eyes off Him—just for a second. The next thing you know, you realize the challenges you face, you take in the threatening wind and waves, and fear bubbles up from the bowels of doubt. You get that sinking feeling then begin to do just that. In desperation, you cry out, "Lord, save me!" And immediately He does, wondering at your lack of faith.

To avoid the sinking feeling of fear, keep your eyes and thoughts on Jesus. And before you know it, you'll be walking on water.

Lord, help me to train my eyes and thoughts to remain on You and Your power—not my fears, obstacles, or challenges!

Day 66

BUNDLED WITH THE LORD

*Though man is risen up to pursue you and to seek your life,
yet the life of my lord shall be bound in the living bundle
with the Lord your God. And the lives of your enemies—
them shall He sling out as out of the center of a sling.*
1 SAMUEL 25:29 AMPC

When life throws you a curveball, when nothing seems to be going right, when you feel as if you can no longer ride the waves of life, stop thinking, stop worrying, stop fearing. And run, as fast as you can, to the arms of the Lord your God.

Allow the Lord of creation to wrap His entire being around you, to bind you to Himself, to erase the margins of where you end and He begins. For in Him you will find the rest you so desperately seek. There your mind will be eased and, once calmed, filled with all the wisdom you need to live the life you were created to live. And all those things that have been hampering you, chasing you down, keeping you from doing what you've been called to do? They will be flung away from your presence.

*Lord, I need to feel Your presence, to bask in Your light,
to share in Your warmth, to seek Your wisdom. Bind me
in a living bundle to You. Then fling all the darkness
away from me as I find my calm in Your closeness.*

Day 67

OUT OF THE DARKNESS

He brought them out of darkness, the utter
darkness, and broke away their chains.
PSALM 107:14 NIV

Do you struggle with depression? It's a state of being, a state of despondency that may be caused by chemical changes in your brain. It's a condition that can shackle your heart and take captive your mind. It's a place in which you feel like a prisoner.

The word *depression* comes from the Latin verb *deprimere*, meaning "to press down," to subjugate or to bring down in spirits. This pressing down can take you to some very dark places. But God never leaves His children in the dark. He is a God of light—and He wants you with Him, standing tall in the Sonshine.

When you are in the abyss, when all you can see is the darkness, God will provide you with a helper, for you were never meant to live life in your own power. God has created physicians, psychologists, counselors, and even friends and family members to help you. So reach out to someone standing outside the pit, someone in the light, who can lift you up and out.

If you are not in such a dark place, take inventory of those around you. Reach out to one who may need help in loosing his or her own chains.

Heavenly Father, thank You for Your promise to rescue those who
are in darkness. You are glorious, everlasting light. Amen.

Day 68

THE WORRY—FREE LIFE

*Jesus said. . ."Therefore I tell you, do not worry about your life,
what you will eat; or about your body, what you will wear.
For life is more than food, and the body more than clothes.
Consider the ravens: They do not sow or reap, they have no
storeroom or barn; yet God feeds them. . . . Who of you by
worrying can add a single hour to your life? Since you cannot
do this very little thing, why do you worry about the rest?"*
LUKE 12:22–26 NIV

What if someone else could handle the stresses and worries of your
health, finances, relationships, work, politics—*all the things* that cause
those pesky worry and frown lines to crease your forehead? No doubt
you'd like to imagine what a worry-free life feels like.

Here's the beautiful thing: not only can you imagine it. . .you can
actually *live* it! How? By giving every anxiety-inducing thought to Jesus.

The direction of your life will always mirror your strongest thoughts
(Proverbs 4:23)—and if those thoughts are worry filled, you'll never
be able to escape overwhelming fear and anxiety. When you create
new pathways of thought, fully trusting the heavenly Father with your
life, then this positive way of thinking will become your default. And
the worry-free life will be yours for the taking!

*Jesus, help me redirect my worried thoughts and fully
trust You in the process. Thank You, Lord! Amen.*

Day 69

UNSHAKABLE LOVE

"For even if the mountains walk away and the hills
fall to pieces, my love won't walk away from you,
my covenant commitment of peace won't fall apart."
The GOD who has compassion on you says so.
ISAIAH 54:10 MSG

As modern women, we seem to be stalked by anxiety. Our newsfeeds mention uprisings, terrorist attacks, market fluctuations, and hurricanes. Fear is a very common reaction to the world's instability, and it can easily cloud our mind and turn us into quaking, terrified children. The question is this: Do we want to dissolve into frightened, anxious women who rarely step outside our comfort zones, or do we desire to be bold, unashamed, fearless women of the Most High King?

God doesn't want us to cower beneath the weight of uncertainty. Instead, through the scriptures, other believers, and the indwelling Holy Spirit, He encourages us to be bold, passionate, and faithful. But how do we bridge the gap between our emotions and His desires for us?

The answer: love. We must rest in God's wild, unbending love for us. He promises in Isaiah that no matter what happens, He will never remove Himself from us. When we believe Him wholeheartedly and rest in His love, we will be filled with fear-busting peace and adventurous faith. That faith allows us to dream big dreams and conquer the worries that keep us chained.

Lord, thank You for Your love, which never leaves me.
Help me to rest in Your love above all else. Amen.

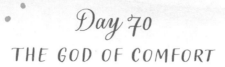

Day 70

THE GOD OF COMFORT

*Blessed be the God and Father of our Lord Jesus Christ,
the Father of mercies and God of all comfort, who
comforts us in all our affliction, so that we may be able to
comfort those who are in any affliction, with the comfort
with which we ourselves are comforted by God.*
2 Corinthians 1:3–4 esv

The apostle Paul knew what it was like to be the recipient of God's supernatural comfort. He and his companions suffered many things to bring to others the good news of a God who loved him—and them—unconditionally. Paul endured a weakness that he pleaded to God to take away, only to find out that God could still use it. At another time, he tells his readers, he and his companions "were completely overwhelmed—beyond our strength—so that we even despaired of life. Indeed, we personally had a death sentence within ourselves, so that we would not trust in ourselves but in God who raises the dead" (2 Corinthians 1:8–10 hcsb). How amazing that even when imprisoned, Paul's thoughts, heart, and actions continually testified of God's goodness.

When you're going through a hard time, remember that you belong to a Lord who also suffered. That the God who delivered you once will do so again. That He will comfort you as no one else can. That you can hope in Him.

*Abba Father, I need Your comfort right now.
Speak to me. Hold me close. May I feel Your presence.*

Day 71
PERMANENCE

"Heaven and earth will pass away,
but My words will never pass away."
LUKE 21:33 HCSB

Jesus makes it clear that His words, His predictions, His promises, will stand against time, against darkness, against trials. And that although the things of this earth may fade and eventually pass away, His words will not.

Through the prophet Isaiah, God claimed the same truth, saying: "The grass withers, the flowers fade when the breath of the LORD blows on them; indeed, the people are grass. The grass withers, the flowers fade, but the word of our God remains forever" (Isaiah 40:7–8 HCSB).

These promises, these truths that God's words will never pass away, give believers a boost in their faith. For it is a reminder that, far from fading or growing weak, God's words of hope and love can continually work to impart life and strength to the weak, joy to the downtrodden, and freedom to those in chains within and without.

Today, sink your mind and heart into this idea that God's words will forever stand, will forever continue to impart their strength and wisdom into your heart and mind, spirit and soul. Take it as a fact, a certainty that God's promises will grow brighter and brighter, shining their power into your life, as you claim each and every one day by day by day.

Thank You, Lord, for Your words that will forever remain,
fueling my prayers, my faith, and my life. In Jesus' name, amen.

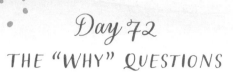

Day 72
THE "WHY" QUESTIONS

*Isaac prayed to the LORD on behalf of his wife because she
was childless. The LORD heard his prayer, and his wife
Rebekah conceived. But the children inside her struggled
with each other, and she said, "Why is this happening
to me?" So she went to inquire of the LORD.*
GENESIS 25:21–22 HCSB

When things don't seem to be going as planned, "why" questions begin creeping into our minds. And if we don't take those "why" questions to God, doubts begin to develop, darkening our hopes and joys.

Rebekah's seeking out God to put her question before Him is the first recorded instance we have of a woman pursuing Him in prayer. Rebekah is a great example to follow in this regard. For she reminds us that God alone holds all the answers, that He alone is the ultimate source of wisdom, and that He alone can and will answer our specific questions.

When you have a question or concern about anything in your life, go directly to God. Head straight to the ultimate source, knowing He will give you whatever guidance you need just when you need it.

*Lord, You are the source of all wisdom. So I come to You now,
asking why this is happening to me—knowing that You will
answer and give me whatever guidance I need. Amen.*

Day 73
JESUS DOES
THE UNEXPECTED

*When the Lord saw her, his heart overflowed
with compassion. "Don't cry!" he said.*
LUKE 7:13 NLT

A crowd followed Jesus and His disciples when they reached the village of Nain. There He noticed the funeral procession of a young man, a widow's only son.

When Jesus saw her, He couldn't help but be deeply touched by her grief and her dire situation. Without her asking anything of Him, He first told her not to cry and then, amazingly, brought her dead son back to life! After the boy sat up and began to talk, "Jesus gave him back to his mother" (Luke 7:15 NLT).

When you are at your wit's end, when it looks like there's no hope for you, when you find yourself walking in a daze, struck with sadness, remember this story.

Know that Jesus sees what you are going through. That His heart overflows with compassion for you.

So don't cry. Don't be discouraged. Don't despair. Don't grieve. Only believe. At the last minute, Jesus just may surprise you beyond anything you ever imagined or expected and turn your entire life around by doing the impossible.

*Jesus, You never cease to amaze me. Thank You for the
reminder that I need never despair. For You see what is
happening in my life. I feel Your love and compassion
surround me! I will not grieve—only believe.*

Day 74

JOSEPH MOMENTS

O LORD, hear my plea for justice. Listen to my cry for help.
Pay attention to my prayer, for it comes from honest
lips. . . . You have tested my thoughts and examined my
heart in the night. You have scrutinized me and found
nothing wrong. . . . My steps have stayed on your path.
PSALM 17:1, 3, 5 NLT

Every woman will, at some point in her life, experience a string of Joseph moments (Genesis 39–40), times when she just can't seem to get a break, when she believes herself a wretched victim of circumstance. These may be moments when her friends or family disappoint her. When she's forced to move into an unpleasant situation. When dungeon-like darkness threatens to overwhelm her. When people she has helped are restored then leave her behind.

Yet even during the darkest of days, the worst of circumstances, it would behoove a woman to remember God is with her. And because He's with her, there's hope. There's light. There's love. There's comfort. And because of those things, she will find favor. She will be raised up, succeed, and prosper—because through it all, she stuck with the God who stuck with her!

Dear Lord, "I am praying to you because I know you will
answer, O God. Bend down and listen as I pray. Show me
your unfailing love in wonderful ways. . . . Guard me as
you would guard your own eyes" (Psalm 17:6–8 NLT).

Day 75
PEACE THROUGH PRAYER

*Be anxious for nothing, but in everything by prayer and
supplication, with thanksgiving, let your requests be made known
to God; and the peace of God, which surpasses all understanding,
will guard your hearts and minds through Christ Jesus.*
PHILIPPIANS 4:6–7 NKJV

Some days it is easy to be thankful. We nearly bubble over with thanksgiving. These are mountaintop days—a graduation day, a wedding, or a reunion with old friends. The day comes to a close, and we whisper a prayer. It flows easily off the tongue. "Thank You, God," we say, "for a perfect day."

There are days when thankfulness is not as natural, not as easy. These are valley days—in the hospital room, at the graveside, or when we are distraught about a relationship or work issue. It is in these times that the Father wants us to give Him our burdens through prayer. It seems impossible to be thankful for the pain, the confusion, or the longings in our lives. We can be thankful, though, that we have a loving heavenly Father who stands ready to help.

The peace of God cannot be explained. It cannot be bought. The world cannot give it to us. But when we release our cares to the Lord in prayer, His peace washes over us and fills our hearts and minds. What a comfort is the peace of God when we find ourselves in the valley.

*Sovereign God, You are the same yesterday, today, and tomorrow.
You are with me through the good and the bad. Draw near
to me and replace my worry with Your peace. Amen.*

Day 76

GOD OF ALL THE EARTH

Shout for joy to God, all the earth; sing the glory of his name; give to him glorious praise! Say to God, "How awesome are your deeds! So great is your power that your enemies come cringing to you. All the earth worships you and sings praises to you."

PSALM 66:1–4 ESV

Do you tend to reserve your songs of praise for Sunday morning? Or do you sing praises for God's goodness throughout the week too?

In the verses above, the psalmist is calling *everyone* to joyfully praise God—after all, God is the God over all the earth, not just the God of Israel. The psalmist then follows with instruction on *how* to praise God: "Say to God, 'How awesome are your deeds!'" Praise involves telling God how amazing He is. . .what wonderful things He has done in your life. Praise celebrates His awesome power.

If praise doesn't come easy or naturally because your mind runs amok with thoughts of doubt and fear, ask God to remind you that He's in control and will protect and care for you always. When you invite Him to take complete control, your worries will be replaced with joy—and, as thoughts of thanksgiving and hope fill your mind, praise will spill from your heart and lips!

Father God, You are God of all the earth. And I am so thankful. I will praise You every day of my life! Amen.

Day 77
CLOSER THAN BREATHING

"This time I will spare the region of Goshen, where my people live. No flies will be found there. Then you will know that I am the LORD and that I am present even in the heart of your land. I will make a clear distinction between my people and your people."
EXODUS 8:22–23 NLT

God brought the ten plagues upon Pharaoh and his people so that they would know that He is the God of all gods, even those the Egyptians worshipped. That He was present, even in the heart of their land.

God continues to go to great lengths to let His people know not just who He is but *where* He is. He once inspired the poet Alfred, Lord Tennyson to write these insightful words about Him: "Closer is He than breathing and nearer than hands and feet." The apostle Paul agreed, saying, "He is actually not far from each one of us, for 'In him we live and move and have our being'" (Acts 17:27–28 ESV).

God wants you to know the same thing. He sees you rushing through life, stranded at a crossroads, or very alone, longing for love and companionship. And He wants you to realize that He—as well as His wisdom, help, and strength—lives in the very heart of you.

Know, believe, live a full life knowing God is closer than your breathing.

Lord, my breath and hope, thank You for being so near.

Day 78

TRUST THE GOOD NEWS

*We also have the prophetic message as something
completely reliable, and you will do well to pay attention
to it, as to a light shining in a dark place, until the day
dawns and the morning star rises in your hearts.*

2 PETER 1:19 NIV

The beauty of the Old Testament is that it foreshadows the coming of Jesus through the histories that depict humanity's great need for God as rescuer. The apostle Peter knew that God's message was true. Like any good Jewish boy, he had learned the Torah, the first five books of the Bible, and then he actually saw Jesus as the one who made all those images and promises come true. However, there was a time when Peter doubted the role of Jesus as Savior. His denial was the darkest moment of his life. Peter's letters were most likely written to other Jews of his time who also were well acquainted with the Old Testament prophecies about the Messiah. Peter tells the readers to believe the good news of Jesus Christ. It is completely reliable. In the darkest moment of Peter's despair, Jesus—as the incarnate Word of God, Divinity in the flesh—broke the chains of sin holding humans captive since the fall of Adam and Eve. In Jesus' death and resurrection, the awesomeness of God's mysterious rescue plan was revealed. Light came into the hearts of humankind and gave them life.

*Indelible Light, guide us to trust and live out Your message
so that Jesus can fight the darkness within and give us life anew.*

Day 79
JOYFUL ANTICIPATION

The lines of purpose in your lives never grow slack, tightly tied
as they are to your future in heaven, kept taut by hope.
Colossians 1:5 msg

Hope isn't just a warm fuzzy feeling that makes us feel good about life. When the Bible speaks of hope, it's not referring to an emotion. Instead, the Greek word our English Bibles translate as *hope* meant, literally, "confident expectation" or "joyful anticipation." It's similar to the way we might feel as we wait for a beloved friend to arrive at our house, confident she will not disappoint us. Or we could compare the biblical meaning of *hope* to the way a child feels before Christmas: no matter how dismal life may be at this moment, Christmas always comes!

In today's verse, the apostle Paul tells us that as we live our lives with our minds filled with the joyful anticipation of eternity, that awareness will shape our actions today. It will give us a greater sense of perspective, allowing us to rise above the negative emotions that so often overcome us. No matter what happens today, we can be confident that something wonderful lies ahead.

Thank You, beloved Lord, that You have tied my life
to heaven. May I live each day in joyful anticipation
of all You will do, in me and around me. Remind me
to always look at life through the eyes of eternity.

Day 80

KEEPING TRACK OF GOD'S GOODNESS

*He quieted the wind down to a whisper, put a muzzle on
all the big waves. And you were so glad when the storm
died down, and he led you safely back to harbor. So thank
GOD for his marvelous love, for his miracle mercy to the
children he loves. Lift high your praises when the people
assemble, shout Hallelujah when the elders meet!*

PSALM 107:29–32 MSG

Every time God does something wonderful in your life, write it down.
Maybe you make a note in your Bible or write in a journal, but find
a way to memorialize the moments when God has shown up in your
life in meaningful ways.

Why is this important? Because we will need to revisit these
moments again and again. When we're facing a situation that seems
hopeless or a circumstance that feels overwhelming, we will need to
remember the times God intervened. We will need to remember that
He is good all the time.

Nothing breeds hope more than a positive past experience. So be
quick to write down the times He quieted the wind or calmed the
tumultuous waters in your life. And keep track of the powerful ways
God has shown His unconditional love.

*Lord, I see You moving in my life and I'm grateful You've
chosen to love me the way You do. Help me remember
Your goodness so I'm encouraged to look for it again.*

Day 81

CALM YOURSELF

Anxiety weighs down the heart,
but a kind word cheers it up.
PROVERBS 12:25 NIV

How could there be a garbage truck and a school bus in front of her on the same morning? Sara finally got to the parking lot, zipping into a spot. She threw the car into PARK and quickly gathered her file bag, purse, and coffee. After pushing the door shut with her foot, she walked swiftly toward the office, going over in her head all the things that needed her attention that day.

She realized she was taking shallow breaths when she nearly gasped for air, and she felt her tenseness all of a sudden. "Lord," she prayed quickly, focusing her mind for a moment. Remembering His promise to provide peace, she slowed her steps, took a deep breath, and looked around at His creation for the bit of time she had before getting to work. She hadn't noticed until then the symphony of birds or the sound of the leaves rustling in the gentle breeze of summer.

It was just like God to help her get to a place of calm and clear thinking. Her mind turned to thanking Him for many things rather than getting anxious over the issues she was facing.

Lord, thank You for Your faithfulness to remind us
of the peace that passes all understanding. You are
the only one who can provide it for us. Amen.

Day 82

SEARCHING FOR THE GOOD

*He who deals wisely and heeds [God's] word and counsel
shall find good, and whoever leans on, trusts in, and is
confident in the Lord—happy, blessed, and fortunate is he.*
PROVERBS 16:20 AMPC

As Christians, each morning (hopefully) we are on the hunt for what is good. We like good things to eat for breakfast. We like to hear words that are lovely rather than words full of anger. We like a hug before we head out for the day. We like to plan for hopeful and excellent things that will happen at the office or home or wherever we will be. If there are major problems, we spend time trying to transform them into what is true and helpful. In other words, as Christ followers, our souls long for what is good.

If we find ourselves turning away from that godly ideal, it could be that we have fallen into some kind of snare. But with the help of the Holy Spirit, we can be freed of the unhealthy patterns and negative traps we may find ourselves in. We can learn to live the words of today's verse, and we can discover how to be free and happy in the Lord!

*Lord, Your Holy Word is a wonderful guidebook for
living a healthy and satisfying and hope-filled life in You.
Thank You for that—and for so much more besides! Amen.*

Day 83

GREAT CONFIDENCE AND HOPE

God also bound himself with an oath, so that those who received the promise could be perfectly sure that he would never change his mind. So God has given both his promise and his oath. These two things are unchangeable because it is impossible for God to lie. Therefore, we who have fled to him for refuge can have great confidence as we hold to the hope that lies before us.
HEBREWS 6:17–18 NLT

Ever get discouraged, wondering if God is going to make good on all the promises He has made to His children? Consider Abraham. He had to wait twenty-five years for the promises of a son to become a reality!

So, woman of the Way, hang on! God *will* come through. He will not change His mind. He cannot, does not, lie. Those promises God made all those thousands of years ago will be fulfilled, some in your own lifetime. Because God said, "I am the LORD! If I say it, it will happen" (Ezekiel 12:25 NLT).

If there's any person you can take at His word, who's honest as the day is long and a tried-and-true keeper of promises, it's the Lord of the universe, your Creator and sustainer. Yahweh. So hang on to that great confidence and hope you have in Him.

Thank You, Lord, for being true to Your word and promises. Because You do what You say, I have confidence and hope!

Day 84
A CHOICE

I'm singing joyful praise to GOD. I'm turning cartwheels
of joy to my Savior God. Counting on GOD's Rule
to prevail, I take heart and gain strength. I run like
a deer. I feel like I'm king of the mountain!
HABAKKUK 3:18–19 MSG

Many days, life seems like an uphill battle, where we are fighting against the current, working hard to maintain our equilibrium. Exhausted from the battle, we often throw up our hands in disgust and want to quit. That's when we should realize we have a choice. We can choose to surrender our burdens to the Lord!

What would happen if we followed the advice of the psalmist and turned a cartwheel of joy in our hearts—regardless of the circumstances—then trusted in His rule to prevail? Think of the happiness and peace that could be ours with a total surrender to God's care.

It's a decision to count on God's rule to triumph. And we must realize His Word, His rule, never fails. Never. Then we must want to stand on that Word. Taking a giant step, armed with scriptures and praise and joy, we can surmount any obstacle put before us, running like a deer, climbing the tall mountains. With God at our side, it's possible to be king of the mountain.

Dear Lord, I need Your help. Gently guide me so I might learn
to lean on You and become confident in Your care. Amen.

Day 85

PREPARING FOR THE JOURNEY AHEAD

The LORD your God has blessed you in all the work of your hands. He has watched over your journey through this vast wilderness. These forty years the LORD your God has been with you, and you have not lacked anything.
DEUTERONOMY 2:7 NIV

If you've ever packed for a vacation, you know what it's like—you stare at mounds of clothes in your suitcase and wonder, "How much of this am I really going to need?"

The truth is some women overprepare. We pack too many shoes, too many blouses, too many pieces of jewelry. We're so overburdened with stuff that the journey gets off to a rocky start.

Now think about this from a spiritual perspective. Picture the Israelites in the wilderness. They could only take with them what they could carry for the journey. Too much baggage and the journey would be slow going.

If you knew the Lord was about to lead you into a new experience with Him, what would you take with you? Maybe it's time to scale back. Ask God what's important to keep—and what to get rid of. Shake off the nonessentials (things like bitterness, unforgiveness, and anger) and move forward into a new place with the Lord. He will replace those missing items with things like peace, joy, and love. Ah, now that's traveling light!

Lord, I don't want to make my journey harder than it already is. I don't want to drag around weighty things like bitterness, jealousy, pain, and frustration. Today I lay those things down. Please refill my spiritual luggage with peace, joy, hope, and gentleness.

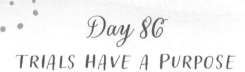

Day 86

TRIALS HAVE A PURPOSE

*Then Joseph said to his brothers, "Please come closer
to me." And they came closer. And he said, "I am your
brother Joseph, whom you sold to Egypt. Now do not be
grieved or angry with yourselves because you sold me
here, for God sent me ahead of you to save lives."*

GENESIS 45:4–5 NASB

How many of us could forgive as Joseph did? His jealous siblings had kidnapped him, thrown him into a pit, and then sold him into slavery. Yet Joseph trusted that from God's perspective, not his own, his trials had a purpose.

Joseph walked through his humiliating ordeal with his eyes focused on the Lord. He continued not only to love his brothers but to find forgiveness in his heart for them. Studying his life can enable us to look at our own situations differently: God can accomplish miracles in the midst of trials.

Is there a hurt so deep inside that you have never shared it with another human being? Perhaps someone in your own family has rejected or betrayed you. Remember the pain suffered by Joseph; remember the anguish of Jesus Christ, who was betrayed by one as close as a brother, Judas Iscariot. God knows your pain, and He is strong enough to remove any burden.

*Lord, sometimes I want to enjoy my agony awhile longer.
Show me the brilliance of Your forgiveness that I might trust
You in the trial and not miss the outcome You've planned.*

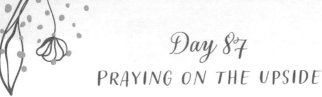

Day 87
PRAYING ON THE UPSIDE

"O Lord, . . .give us. . .great boldness in preaching your word.
Stretch out your hand with healing power; may miraculous
signs and wonders be done through the name of your
holy servant Jesus." After this prayer, the meeting place
shook, and they were all filled with the Holy Spirit.
ACTS 4:29–31 NLT

Sometimes we may find ourselves somewhat casual in our prayer frequency and intensity. Other days, our burden is so great, our crisis so deep, we find ourselves driven to our knees in pleading before God. But how often do we pray intensely for more of what we already have?

That's what the apostles did. They'd already performed lots of miracles (see Acts 2:43; 3:7–11). They'd already demonstrated their courage and boldness before many people, including the Jewish courts. But they didn't rest on their reputations. Instead, they asked God for more boldness in preaching, more healing, more signs, and more wonders. Afterward, the place where they were meeting in prayer shook, they were filled by the Holy Spirit, and they began preaching God's Word with boldness.

Consider putting all your faith and trust in God and praying on the upside. When things are going well, pray even harder for God to work His will in your life. Shake up your world!

Make me bolder, Lord. Stretch out Your hand to heal. Show Your
presence and power in my life. Shake up my world—for You!

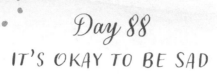

Day 88

IT'S OKAY TO BE SAD

They mourned and wept and fasted till evening for Saul and his son Jonathan, and for the army of the LORD and for the nation of Israel, because they had fallen by the sword.

2 SAMUEL 1:12 NIV

Sometimes we think we must be brave when the storms of life hit. We put a smile on our face as if nothing is wrong. We see sadness as weakness, and we don't want that adjective to define us.

Yet life is rough, friend. We face heartache on a regular basis. Maybe it's working through divorce, death, or disease. It could be an unexpected betrayal or a child having to suffer the natural consequences of making bad decisions. There are addictions, lawsuits, cross-country moves, and the loss of a job.

Life isn't fair or easy for anyone. Sorrow is something we all face. And it's okay to be sad. It's healthy to mourn. God gave you that powerful emotion to help you process upsetting situations. It's in those sad times that He will help heal your heart.

But you can't live there. Life moves forward and so must you.

Embrace the sadness. Invite God into it. Ask for Him to heal your heart. And know that, in time, you will smile again.

Lord, it's hard for me to be honest about my sadness. I don't want to be a burden or seen as overly dramatic. Will You give me courage to feel those emotions and trust You for healing?

Day 89

MERCIFUL HEAVENS!

I love the LORD, for he heard my voice;
he heard my cry for mercy.
PSALM 116:1 NIV

The days when nothing goes according to plan are frustrating beyond belief. Worst are the surprises. Summer storms bring down power lines; the computer crashes before important work is saved; a fresh pot of coffee splatters on the floor. No one was planning to spend the day huddled indoors listening to raging winds. The frazzled engineer still has to turn in her report by 5:00 p.m. And Sarah will have to mop the whole kitchen *before* she can go out for her much-needed cup of joe.

It's a good thing our heavenly Father is compassionate toward His children. Heaven knows we need mercy when even a small thing going wrong can ruin our thankful attitudes for the day, and we definitely need His kindness when we stagger under huge disappointments.

Thankfully, our Father is never surprised at what happens, because all events fit in with His eternal plan (Romans 8:28). He knows His children can't see all the details, but He does know how much they can handle (1 Corinthians 10:13). Best of all, they can call on Him to shower down compassion upon the situation. "Mercy, Father! I can't handle this alone." "Mercy, Lord Jesus! Lift this burden—it's so heavy." The psalmist praises God for hearing and answering his prayer for mercy. God is more generous with His mercy than we suspect— ask Him in faith and see.

Father God, I love You because You keep pouring
out mercy upon me when I need it. Help me
continually draw my strength from You. Amen.

Day 90
THIS IS GOD

Walk about Zion, go around her, number her towers,
consider well her ramparts, go through her citadels,
that you may tell the next generation that this is God,
our God forever and ever. He will guide us forever.
PSALM 48:12–14 ESV

In Psalm 48, we see two very different responses to Zion. Those who were against God panicked; they trembled and fled. But the people of God praised Him. In God's great city, His people saw God's greatness. In Zion's citadels and temple, they saw proof of His protection and love. They were to look at Zion and think of their God.

As we walk this earth, our responses to life could run the gamut—from wonder and joy to apathy, gloom, fear, and so on. Regardless of what we face, positivity and praise are possible if we keep our thoughts fixed on God.

What "landmarks" can you recall—times when God has shown who He is or come through for you or others in little or big ways? Where have you seen God's hand in the past—His generosity, compassion, and power? Touch upon those times in your mind every day. And when you have a burden to bear, don't dwell on the burden. Give it to God! Be assured that He will take care of you as He has always done (Psalm 55:22).

Lord, help me focus on the many evidences of You.
You are God, and I praise You. Amen.

Day 91
TRIBULATIONS TO TRANSFORMATION

*After preaching the Good News in Derbe and making many
disciples, Paul and Barnabas returned to Lystra, Iconium,
and Antioch of Pisidia, where they strengthened the believers.
They encouraged them to continue in the faith, reminding them
that we must suffer many hardships to enter the Kingdom of God.*
ACTS 14:21–22 NLT

As a daughter of Jesus, have you noticed something about seasons
of testing? When you feel like you're under a lot of pressure, going
through one trial after the next, you might feel weighed down and
burdened. But with the eyes of faith, you can stand encouraged that
God really is at work. For the good news reminds you that on the
other side of tribulation comes transformation, and on the other side
of a test comes a testimony.

When you're in the midst of the battle, cry out to God and He'll
give you victory, as He always does for those who rely on, cling to,
and trust in Him (1 Chronicles 5:20 AMPC).

Whatever you might be going through, cry out to Jesus. Cling to
Him. Trust that He's moving mountains on your behalf. That He is
all you need.

*Lord, lead me on the pathway to be encouraged by You
and other followers in the faith. Help me stand firm in
what You say about me. May I cling to You and Your
Word. May I rely on You and trust in You alone.*

Day 92

OUR STRONG ARM

But LORD, be merciful to us, for we have waited for you. Be our strong arm each day and our salvation in times of trouble.
ISAIAH 33:2 NLT

At times we may feel weak and discouraged. We don't even have the energy to lift our heads up and take on the next challenge. But God can turn us around. When we go to Him, when we seek His face, when we put all our cares on His shoulders, He comes to our rescue. He not only willingly takes our burdens away but also becomes our arm of strength. Through Him, we find more than enough energy to change the next diaper, tackle another project at work, seek a new path for our lives, deal with our teens and aging parents, cope with an illness, and find a way through a difficult relationship. Only God can turn our challenges into opportunities for Him to show His power. Just be patient. Wait on Him. And He will do more than see you through.

Lord, I am facing so many challenges, I don't even know where to start, what to do, how to approach them. And I feel so weak and powerless. My mind is confused, my emotions jumbled. So I am looking to You, waiting on You in this very moment. Be my strong arm. Fill me with Your awesome, mountain-moving power. Rescue me from these troubles. Make a path through this debris. Be my defense so that I can catch my breath. I rest in You now, knowing in You I am as safe as a babe in a mother's arms. Amen.

Day 93
ARMED AND READY

Finally, my brethren, be strong in the Lord and in the power of His might. Put on the whole armor of God, that you may be able to stand against the wiles of the devil.
EPHESIANS 6:10–11 NKJV

The enemy is skilled at surprise attacks. Many times, he lashes out when we least expect it and when we're ill prepared. That's why it's important to be armed and ready at all times, not just in obvious battles. When he kicks our knees out from under us, we don't have to crater. If we're fully suited up to fight, the enemy won't get far.

God doesn't want us to be armed out of fear or intimidation. His goal isn't to weigh us down with burdensome armor. Ultimately, God longs to free us up. His armor isn't heavy—it's life-sustaining, life-giving. It does the job without driving us to our knees.

What enemies are you facing today? What opposing forces threaten to undo the work God is doing in your life? Suit up, my friend! You can take down this foe in the name of Jesus!

Lord, I want to be armed and ready. Today I choose to step into the armor You've provided so that I'm ready for the battle ahead. No cowering. No cratering. I'm strong when I'm suited up, Lord. . .ready to fight in Your name, strength, and power. Amen.

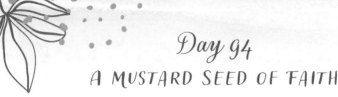

Day 94

A MUSTARD SEED OF FAITH

The kingdom of heaven is like a grain of mustard seed,
which a man took and sowed in his field. Of all the seeds
it is the smallest, but when it has grown it is the largest
of the garden herbs and becomes a tree, so that the birds
of the air come and find shelter in its branches.
MATTHEW 13:31–32 AMPC

Have you ever planted seeds in the ground? It's awe-inspiring to watch that teensy-tiny little seed blossom into a lovely plant. The process is remarkable, if you pause to think about it.

Jesus shared the story about the mustard seed to remind His followers that the burden of proof isn't on them. You don't have to have massive amounts of faith to witness a miracle in your life. You just need a teensy-tiny bit of faith in the one who's capable. If it were up to you (and aren't you glad it's not?), you could never grow your faith to the necessary proportions. But the weight is on God's shoulders, not yours. He's the miracle worker. He's the seed blossomer. He's the one who can take your impossible situation and (with a smidgen of faith from you) completely turn it around.

What are you facing today? Take your mustard seed and plant it deep, and then watch God intervene. He longs to grow your faith as He steps in to take control.

Lord, thank You for growing my faith. I'll plant my little
mustard seed today and watch You work on my behalf. Amen.

Day 95
HE'LL CARRY IT FOR YOU

Praise be to the Lord, to God our Savior,
who daily bears our burdens.
PSALM 68:19 NIV

So many times, we hyperfocus on our burdens. It's almost as if we choose to trust in the burden, not the burden bearer. Our gaze remains fixed on the problem, not the problem solver.

It's time to shift our focus! God has promised in His Word that He will bear our burdens, not just occasionally, but daily. Every problem we face can be placed into His mighty hands. He's more than capable. When we shift our attention away from our trials and onto Him, our perspective changes completely. The weight is gone! And when the weight is gone, we're better able to lift our hands and hearts in praise, which further strengthens our faith.

No matter what you're going through today, praise God! He's ready and willing to carry the load on your behalf. What a trustworthy and faithful God we serve!

Lord, there are so many days when I feel weighed down by life's burdens. How freeing to know You want to lift those weights from my shoulders, to carry them for me. What a gracious and kind Father You are! I'm so grateful to You, my burden bearer. Amen.

Day 96
HOLY SPIRIT PRAYERS

*We do not know what to pray for as we should, but the Spirit
Himself intercedes for us with groanings too deep for words;
and He who searches the hearts knows what the mind of the Spirit
is, because He intercedes for the saints according to the will of God.*
ROMANS 8:26–27 NASB

Many times the burdens and troubles of our lives are too complicated to understand. It's difficult for us to put them into words, let alone know how to pray for what we need. And unless we know someone who has been through similar circumstances, we can feel isolated and alone.

But we can always take comfort in knowing that the Holy Spirit knows, understands, and pleads our case before the throne of God the Father. Our groans become words in the Holy Spirit's mouth, turning our mute prayers into praise and intercession "according to the will of God."

We can be encouraged, knowing that our deepest longings and desires, maybe unknown even to us, are presented before the God who knows us and loves us completely. Our names are engraved on His heart and hands. He never forgets us; He intervenes in all things for our good and His glory.

*Father, I thank You for the encouragement these
verses bring. May I always be aware of the
Holy Spirit's interceding on my behalf.*

Day 97

THE LORD HIMSELF
GOES BEFORE YOU

*"The LORD himself goes before you and will be
with you; he will never leave you nor forsake you.
Do not be afraid; do not be discouraged."*
DEUTERONOMY 31:8 NIV

How comforting and freeing when we allow God to go before us!
Stop and consider that for a moment: you can relinquish control of
your life and circumstances to the Lord Himself. Relax! His shoulders
are big enough to carry all of your burdens.

The issue that has your stomach in knots right now? Ask the Lord
to go before you. The problem that makes you wish you could hide
under the covers and sleep until it's all over? Trust that God Himself
will never leave you and that He is working everything out.

Joshua 1:9 (NIV) tells us to "be strong and courageous. Do not be
afraid; do not be discouraged, for the LORD your God will be with
you wherever you go." Be encouraged! Even when it feels like it, you
are truly never alone. And never without access to God's power.

If you've trusted Christ as your Savior, the Spirit of God Himself is
alive and well and working inside you at all times. What an astounding
miracle! The Creator of the universe dwells within you and is available
to encourage you and help you make right choices on a moment-by-
moment basis.

*Thank You, Lord, for the incredible gift of Your presence in
each and every situation I face. Allow me to remember this
and to call upon Your name as I go about each day. Amen.*

Day 98

STRENGTH IN THE LORD

The LORD is my light and my salvation—
whom shall I fear? The LORD is the stronghold
of my life—of whom shall I be afraid?
PSALM 27:1 NIV

Even when it seems that everything is piling up around you, Christ is there for you. Take heart! He is your stronghold, a very present help right in the midst of your trial. Regardless of what comes against you in this life, you have the Lord on your side. He is your light in the darkness and your salvation from eternal separation from God. You have nothing to fear.

At times, this world can be a tough, unfair, lonely place. Since the fall of man in the garden, things have not been as God originally intended. The Bible assures us that we will face trials in this life, but it also exclaims that we are more than conquerors through Christ who is in us! When you find yourself up against a tribulation that seems insurmountable, *look up.* Christ is there. He goes before you, stands with you, and is backing you up in your time of need. You may lose everyone and everything else in this life, but nothing has the power to separate you from the love of Christ. Nothing.

Jesus, I cling to the hope I have in You.
You are my rock, my stronghold, my defense.
I will not fear, for You are with me always. Amen.

Day 99
POWER TOOL

Then the king said to me, "What do you request?"
So I prayed to the God of heaven.
NEHEMIAH 2:4 NKJV

When Nehemiah, cupbearer to the king of Persia, received news of the destruction of Jerusalem, he wept for days. With a heavy heart, he fasted then prayed to God (Nehemiah 1:4–11), speaking of His kindness for His people who love Him and keep His commandments. He asked God to hear his prayer for the Israelites, acknowledging they'd behaved badly. Then Nehemiah reminded God that He'd promised to bring them back if they changed their ways.

The following day, the king noticed Nehemiah's sadness. Knowing there was something on his cupbearer's mind, he said, "How can I help?" Before speaking, Nehemiah "prayed to the God of heaven." Then he asked the king to send him to Jerusalem to rebuild it.

Prayers come in all different shapes and sizes. That's because different situations require different prayers. Nehemiah's first and longer prayer was his way of unburdening himself. It also allowed him to remind God (and himself) of His promises—and to ask for help. But the next day, before the king, Nehemiah wisely used an arrow prayer, a quick opening up to God for help to speak wisely.

No matter what the length or content of your prayer, be assured of its power to transform you, your words, and the situation at hand.

Thank You, God, for gifting me
with the tool and power of prayer.

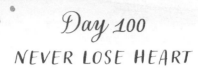

Day 100

NEVER LOSE HEART

I would have lost heart, unless I had believed that I would see the goodness of the LORD in the land of the living. Wait on the LORD; be of good courage, and He shall strengthen your heart.

PSALM 27:13–14 NKJV

When things don't seem to be going our way, it's easy to lose heart. This is especially true when our difficulties revolve around life-changing losses. The sudden death of a loved one can be heartbreaking, leaving us gasping for breath, wondering how it happened and how we will ever find peace again. A devastating illness, a dashed dream, an ugly divorce, an alienation from a family member can leave us feeling untethered, without hope. When we're still reeling, having difficulty finding our feet, it's hard to stand up to even the littlest of daily challenges. Meanwhile, everyone else's life goes on as before and we feel as if we've been left behind in the dust of despair. But you *can* find a rainbow in the midst of these storms. It comes with the power of God and the belief that you will one day see His amazing goodness in your life. All you need to do is take courage and wait on Him. He will not only see you through but also give you whatever strength you need to find your feet and walk on stronger than ever before.

I've lost all hope that things will ever be normal again, Lord. So I'm hanging on to Your promise that I'll one day see Your goodness come streaming through. I'm waiting on You. Give me courage, hope, patience, and the strength I need to find my feet. Amen.

Day 101

PERSISTENTLY PRESENTED PETITIONS

"O woman, great is your faith! Let it be to you as you desire."
MATTHEW 15:28 NKJV

When our loved ones are troubled—emotionally, spiritually, financially, physically, mentally—our hearts are heavy and we feel helpless. But with Christ's ear within reach of our voice, we are anything but powerless. We have an interceder, someone to whom we can continually go and present our petitions.

In Matthew 15:21–28, a Canaanite woman asked Jesus for mercy and to heal her demon-possessed daughter. At first Christ seemed not to hear her pleas. The disciples, irritated with her persistence, told Jesus to send her away.

Yet this woman had dogged determination. She *knew* that the Son of God could heal her daughter. She continued to plead, driven by love for her child and faith in Christ's power.

Her insistence was met by a reproach from Christ, who told her He did not come to help the Gentiles but the Jews. This had to have crushed her expectations. Yet even then she persisted. She did not despair but continued running after Him, worshipping Him, pleading with Him, begging for mercy.

Jesus reproached her again. But still she was undeterred. Finally, Jesus said the words we all long to hear: "Woman, great is your faith! Let it be to you as you desire."

May we live our lives as persistent in our petitions as the Canaanite woman. And may God see our faith and honor our requests as we boldly bring the needs of others before His throne!

Lord, have mercy! Help others in their hour of need. Amen.

Day 102
THE FAITH ADVANTAGE

"If you embrace this kingdom life and don't doubt God,
you'll not only do minor feats like I did to the fig tree,
but also triumph over huge obstacles. This mountain,
for instance, you'll tell, 'Go jump in the lake,' and it
will jump. Absolutely everything, ranging from small
to large, as you make it a part of your believing
prayer, gets included as you lay hold of God."
MATTHEW 21:21–22 MSG

Jesus admitted that in this life you will have problems (John 16:33). Who doesn't? Even those who have money and treasures to fill twenty vacation homes have troubles. But those who are believers have an advantage over all the rest: their faith.

Jesus made sure His followers understood that as long as they had faith, as long as they didn't doubt the strength, the love, and the power of the God who created the universe, the visible and the invisible, they would overcome any obstacles that stood in their way—no matter how huge they appeared!

Some people see their obstacles as something they will never be able to overcome. Their doubts make them stop short, reconsider, then turn and run (Numbers 13:30–33). They see their obstacles as bigger than their own God!

Yet you're different. You know that nothing—no barrier, problem, trouble, or burden—is bigger than your God. You have the faith advantage.

I'm praying my believing prayer, Lord. Help me
triumph over any obstacles that come my way,
for nothing is bigger or more powerful than You!

Day 103
WHOLENESS

For in Christ all the fullness of the Deity lives in bodily form, and in Christ you have been brought to fullness. He is the head over every power and authority.
<small>COLOSSIANS 2:9–10 NIV</small>

Self-talk reveals more about a woman than she may realize. Does she speak to herself with positive words or words of self-loathing? Truthfully, it is much easier to focus on her broken parts, whether it is bodily imperfections, struggles with sins, or circumstances that can't be changed. The mirror and the mind become battlegrounds, thoughts launching inward like grenades.

When a woman trusts Jesus, she is more than her mistakes or her victories. She is *whole* in her Savior. She is whole because Christ gave her His all—His righteousness, His riches of wisdom, His perfect life for hers. He called her to follow Him so that she could share in His abundant life. His love lets her deflect the cruel words she had aimed at herself.

In Christ, she is no longer condemned because of her sin—He has wiped it away (Romans 8:1). In Christ, she is never alone—He has given her His Spirit to comfort her (Romans 8:26–27). In Christ, she can stand bravely, content in whatever situation she finds herself—His hand is there to sustain her (Philippians 4:12–13; Psalm 89:21). Nothing—good or bad—can change His love for and complete acceptance of her. He looks at her and sees His beloved for whom He died—His bride, His delight.

Father God, thank You that Your love never changes. Help me see myself the way Christ does and draw strength and confidence from His love. Amen.

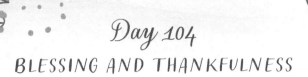

Day 104

BLESSING AND THANKFULNESS

Give thanks in all circumstances; for this
is God's will for you in Christ Jesus.
1 THESSALONIANS 5:18 NIV

"Count your blessings, name them one by one. Count your blessings, see what God has done." As the hymn says, being thankful is a practice. We should take time to contemplate God's blessings to us, especially when there seems to be more trouble than peace in our lives.

No matter how difficult life becomes, God's gifts are still there, abundant and gracious. I knew an artist whose medical conditions caused such terrible pain that she could only stand and walk for a limited time each day. Despite her situation, she made a practice of tracing the threads of God's blessing in her life. If she ate a peach, she would thank God for the peach, for the store that sold it, for the store's employees, for the truck driver, for the orchard workers, for the farmer who had cared for the trees, and for the soil, air, water, and sunlight. Her spirit radiated thankfulness in the midst of her suffering, even for something as small as a peach.

Our thankfulness is founded on God—He has promised to take care of our needs and to comfort us in our distress. Name what the Father has done for you, blessings big and small, in joyous and in troubled times. All good gifts are from Him (James 1:17). Can you trace the thread of His love in your life?

Dear heavenly Father, open my eyes to Your many blessings
so I may praise Your name! Teach my heart to focus on
Your goodness, no matter the circumstances. Amen.

Day 105
SAFE PLACE

*O God, be merciful and gracious to me, for my soul takes
refuge and finds shelter and confidence in You; yes, in the
shadow of Your wings will I take refuge and be confident
until calamities and destructive storms are passed.*
PSALM 57:1 AMPC

Where can a woman run when the thunderclouds begin rolling in?
Where can she hide when feeling blue? Where can she find sleep
when the night seems endless? Where can she go when there is
danger? To God.

God is the only really safe place to go when threatened, sad, troubled, or in need of safety. In Him, a woman of the Way has a true
sanctuary. Beneath His precious, soft, silky, massive wings, her soul
can rest in comfort. In the midst of that wingspan, no destructive
force can touch her. In that safe place, she can regain her confidence,
rethink her game plan, consult God, glean His wisdom, and come
away with a new perspective.

God says, "I carried you on eagles' wings and brought you to myself"
(Exodus 19:4 NLT). He has done so over and over again. That is part
of God's character. That wingspan is real. That feathery fortress can
hold each and every person. There, and only there, are His daughters
safe during the worst of storms.

*Thank You, Lord, for being my safe place. I come to You now,
ready to find shelter, love, protection, and confidence
before, during, and after the storms of this life.*

Day 106
RELY ON HIM

Do not let your hearts be troubled (distressed, agitated).
You believe in and adhere to and trust in and rely on God;
believe in and adhere to and trust in and rely also on Me.
JOHN 14:1 AMPC

Some days are full of joy and peace; others are not. When we face the inevitable dark days in life, we must choose how we respond. We bring light to the darkest of days when we turn our face to God. Sometimes we must let in trusted friends and family members to help on our journey toward solving our problems.

David knew much distress and discomfort when he cried out, "God is our Refuge and Strength" (Psalm 46:1 AMPC). Matthew Henry's commentary says of Psalm 46, "Through Christ, we shall be conquerors. . . . He is a Help, a present Help, a Help found, one whom we have found to be so; a Help at hand, one that is always near; we cannot desire a better, nor shall we ever find the like in any creature."

Knowing that Christ is at the center of our battles—and that we can trust Him—lends peace and stills the weakest of hearts. Rely on Him to lead you through the darkest days.

Oh Lord, still my troubled heart. Let me learn to rely on You in all circumstances. Thank You, Father, for Your everlasting love.

Day 107
AN EXTRAVAGANT GOD

*Change your life, not just your clothes. Come back
to GOD, your God. And here's why: God is kind and
merciful. He takes a deep breath, puts up with a lot,
this most patient God, extravagant in love.*
JOEL 2:13 MSG

There are times when we are exhausted and discouraged and we allow
our minds to roam to dark places. Despair and disappointment set in.
A woe-is-me attitude prevails. How do we rise from the doldrums?
How do we continue? We turn our faces toward the Lord God and
know that He is in control.

Scripture tells of God's mercy and loving-kindness. It speaks to
us to come back to God. This doesn't necessarily mean a change of
circumstances, but a change of heart. And this change is a choice we
intentionally make. It's not necessary to be in a church building or
revival tent. While many changes happen there, ours can be in our
closet, our car, our office. We reach inwardly to the Highest and ask
for His mercy. And scripture says He is merciful.

Focusing on the negative—choosing despair—doesn't bring life.
Voluntarily focusing on Jesus will. Praise Him for all your blessings:
They are there; look for them! Some might be tiny, others magnificent.
But they're all because of our Lord Jesus Christ. He is a most patient
God and extravagant in His love.

*Heavenly Father, I praise Your name. You are
extravagant in Your love, filling me to overflowing!
I am grateful for all You've done.*

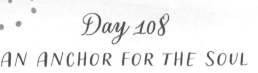

Day 108

AN ANCHOR FOR THE SOUL

We have this hope as an anchor for the soul, firm and secure.
It enters the inner sanctuary behind the curtain.
HEBREWS 6:19 NIV

In just a few words, Hebrews 6:19 paints a rich word picture to comfort us. "This hope" refers to verses 13-18, where God swore to Himself to secure His promise to Abraham. Like the great patriarch, we who walk in faith today have two trustworthy things in which to place our hope: God's Word and Himself.

Anchors are also a symbol of hope. During a storm, a strong anchor locked into a solid foundation keeps the boat from being blown off course or onto the rocks. Sailors' hope during a storm is the anchor.

"The inner sanctuary behind the curtain" would be familiar to these Jewish Christians—the audience of the book of Hebrews—as the Holy of Holies where the high priest went once a year, after the sin sacrifices were offered, to enter the presence of God. When Christ died on the cross, the curtain separating the two areas tore from top to bottom, symbolizing direct access to God for all believers. So instead of anchoring into solid rock, like a ship would, we anchor our hope directly to God.

Our hope is founded in the unshakable character of God, who loves us so much He sent His Son to die for us. His Word is true. He will do what He says He will do.

> *Heavenly Father, we are grateful for the sacrifice*
> *of Your Son, making it possible for us to have a*
> *relationship with You. Remind us we can trust You*
> *completely, and help us to rest in that truth. Amen.*

Day 109
NO MORE TEARS

*" 'He will wipe every tear from their eyes. There will
be no more death' or mourning or crying or pain,
for the old order of things has passed away."*
REVELATION 21:4 NIV

This world is sadly full of sorrow and disappointment. But God doesn't allow our pain to be purposeless. It helps us need Jesus more. It drives us to a closer, more dependent relationship with Him, even when we can't possibly understand the reason for the pain we are experiencing.

Pain, especially when it's seen in our rearview mirror rather than in front of our faces, helps us have greater compassion for others' suffering. It also gives us common ground to give comfort and empathize with others who are in painful circumstances.

It won't always be like this. Someday we will live with Jesus in a perfect life with no sorrow, pain, or disappointment. And we get a "no more tears" promise that is greater than any baby shampoo could deliver. Someday we will have joy greater than anything this earth can offer because it won't be tinged by sin and death. And that is a promise we can hold on to.

*Heavenly Father, thank You so much for defeating death and sin so
we can have a glorious future with You in heaven, where we will
truly have no more tears. Help us to cling to Your promises and to
comfort others who are going through painful situations. Amen.*

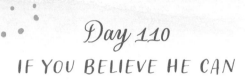

Day 110
IF YOU BELIEVE HE CAN

*"What do you want me to do for you?" Jesus asked him.
The blind man said, "Rabbi, I want to see." "Go,"
said Jesus, "your faith has healed you." Immediately he
received his sight and followed Jesus along the road.*
MARK 10:51–52 NIV

Do you remember the 1930s children's book *The Little Engine That Could*? This American folktale, as related by Watty Piper, was meant to teach children optimism and belief in themselves. It was about a little train engine tasked with pulling a long train of stranded freight cars over a steep mountain. Larger engines declined to try, but this little engine took on the seemingly impossible task. What separated this little guy from the rest? He had faith. He believed. His mantra, "I think I can," resonated throughout his journey.

In the verses above, the blind man was healed by his faith in Jesus, not by medicine, not by treatments, not by specialists. He was healed only because he believed in God's Son, *who could do anything.*

Faith in God can help you get through any weighty issue. Nothing is too heavy for God to handle if you truly believe He can.

*Dear God, some days the load seems so heavy, the burdens so great,
the afflictions insurmountable. Please help me to keep my faith
strong, to know that You will help me with any and all challenges
if I simply trust in You, convinced that You can do anything.*

Day 111

LOOKING BEYOND EARTHLY REASSURANCES

Some nations boast of their chariots and horses,
but we boast in the name of the LORD our God.
PSALM 20:7 NLT

David, the writer of this psalm, did not find his hope in things that came from this earth—things he could see with his own eyes or create with his own hands. He did not find it through a solution his mind could conjure. He had faith in the Lord, and that was enough. We can only imagine how comforting it would be to look upon our defending army during a time of war, but he chose to look beyond the army and instead fix his eyes on the Lord.

Through any trial or pain, the Lord sees all, and He loves His people in a deep, unfailing way. Although a thousand may fall, our fate and lives rest in Him and Him alone. We cannot look to earthly things to predict our future, finances, employment, etc. God's plans far exceed anything we could plan, and if we trust and follow Him, we will end up in a place we never would have come up with on our own.

Breathe in. Breathe out. Rest and believe. It is through fixing our eyes on God and looking to Him for direction that we are reassured and can experience peace.

Lord, please set my eyes on You. Help me not to seek
reassurance through earthly things but to understand on
a deeper level that You control all. You hold my heart and
care about each step I take. My hope is in You alone.

Day 112

HIS RIGHTEOUS RIGHT HAND

*"Do not fear, for I am with you; do not be afraid, for I
am your God. I will strengthen you, I will also help you,
I will also uphold you with My righteous right hand."*
ISAIAH 41:10 NASB

It was first discovered in animals, but humans have it too. When we sense danger, our bodies and brains are flooded with stress chemicals that cause us to either fight or flee. These chemicals turn off rational thought and focus on physical strength. It's the stuff that allows mothers to lift cars off children or carry a loved one from a burning building. The moment the danger has passed, these chemicals subside and allow us to return to our regular activities.

Unfortunately, because of sin in the world, these chemicals can be activated even when we are not in immediate danger. We can become fearful—fighting the feeling that something horrible is about to happen. This is called anxiety. Anxiety can be crippling and cause us to look around fearfully, waiting for a crisis. When we are plagued by anxiety, we feel weak, like we could fall. With God as our Father, we never have to fear. Anxiety is completely unnecessary because He promises to strengthen us and uphold us with His righteous right hand.

*Lord Jesus, I confess that I get anxious. I'm sometimes afraid
and distracted by worrisome thoughts. Help me to rest in
Your strength. Take my hand and help me. Amen.*

Day 113
LET GOD REIGN!

Oh, how great are God's riches and wisdom and knowledge!
How impossible it is for us to understand his decisions and his ways!
For who can know the LORD's thoughts? Who knows enough to give
him advice? And who has given him so much that he needs to pay
it back? For everything comes from him and exists by his power
and is intended for his glory. All glory to him forever! Amen.
ROMANS 11:33–36 NLT

It's easy for us to believe that we carry the world on our shoulders. We tend to believe, though we may not admit it, that we alone make the world turn. We convince ourselves that worry, finances, or power will put us in control. But in truth, God is the one who controls all.

What a blessed peace awaits us! As you go about your day, rest in the assurance that God, not you, is in control. God understands every feeling you experience, and He can comfort you. God knows the best steps for you to take in life, and He is willing to guide you. He is above all and knows all, yet He is not out of reach.

Set your eyes firmly on the Lord, and He will care for you.

Lord, please let this truth sink deep into my heart
today so that I may live in joy and peace. Please guide
me by Your wisdom and provide for me according to
Your riches. I praise You because You are good!

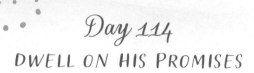

Day 114

DWELL ON HIS PROMISES

*Tell everyone about God's power. His majesty shines
down on Israel; his strength is mighty in the heavens.
God is awesome in his sanctuary. The God of Israel gives
power and strength to his people. Praise be to God!*
PSALM 68:34–35 NLT

Do you ever find yourself dreaming of a place of safety? A place where
you can close your eyes, rest your head, and let go of the stress and
angst that follow you around like a shadow? It rarely matters what
kind of season you are in—busy or calm—you always seem to feel
an inner longing to find a place where there is nothing but peace.

Before you move on to the next thing on the list, take a moment to
close your eyes. Don't reach for a book. Refuse to look at your phone.
Keep your thoughts from wandering away. And simply fix your heart
on the one who loves you. Think about His compassion. Dwell on His
promises. Consider His majesty and the army of angels He commands.
Have faith in the one He sent so you can forever be with Him.

Whether you need comfort, encouragement, or protection, He is
the answer. Look first in His direction for clarity and understanding.
He is close at hand and forever unchanging.

*Lord, thank You for showing me that You are my everything.
Through every day, through every year, I need only to fix
my eyes on You—the author and perfecter of my faith.*

Day 115
MORE JESUS

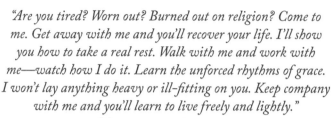

"Are you tired? Worn out? Burned out on religion? Come to me. Get away with me and you'll recover your life. I'll show you how to take a real rest. Walk with me and work with me—watch how I do it. Learn the unforced rhythms of grace. I won't lay anything heavy or ill-fitting on you. Keep company with me and you'll learn to live freely and lightly."
MATTHEW 11:28–30 MSG

When was the last time you had a real, honest-to-goodness rest? The kind that refreshes you both mentally and physically, that makes you feel completely revitalized and alive?

If that sounds like wishful thinking...if your mind tells you, *Yeah, right! I haven't had a good rest in at least ten years—and there's no end in sight for me!* ...take these words from Matthew 11 to heart. Jesus says, "Get away with me. . . . I'll show you how to take a real rest." What a promise!

Instead of more *busy* in your life, get more of *Jesus*. He is just what your weary soul needs. He will pull you from the depths of your day-to-day burnout and give you rest like you've never experienced it before—a rest that leads to free and light living! Praise Him!

Father God, rest giver, comfort my world-weary soul today. I am exhausted! I trust You to show me the way to refreshing rest. Thank You!

Day 116

SPIRIT — ENABLED

Declare his glory among the nations,
his marvelous works among all the peoples!
PSALM 96:3 ESV

"Sing to the LORD, praise his name; proclaim his salvation day after day," the psalmist said (Psalm 96:2 NIV). But, let's face it, some days we don't feel much like singing. We know God is great, yet our burdens seem greater. We lug their heavy weight with us everywhere until the burdens are the biggest thing in our lives. They would stay that way too if we were left on our own. But we are not on our own, not since one day centuries ago.

It was the day of Pentecost. Earlier, Jesus told His followers that they would be baptized with the Holy Spirit. Just what He meant, they likely didn't know. Then on that day they heard a sound like rushing wind, and flaming forked tongues rested on each of them. They were filled with the Holy Spirit! If that wasn't amazing enough, they also began speaking in different languages as the Spirit prompted them, declaring God's mighty works (Acts 2:1–4, 11). What they never imagined doing, the Spirit enabled them to do.

Still today, the Holy Spirit fills believers. Still the Spirit enables us to declare God's glory even in the bleakest times. Still He who is in us is greater than anything we encounter in life (see 1 John 4:4).

Holy Spirit, fill me so full that I can't help but sing out!

Day 117
HE CARRIES US

In his love and mercy he redeemed them. He lifted
them up and carried them through all the years.
Isaiah 63:9 nlt

Are you feeling broken today? Depressed? Defeated? Run to Jesus
and not away from Him.

When we suffer, He cries. Isaiah 63:9 (nlt) says, "In all their
suffering he also suffered, and he personally rescued them. In his love
and mercy he redeemed them. He lifted them up and carried them
through all the years."

He will carry us—no matter what pain we have to endure. No
matter what happens to us. God sent Jesus to be our Redeemer. He
knew the world would hate, malign, and kill Jesus. Yet He allowed
His very flesh to writhe in agony on the cross—so that we could also
become His sons and daughters. He loved me and you that much.

One day, we will be with Him. "Beloved," He will say, "no more
tears. No more pain." He will lift us up and hold us in His mighty
arms, and then He will show us His kingdom, and we will finally be
whole.

Lord Jesus, thank You for coming to us—for not abandoning us
when we are broken. Thank You for Your work on the cross, for Your
grace, mercy, and love. Help me to seek You even when I can't feel
You, to love You even when I don't know all the answers. Amen.

Day 118
A DEEP WELL

Love means doing what God has commanded us,
and he has commanded us to love one another,
just as you heard from the beginning.
2 JOHN 1:6 NLT

Trying to discover how best to serve and love God can sometimes be a struggle. The list of Christian duties can appear overwhelming: daily quiet time, prayer, church services, serving the community, evangelizing. And the list goes on. There might be times in your life when the most you can do is get out of bed in the morning and survive the day, let alone attempt these other tasks.

Thankfully, John boils it down for you in his second letter. In its simplest terms, loving God means doing as He commands. And He has commanded you to love others with long-suffering and selflessness.

But isn't this just another item on the list of duties? At first glance, it may seem like another burdensome task you will have to bear. However, you must never forget that the first step to truly fulfilling this command is accepting God's great love for you. Then you can take His hand and love Him right back. By drawing from this deep well of love, you will find that you are able to pour it into the lives of those around you. Because God first loved you, you now have the power to love others radically.

Let Your love fill my heart and spill over onto
others, God. Thank You for first loving me.

Day 119

EVERLASTING PEACE

*Peace I leave with you; My [own] peace I now give
and bequeath to you. Not as the world gives do I give to
you. Do not let your hearts be troubled, neither let them
be afraid. [Stop allowing yourselves to be agitated and
disturbed; and do not permit yourselves to be fearful
and intimidated and cowardly and unsettled.]*
JOHN 14:27 AMPC

Do you want to be free from worry and fear? Want to live a life filled
with peace and calm? Jesus holds the answer!

Yes, Jesus has left His peace with you. And this peace, *His* peace,
is not the kind of peace the world holds. His is a supernatural peace.
And it is found in the presence and strength of God and His Word.
But, you may be asking, *how can this be? How can I access this amazing
and unsurpassed peace Jesus talks about?* By calling on the Comforter,
a.k.a. the "Counselor, Helper, Intercessor, Advocate, Strengthener,
Standby" (John 14:26 AMPC). You know, the Holy Spirit, the one God
sent down in Jesus' name to teach you and remind you of things Jesus
has already told you in His Word (John 14:26).

Today, stop allowing yourself to be frightened and freaked out.
Instead, seek God's presence and receive His peace.

*Here I am, Lord, before You. Bless me,
pour upon me, Your everlasting peace.*

Day 120

IN THE DETAILS

He also asked, "What else is the Kingdom of God like?
It is like the yeast a woman used in making bread.
Even though she put only a little yeast in three measures
of flour, it permeated every part of the dough."
LUKE 13:20–21 NLT

Where is God? Where is His majesty, His miracles, the work of His hands in your life?

God is the morning sunrise when it's hidden by dewy fog. He's the oldest evergreen tree in the woods and the budding flower in spring. He's the comforting touch between spouses, the laughter with friends, and the kindness of strangers.

Jesus says the kingdom of God is in everything you see, touch, hear. His kingdom is in everything good. Like the yeast in bread, once it's added, it cannot be taken out or seen and counted, but you can see its effects. The dough rises with help of the yeast, whether it's seen or unseen.

God is like that yeast. He's always working in your life even when you don't see it or feel it. You simply have to trust that His will, His hand, and His way are in the details.

Dear God, I know You are with me. Even when I can't see
You. Even when I can't feel You. I trust that You have gone
ahead of me and are planning the way and guiding my
steps. I trust You, Lord, to know what is best. Amen.

Day 121
TESTED

Praise our God, all peoples, let the sound of his praise be heard;
he has preserved our lives and kept our feet from slipping.
PSALM 66:8–9 NIV

This is one of those psalms that sounds lovely—until you read a little bit further. The verses begin by rejoicing in the God who has "preserved our lives and kept our feet from slipping." But how did God do this? By testing His people: "You brought us into prison and laid burdens on our backs. You let people ride over our heads; we went through fire and water" (Psalm 66:11–12 NIV).

Doesn't sound like much fun, right? And surely those actions would not be on anyone's list of Top 10 Ways to Prevent Slips and Falls. But God works in mysterious ways indeed. Sometimes He carries you. But other times He pushes you to grow the strength you need to carry yourself. He's the ultimate trainer—seeing all your weaknesses and knowing exactly which muscles must be stretched to get you to your goal. Yet He pushes you even past that—past the small dreams you have into a place of abundance you could never imagine.

As you walk with Him today, consider the many times He has kept you from falling. Praise Him for testing you and refining you. Thank Him for laying burdens on you that in the end made you stronger.

God, stretch me, move me, push me, test me. Amen.

Day 122

UNSEEN BEAUTY

"Don't call me Naomi," she told them. "Call me Mara, because the Almighty has made my life very bitter. I went away full, but the LORD has brought me back empty. Why call me Naomi? The LORD has afflicted me; the Almighty has brought misfortune upon me."

RUTH 1:20–21 NIV

God has unseen beauty hidden amid trials. Naomi, whose name means "pleasant," poured out her sorrow to the women of Bethlehem, her hometown, in the scripture passage above. She lost her husband, her two sons, and her home for a second time. However, God shows throughout history that He heals both physically and spiritually. He gives beauty for ashes and joy for the spirit in distress. For Naomi, the answer was right beside her: her loyal daughter-in-law Ruth. Naomi, this old and tired woman, did not realize what happened would be used by God in His great rescue plan for humanity. In her confusion and despair, she was bitter; but El Shaddai, God Almighty, had everything under control. He used the death of Naomi's sons and her return to Bethlehem to bring Ruth and Boaz together. Otherwise, God would have used another family to be the ancestors of Jesus. God once again brought pleasantness to Naomi by giving her a new home and hope. Although she did not personally see the blessing of kingship that came to Boaz's great-grandson David, Naomi was an important part of God's great plan for the little town of Bethlehem.

El Shaddai, give Your daughters perseverance to trust in Your greater plan. Turn bitter and angry hearts to see Your work of redemption and reconciliation.

Day 123
WHAT ABOUT EVIL?

Let those who love the LORD hate evil, for he guards the lives of his faithful ones and delivers them from the hand of the wicked. Light shines on the righteous and joy on the upright in heart.
PSALM 97:10–11 NIV

We can pretend it isn't there. We can soften its blow by looking on the bright side. We can even escape it for brief moments via entertainment. But evil still exists—an undeniable, sad fact of a fallen world. If we can't deny it, how do we deal with it?

While we will never be okay with evil—we are in fact told to *hate* it—evil doesn't have to make us quake in our boots. When confronted with evil, we can find comfort in God. The Most High is watching over us. He is a guarding presence, a source of light and joy. He is the *only* lasting answer to evil. Social programs fail. Leaders let us down. The "gods" of money and ambition and stuff leave us empty. But those who trust in the Lord will not be put to shame.

Hold fast to the God who takes evil and redeems it (Genesis 50:20). Hold fast to the God who treads the heights and will one day trample evil for good.

Lord, these days it seems there's no stopping evil, yet evil is no match for You. Keep us safe in the evil days and hasten the good days ahead.

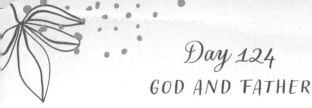

Day 124

GOD AND FATHER

The LORD reigns, let the nations tremble; he sits
enthroned between the cherubim, let the earth shake.
PSALM 99:1 NIV

God is our heavenly Father. He is a God who dries tears, who sends His Spirit to comfort us, who enfolds us in the shelter of His wings. He calls us to His side as a dad calls his children, and we can call back, "Abba—Daddy!" Yet He is more. He is God Almighty. "Great is the LORD," the psalmist wrote. "The LORD our God is holy" (Psalm 99:2, 9 NIV). God is lofty, and down here entire nations tremble and the earth shakes as a result.

When the Bible speaks of fearing God, it doesn't mean better-run-and-hide fear; it means the awe and respect that overcome us in God's presence. And that kind of fear actually ends the run-and-hide kind, no matter where it surfaces in our lives. How can that be? Because God is *both* mighty God *and* loving Father. He has the ability and desire to hear us whenever we pray—as well as the power and compassion to answer. He is holy and He is forgiving. He is the steady pillar that points out the way, all the while reminding us that we are not alone along the way. There's just no other God like Him!

God, I am amazed by all You are. And I am
so glad that You are my God and Father.

Day 125
X = JESUS

Thank God! The answer is in Jesus Christ our Lord.
ROMANS 7:25 NLT

In chapter 7 of Romans, Paul's words read like a long-winded and complicated word problem in a math textbook. Paul + Law + Sin = Bad. Paul + Law - Sin = Good. He continues to say he knows what's right but his human nature forces him to do wrong. It's an unending cycle of Good to Bad to Redemption to Good again and so on. . . . Paul asks helplessly if anyone will save him from this vicious circle of misery and death.

Then the apostle shares the answer he's found. The missing part of every equation Paul posed is Jesus. Jesus can save Paul from the cycle. Jesus + Paul = Forgiven and Saved. Jesus is the x, the cross that changes everything.

Jesus can be your answer too. He can be the answer to the grasp a sin has on your life. He can be the answer to that unending cycle of heartbreak, loneliness, anger, or sadness. He can encourage you toward the help you may need and the comfort you crave.

All you have to do is start adding Jesus to the equation.

Father, thank You for Jesus and what He's done—
saving me from eternity without You. And He now
wants to save me from the brokenness of this world.
Lord, although I might not get every answer I want on
this side of life, I know Jesus is the ultimate solution. Amen!

WORTH THE RISK

*All these died in faith, without receiving the promises. . .
having confessed that they were strangers and exiles on the
earth. For those who say such things make it clear that they are
seeking a country of their own. . . . That is, a heavenly one.*
HEBREWS 11:13–14, 16 NASB

On October 12, 1492, a sailor on the *Pinta* spotted land. Christopher
Columbus named it San Salvador, meaning "Holy Savior," to honor
the one who answered their prayers. By sailing to an unknown destination, Columbus braved the ocean with no assurance that he would
ever return home. He risked everything, trusting in Providence.

Several Bible people did likewise, as Hebrews 11 points out. We
can imitate their faith and risk our earthly lives for God and His
promises. Like Sarah, who considered God faithful (verse 11). Or
Moses, who considered "the reproach of Christ [to be] greater riches
than the treasures of Egypt" (verse 26 NASB).

Columbus' mission was also a journey of faith. Toward the end,
the needle on his compass had started pointing northwest instead
of to the North Star. His pilots grew fearful and anxious. Allegedly
they threatened to sail back to Spain, but Columbus convinced them
to press on.

In our spiritual voyage, we too are prone to fear. When the circumstances we see make us anxious, we must push on, "as though
seeing Him who is unseen" (verse 27 NASB). Someday we will land on
heavenly shores and know our hardships and hazards were worthwhile.

*Faithful Father, You promise to reward those who
diligently seek You. May I be one whose faith
pleases You and who endures to the end.*

Day 127
ONLY GOD

*For God alone my soul waits in silence; from him comes
my salvation. He alone is my rock and my salvation,
my fortress; I shall not be greatly shaken.*
PSALM 62:1–2 ESV

David, the author of today's psalm, knows only the Lord can save him from his enemies. He seeks rescue from nowhere, nothing, and no one else. Not allies. Not his own means. From God. Only God. And he believes God will come through for him.

David explains his situation: "Surely they intend to topple me from my lofty place; they take delight in lies. With their mouths they bless, but in their hearts they curse" (Psalm 62:4 NIV). Rumors are being spread about him. Nasty talk that will diminish his image, damage his relationships, and weaken his kingly rule.

Yet David understood that only God is his fortress of safety. The Lord is David's only firm foundation, the only place where he can stand strong in the midst of turmoil and "not be greatly shaken."

Just as God comforted David, God comforts us. If we continue to trust Him and follow His path, God's truth will prevail. He will show those that curse us, those that spread lies—and the ones that believe them—the truth of the matter.

> *Father, thank You for always looking out for me.
> You alone are my rock, salvation, fortress.
> With You in my life, I will not be shaken. Amen.*

Day 128

EVERLASTING LIGHT

In him was life, and that life was the light of
all mankind. The light shines in the darkness,
and the darkness has not overcome it.
JOHN 1:4–5 NIV

We all experience times of darkness in our lives. Depression may seep in through a crack of doubt, fear, or worry; and we spiral downward, focusing on the situation. It's not easy to lift our voices in anything but a moan and a plea for God's help. And He hears those cries; He wants to carry our burdens for us. He listens. It's we who should shift our gaze.

Focus on the fact that Jesus is the Light of the World who holds out wonderful hope for us. Set your prayer life to start with praise and adoration of the King of kings. Lift your voice in song, or read out loud from the Word. The light will eliminate the darkness every time. Keep your heart and mind set on Him as you walk through the day. Praise for every little thing; nothing is too small for God. Did you get a great parking spot? Thank Him. A raise at work? Thank Him. A terrible headache? Praise anyway. Concentrate on His goodness instead of your pain.

A grateful heart and constant praise will bring the light into your day.

Dear Lord, how we love You. We trust in You this day to
lead us on the right path lit with Your light. Amen.

Day 129
SHOUT FOR JOY

The desert and the parched land will be glad; the wilderness
will rejoice and blossom. Like the crocus, it will burst
into bloom; it will rejoice greatly and shout for joy.
ISAIAH 35:1–2 NIV

Is there any season as joyous as spring? The trees unfurl thousands of tiny, juicy green flags to wave hello to the world. Flowers make that final push through the dark soil and stretch out their bedecked arms to embrace the sun-warmed air. Farmers plant seeds of promise into the brown, barren land—measuring out hope by the bushel.

You are human. You will go through times of sorrow and despair, times of suffering and boredom. You will work through long days and toss and turn through longer nights. You will worry and fret and stew. You will look around and see only gray.

But spring is our annual reminder that the story isn't over. It's never over. It starts up from page 1 again every year, ready to be filled with characters and plots and dialogue. No, the story won't always be happy, and the characters won't all get along. But isn't it amazing that it happens at all? That our Creator God is willing to keep writing new chapters for us? And that He never runs out of ideas?

A new story every spring starts right before your eyes. Now that's something to shout about.

Dear Lord, thank You for Your endless creativity that brings
us so much grace and joy. Help me remember in the grayest
times that color is just an inch or so under my feet.

Day 130

LIFE PRESERVERS

My comfort in my suffering is this:
Your promise preserves my life.
Psalm 119:50 niv

It's the law for boaters in many states: always wear your life preserver. The purpose is simple. A life preserver keeps people afloat—and their heads above water—should they accidentally fall overboard. The device's buoyancy can even keep an unconscious person afloat in a face-up position as long as it's worn properly.

In the difficulties of life, God is our life preserver. When we are battered by the waves of trouble, we can expect God to understand and to comfort us in our distress. His Word, like a buoyant life preserver, holds us up in the bad times.

But the life preserver only works if you put it on *before* your boat sinks. To get into God's life jacket, put your arms into the sleeves of prayer and tie the vest with biblical words. God will surround you with His love and protection—even if you're unconscious of His presence. He promises to keep our heads above water in the storms of living.

Preserving God, I cling to You as my life preserver.
Keep my head above the turbulent water so I
don't drown. Bring me safely to the shore.

Day 131
KING FOREVER

You, O God, are my king from ages past,
bringing salvation to the earth.
PSALM 74:12 NLT

Sometimes it seems like every part of our lives is affected by change. From the economy and headline news to friendships and family relationships, nothing ever seems to stay the same. Even our leaders are in a constant state of flux. Every election cycle we see politicians come and go. Generation after generation, monarchs succeed their elders to the throne. Ministers move from one church to the next, and bosses get promotions or transfers.

These changes can leave us feeling unsteady in the present and uncertain about the future. With more questions than answers, we wonder how these new leaders will handle their roles.

It's different in God's kingdom. He's the King now, just as He was in the days of Abraham. His reign will continue until the day His Son returns to earth, and then on into eternity. We can rely—absolutely depend on—His unchanging nature. Take comfort in the stability of the King—He's our leader now and forever!

Almighty King, You are my rock. When my world is in turmoil
and changes swirl around me, You are my anchor and my
center of balance. Thank You for never changing. Amen.

Day 132

THE MOST HIGH

God is within her, she will not fall;
God will help her at break of day.
PSALM 46:5 NIV

Psalm 46 is filled with this beautiful imagery of a city surrounded by "a river whose streams make glad the city of God" (verse 4 NIV).

How do you picture this city? High stone walls? A moat? Guards with arrows ready to attack enemies on sight? When you think of a city that cannot be defeated, you may think of the cautionary and military measure it will take to keep it safe. But the writer doesn't describe the city this way but notes only that "God is within her." No guns or tanks or armies.

The Most High dwells in that city, and because of that, it cannot be destroyed or conquered by any outside forces.

The presence of God anywhere changes everything. He has unlimited power, unending protection; He never sleeps and never falters. He is the ultimate protector of His creation, including His daughters. When the Most High dwells in you, you cannot be defeated. When your heart is full of His love, you cannot be conquered and put down by this world. Hard times will come, and you may be hurt, but you can find comfort that He is with you and fighting beside you.

Great Protector, thank You for fighting for me.
Go before me today into the battles I will face. Amen.

Day 133

OPEN THE BOOK

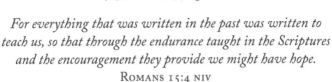

For everything that was written in the past was written to teach us, so that through the endurance taught in the Scriptures and the encouragement they provide we might have hope.

ROMANS 15:4 NIV

"Out with the old and in with the new!" is unfortunately some Christians' philosophy about the Bible. Yet the Old Testament scriptures are vital to every believer. We cannot understand the power of the New Testament until we embrace the teachings, wisdom, and moral laws of God revealed in the Old Testament. After all, the Old Testament points directly to the coming of the Messiah, Jesus, and our salvation.

The apostle Paul reminds us that everything in the Bible was written with purpose—to teach us that through our trials and the encouragement of God's Word we might have hope.

Life is tough, after all. We get discouraged and, at times, disheartened to the point of such despair it's hard to recover. Yet the Word of God ignites the power of a positive, godly fire within.

Reading *all* of God's Word is paramount. It is the source of hope, peace, encouragement, salvation, and so much more. It moves people to take action while diminishing depression and discouragement. As the writer of Hebrews put it, "For the word of God is alive and active. Sharper than any double-edged sword" (Hebrews 4:12 NIV).

Need some encouragement? Open the Book.

Lord, help me read Your Word consistently to empower me with the hope and encouragement I need. Amen.

Day 134

FINDING SHELTER IN THE STORMS

I love you, Lord; you are my strength. The Lord is my rock,
my fortress, and my savior; my God is my rock, in whom
I find protection. He is my shield, the power that saves
me, and my place of safety. I called on the Lord, who is
worthy of praise, and he saved me from my enemies.
Psalm 18:1–3 nlt

How do you typically react when life's storms are raging around you? Imagine receiving a dreaded phone call with someone's news of failing health. Or finding a lifelong friend has unexpectedly turned her back on you. Or discovering a beloved child has made another poor life choice.

Do you cower in fear? Are you drained of all hope, not knowing where to turn for safety and shelter? Or do you look up to your protector—the almighty God—who is a rock, a fortress, a savior who won't allow you to be enveloped by the pelting rain and gale-force winds?

When you have accepted Jesus as Lord and leader of your life, you have a protector on standby. He's waiting and ready to step in and provide shelter, a safe place where you will find strength and security just when you need it most. Call out to Him, and He will see you through the storm. Hold tightly to Him today!

Father, You are worthy of all my praise. In You
I find the peace and protection my soul craves.

Day 135
STAND STILL, FIRST

And as they were going down to the outskirts of the city,
Samuel said to Saul, Bid the servant pass on before
us—and he passed on—but you stand still, first,
that I may cause you to hear the word of God.
1 SAMUEL 9:27 AMPC

We're busy women, not just at home and at work, but in our church and community. Sometimes we may feel like we're being pulled in a thousand different directions, making it difficult to get our minds on God. Yet only when we're focused on Him will we be entertaining the right thoughts, speaking words of healing, and following the plan, walking the road God has set before us.

Today and every day, before you take one step, stand still. Take the time to open up your mind and heart to seek, to hear the Word of God. To pray and ask for His help in playing your part in His plan. Then you will remember who and what the Lord is in your life—your rock, Redeemer, comforter, cheerleader, peace, joy, love, and light. Your reason for being.

Woman of the Way, stand still, first.

Here I am, Lord, standing before You. My mind, heart,
spirit, and soul await You in stillness. Tell me what You
would have me know, think, do, and say today.

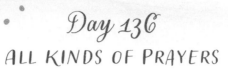

Day 136

ALL KINDS OF PRAYERS

*But you, O Lord, are a God of compassion and mercy,
slow to get angry and filled with unfailing love and
faithfulness. Look down and have mercy on me. Give your
strength to your servant; save me, the son of your servant.
Send me a sign of your favor. Then those who hate me will
be put to shame, for you, O LORD, help and comfort me.*
PSALM 86:15–17 NLT

There are all kinds of prayers. There are those that are filled with praise and thanksgiving. Or perhaps we offer our song or dance or written words as a kind of prayer. There are supplications, asking for various needs to be met. There are appeals for forgiveness, or we might simply bask in the Lord's presence and listen for Him to speak to us. Or we might remind the Lord how much we love Him! Then, sometimes, there are pleas that come from the depths of our being.

Psalms is full of those lamenting kinds of petitions, and always, God is there. When those deepest cries of our souls rise up, when enemies threaten us, and when all seems lost, may we remember and reach out to the one who's known throughout all time for His divine compassion and mercy, His love and faithfulness.

*Thank You, Lord, for Your mercy and
compassion. Please hear my prayer. Amen.*

Day 137
EXCHANGING OUR FAILURE FOR HIS GRACE

This is the day which the LORD has made;
let's rejoice and be glad in it.
PSALM 118:24 NASB

Have you ever wondered how a perfectly good day can get so messed up?

The answer can usually be laid down to human behavior. All it takes is a sharp word to a family member or an unhelpful attitude or an unkind action and the situation quickly degenerates. Personal failure has odd tentacles. The guilty feeling from knowing the problem was self-instigated fosters a desire to shift the blame and then in the end leads to self-incriminating despair at again being the cause of strife.

Human relationships, while having the strength to withstand much trauma, are remarkably fragile when it comes to insult. Friends and spouses and children can be hurt greatly when we are careless with our words and attitudes. So how do we fix the day?

We can turn to our God who is the essence of redemption. Since He sent Jesus to redeem our souls, He is able also to redeem even the smallest earthly concern. Coming to Him for mercy is the first step in righting the wrong. Exchanging our failure for His grace reminds us that all is not lost. The day is His, after all, and He offers the hope we need to live it through to the end.

Father God, thank You for Your abundant mercy and
constant grace. Redeem my failures today and help
me not to repeat them. In Jesus' name, amen.

Day 138

HONESTY IN PRAYER

Hezekiah became terminally ill. The prophet Isaiah son of
Amoz came and said to him, "This is what the LORD says:
'Put your affairs in order, for you are about to die; you will
not recover.'" Then Hezekiah turned his face to the wall and
prayed to the LORD, "Please LORD, remember how I have
walked before You faithfully and wholeheartedly and have
done what pleases You." And Hezekiah wept bitterly.
2 KINGS 20:1–3 HCSB

Sometimes we struggle to embrace what we believe God is telling us. It may feel too scary. It may be miles out of our comfort zone or trigger deep insecurities. It might remind us of other times we've tried and failed. Perhaps we wonder if it's really God's voice we're hearing.

When Hezekiah received a distressing word from God through the prophet Isaiah, he immediately prayed. In that moment, his faith took over and Hezekiah went right to the throne room. Through his tears, this righteous king of Judah took his pain and angst to the only one who could bring comfort. He was vulnerable in his pleading with his Creator.

When you hear a word from God, will prayer be your immediate response? Have you invested in your relationship with God to where you can be honest with Him?

Lord, mature my trust in You and Your Word so that I will
feel confident in being vulnerable before You, even honest
about my feelings about Your plans for my life. Amen.

Day 139
PROMISES HELD TRUE

"For I know the plans I have for you," declares the LORD,
"plans to prosper you and not to harm you,
plans to give you hope and a future."
JEREMIAH 29:11 NIV

Unimaginable. That must describe the hopelessness the disciples felt as they saw their Master die on the cross. All the promises they held dear—all their feelings of hopeful expectation—were shot down with those final words: "It is finished."

Some of Jesus' followers may have remembered His earlier words assuring them of His return. But in the face of certain death, those words of victorious life must have been hard to accept.

We all experience moments of hopelessness in our earthly journeys. The death of our dreams, the crashing down of our hopes, the promises of God seemingly unfulfilled. . . We are no more immune to disappointment than Jesus' disciples were.

In the end, though, Jesus' promises held true—He did prevail no matter how dark that first Good Friday looked. We can always trust the words of our Lord. He knows the plans He has for us, and He has the power to see them through.

Hope and a future, prosperity and peace—we can trust that, even when things seem hopeless, God is still at work, carrying out His promises.

Thank You, Jesus, for being at work in my life.
Thank You for having a perfect plan and for keeping
Your promises. Give me faith to believe in You even
when it seems like everything is going wrong.

Day 140
AMAZING GRACE

I have strayed like a lost sheep. Seek your servant,
for I have not forgotten your commands.
PSALM 119:176 NIV

You have probably sung the classic hymn "Amazing Grace" many times. Its lyrics echo the sentiment of today's verse: "I once was lost but now am found." These words are a comfort because they give hope. The author, like the strayed sheep, was lost. But, through prayer and God's "amazing grace," no one remains alone. His lost and humble servants become found through faith.

If you stray from the right path, you may find yourself confused, disoriented. It is easy to lose your sense of direction in this troubled world. Many are the times you may feel separated from the flock and struggling to find your way back. You may for some time continue to wander further and further away, unaware of how to return.

Little lamb, know this: God will always look for you. Just do what you can to keep the faith, to follow the commands God has laid down in His Word. No matter how alone you may feel, know God is watching for you. Keep His teachings in your heart. And pray. He will hear. He will seek you out.

Dear God, rescue me when I stray from Your path.
Seek me out. Show me the way to return home to You.

Day 141
FILL 'ER UP

May the God of hope fill you with all joy and peace
as you trust in him, so that you may overflow
with hope by the power of the Holy Spirit.
ROMANS 15:13 NIV

Have you ever looked down at your gas gauge while driving and realized your tank was dangerously low? You have two choices in this scenario: you can either fill your tank with gas or keep driving, which means you'll eventually run out of gas completely. Certainly, the former is the best choice.

A similar scenario can occur in your walk of faith. Sometimes your spiritual tank may seem near overflowing. But then something may drastically drain you—maybe some unexpected bad news or a daunting task. Suddenly the low energy indicator light is flashing in your mind and you find you've nothing left to give.

Take heart! The apostle Paul has already put a prayer out there to cover you, asking that God would *fill* you with joy and peace by trusting in God so that your spiritual tank will be *overflowing* by the power of the Holy Spirit.

God is there for you with a spiritual fill-up anytime you need it. To access His supply, simply close your eyes and pray for His Spirit to fill you up—and hope, joy, and peace *will* be restored in you.

Dear God, please keep my tank of hope, joy,
and peace filled to overflowing as I trust in You.

Day 142
NIGHTTIME PRAISE

Now praise the LORD, all you servants of the LORD who stand in the LORD's house at night! Lift up your hands in the holy place and praise the LORD! May the LORD, Maker of heaven and earth, bless you from Zion.
PSALM 134:1–3 HCSB

When you need a faith-lift, when you need to raise your spirit, free your soul, and get closer to God, praise Him. At night. In the wee hours. When it's just you and the Lord.

Lift your hands where you stand.

You don't have to be in a church. Wherever you meet God, wherever you feel the Spirit's presence, wherever you sense the breath of Jesus, you are in a holy place. There in that moment, praise Him. Tell the one who has formed you, the one who walks beside you, the one who protects, provides, blesses, and calms you, how much you love Him, need Him, and are in awe of Him. Perhaps better yet, say nothing at all. Just sense the joy of lingering in His presence, in His light and love. Commune with Him. Hope in Him. Merge with Him. Lose yourself in Him.

Then, when your body urges you to find a place of rest and you head to bed, close your eyes, knowing that the Lord, the Maker of heaven and heart, earth and expectations, has blessed you.

*Lord, Maker of my heart, soul, spirit,
and mind, to You I lift my hands in praise!*

Day 143

JOY OVERFLOWING

*Then will the lame leap like a deer, and the
mute tongue shout for joy. Water will gush forth
in the wilderness and streams in the desert.*
ISAIAH 35:6 NIV

Joy flows when there is something to celebrate—like when a lame man can miraculously run, a mute finds her voice, or water gushes forth in a barren land.

God provides the miracle of streams in the arid patches of our lives. Are you in a desert that appears hopeless? Are there circumstances in your life that seem dry and barren? Are you desperate for faith, hope, and love to splash around you like a river in the desert?

God's love is a constant and steady stream. This is a difficult truth to cling to when grief is the sun that parches you each morning. Trust God to break forth with water in your wilderness. Watch for it with hope. God will show you Himself in all His glory. He'll "strengthen the feeble hands, steady the knees that give way; say to those with fearful hearts, 'Be strong, do not fear; your God will come. . .he will come to save you'" (Isaiah 35:3–4 NIV). When you determine to look to God with hope amid great trials and have learned to trust Him in the process, you'll find you have a greater capacity for joy.

*God, please send those waters of restoration and joy into
my day. Give me strength to watch for Your glory.*

Day 144

THE SON OF GOD STANDS WITH YOU

*Nebuchadnezzar said, Blessed be the God of Shadrach,
Meshach, and Abednego, Who has sent His angel and delivered
His servants who believed in, trusted in, and relied on Him!
And they set aside the king's command and yielded their bodies
rather than serve or worship any god except their own God.*

DANIEL 3:28 AMPC

Stolen from their home and taken into captivity as teens, Shadrach, Meshach, and Abednego were dedicated to God. When commanded to bow down to the king's golden idol, they refused to violate the laws of God—even if it cost them their lives.

These three young men stood shoulder to shoulder in faith, knowing God would rescue them from the flames of the fiery furnace if He chose. Imagine how they drew courage and strength from one another, trusting God in this dreadful situation.

It can be difficult to stand for what you truly believe and trust God, but it makes it a little easier when you don't have to go it alone. Shadrach, Meshach, and Abednego walked through the flames together, and though they had each other, they had another with them who, to the king, looked like the Son of God.

You never have to walk through flames alone. Trust that the Son of God stands with you.

*Heavenly Father, thank You for sending Your Son
to stand with me in the fiery times of my life. I trust
that I never have to go through anything alone.*

Day 145
DESPERATE FAITH

And He said to her, "Daughter, your faith has made you
well. Go in peace, and be healed of your affliction."
MARK 5:34 NKJV

When Jesus healed the woman with the hemorrhage, He commended her faith. She had exhausted all her resources on doctors to no avail. Without addressing Jesus at all, she simply got near Him in a crowd and touched His clothes. Instantly His power healed her, and He knew that she had reached out to Him in a way no one else in the pressing throng had. What was unusual about this woman's touch? Why would Jesus commend her faith?

Maybe in her touch He felt her complete emptiness and need. She had nowhere else to turn. He was the source of healing power. Her faith was an act of utter dependence; it was Jesus or nothing.

Proverbs 3:5 tells us to trust in the Lord with all our hearts and not lean on our understanding. This is hard to do, since we prefer to trust in the Lord along with our own understanding of how things should work out. Though we are given minds to read, think, and reason, ultimately our faith comes from abandoning hope in ourselves and risking all on Jesus.

Lord, I am often blind to my own weakness and my need
of You. Help me to trust You the way this sick woman did.

Day 146

THE LIGHTNESS OF JOY

*He gets angry once in a while, but across a lifetime
there is only love. The nights of crying your eyes out
give way to days of laughter. . . . You changed wild
lament into whirling dance; you ripped off my black
mourning band and decked me with wildflowers.*

PSALM 30:5, 11 MSG

Because you have God in your life, any sorrows you may suffer are
transient, temporary. But the joy you have in God, in Jesus, and in
the Spirit is persistent, eternal. And all you can do is laugh! For you
know that your tears will fade. They will quickly dry up in the light
of the morning. You'll find yourself willingly and easily praising God
for bringing you out of the darkness of troubles and sorrow and back
into the peace and lightness of joy.

How wonderful that after you pray to God, relating all your worries
and woes, He turns things around for you. He changes your funeral
dirge into a song and dance of celebration. He tears off your black
mourning band and showers you with flowers. Next thing you know,
you're bursting into songs of thanksgiving and praise of Him.

If you find yourself in the depths of sorrow and despair, go to
the one who can pull you up out of darkness and into the joy of the
morning light.

*Lord, as I pray, take away my sorrows of the night and
lead me with the joy of Your morning light. Amen.*

Day 147
DEEP WATERS

*He reached down from on high and took
hold of me; he drew me out of deep waters.*
PSALM 18:16 NIV

Have you ever been in a really dark place? Maybe you lost a husband or a child and drifted into a deep depression, one you couldn't seem to pull yourself out of. Or maybe you were badly hurt by someone you trusted and sank to the depths after the fact.

Life has a way of tugging us downward. And sometimes, despite our best efforts, we have a hard time digging our way out. That's why it's so comforting to read today's verse. What we cannot do, God can.

Don't you just love the imagery here? God takes His hand, reaches down, and grabs hold of you when you're in the depths. He doesn't leave you there. He offers a way out. Then, (no matter how hard you kick or scream) He "draws" you out.

There's something special about that word *draws*, isn't there? God doesn't yank you out. He doesn't holler and say, "Get out of there!" He gently, lovingly eases you out of the pit and sets your feet on solid ground. And when you're standing on the rock (Jesus), you won't be shaken!

*Oh Lord, I'm so grateful for the many times You extended
a hand my way. When I couldn't lift myself, You were right
there, drawing me out. It's Your name I praise. Amen.*

Day 148
YOUR RESCUER

Break the arms of these wicked, evil people! Go after them until the last one is destroyed. The LORD is king forever and ever! The godless nations will vanish from the land. LORD, you know the hopes of the helpless. Surely you will hear their cries and comfort them. You will bring justice to the orphans and the oppressed, so mere people can no longer terrify them.
PSALM 10:15–18 NLT

Have you ever felt completely and utterly helpless because of the hurt someone has caused you? Just. . .stuck. With nowhere to turn?

Maybe you've been bullied. . .cheated on. . .beat down. . .by someone you love or by an acquaintance or even by a stranger. And maybe you felt like no one had your back. No one was there to pick you up, dust you off, and breathe new life into your weary soul. If this is part of your story, sister, there is hope! As Psalm 10 states: "LORD, you know the hopes of the helpless. Surely you will hear their cries and comfort them" (verse 17 NLT).

And this same Lord Jesus promises to deliver you today. For He is your rescuer. . .the justice bringer. When you know Him as your Lord and Savior, you never need to feel helpless or hopeless again. Thank Him today for bringing you peace and comfort. . .for offering the ultimate deliverance from hard things: heaven, your glorious and final destination!

Lord Jesus, I look forward to the promise of heaven!

Day 149
REFUSE TO QUIT

*And I will pray the Father, and he shall give you
another Comforter, that he may abide with you for ever;
even the Spirit of truth; whom the world cannot receive,
because it seeth him not, neither knoweth him: but ye know
him; for he dwelleth with you, and shall be in you.*
JOHN 14:16–17 KJV

There are days when it seems that nothing goes right and you struggle just to put one foot in front of the other. The good news on a day like that is the truth that you are not alone. Whatever obstacle is in your way, you don't have to overcome it in your own power. God is with you. Jesus sent the Comforter. The Holy Spirit is your present help in any situation.

The Holy Spirit is the very Spirit of God Himself. He is with you always, ready to care for and guide you. By faith you can rest and rely on the Holy Spirit for strength, wisdom, and inspiration.

The next time you feel like giving up, refuse to quit. Ask the Holy Spirit to intervene, to provide you with the strength and wisdom to continue your journey.

*Jesus, You have sent the Comforter to me. I believe He is
with me always, providing what I need today to refuse
to quit. I take the next step in my journey knowing He
is with me. I can press on by faith today. Amen.*

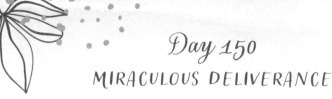

Day 150
MIRACULOUS DELIVERANCE

He brought me out into a spacious place;
he rescued me because he delighted in me.
PSALM 18:19 NIV

God miraculously delivered the Israelites from the waters of the Red Sea. He took them to the promised land of Canaan, which was rich and flowing with milk and honey. But He did not do this immediately. The Israelites had been in bondage for four hundred years in Egypt. God heard their cry. He saw their oppression. The Bible tells us that the Lord came down and rescued them. He does the same for us today. It may be that you have been in a hard place for a long time, so long that you have nearly given up on God. You may not believe that He will come for you, that He even wants to rescue you. The Israelites felt this way also. God is still in the business of rescuing His own today. When He saves you out of a depressed and sorrowful situation, He will take you to a new place. From Egypt to Canaan, so to speak. Have you sought God's deliverance? Be diligent in prayer. In His timing, God will answer your plea, just as He did for the Israelites. You are His child. Even while you remain in the desert, He can refresh your soul. Seek Him. He delights in you.

Father, help me to have faith that You know what is
best for me. Hear my cry from my own personal Egypt
today. I need to know that You delight in me. Amen.

Day 151
G.R.A.C.E.

Because he was full of grace and truth,
from him we all received one gift after another.
JOHN 1:16 NCV

Perhaps you've seen the acronym for G.R.A.C.E. (God's Riches at Christ's Expense). What does that mean to us, His daughters? We face all sorts of challenges and sometimes feel depleted. Dry. In those moments, all of God's riches (peace, joy, long-suffering, favor, help) are ours. What did we do to deserve them? Nothing. That's the point of grace: someone else paid the price so that we could receive God's gifts for free.

Take a good look at today's scripture. God promises not only to give grace and truth but one gift after another. Picture yourself as a little girl at your daddy's knee. Now picture him giving you not one gift. . .not two. . .but one on top of the other on top of the other. He overwhelms you with his beautifully wrapped gifts, topped off with ribbons and bows. Talk about blowing your socks off!

God does the same thing when He "gifts" us with things we don't deserve: forgiveness, comfort, satisfaction, provision. What a generous God we serve!

Father, I know that I haven't done anything to deserve
Your grace. . .Your gifts. And yet, You continue to pour these
things out on my life anyway. Thank You for Your grace,
Lord. You give, and give, and then give some more.

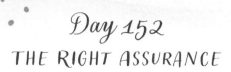

Day 152
THE RIGHT ASSURANCE

And we know that all things work together for good to them that love God, to them who are the called according to his purpose.
Romans 8:28 KJV

"God won't give me more than I can handle." You hear this phrase a lot. Is it true? Does the Bible say this?

The origin of this phrase is 1 Corinthians 10:13 (NKJV), which is actually dealing with the idea of temptation and says that God "will not allow you to be tempted beyond what you are able, but with the temptation will also make the way of escape, that you may be able to bear it."

Sadly, this verse is used by many who do not know Christ but find some measure of mental comfort in the idea that, no matter what they are experiencing, even if it is the consequences of sinful choices, God is not allowing them to bear too much. This just isn't so. Proverbs 13:15 (KJV) declares that "the way of transgressors is hard." The crushing consequences of sin will break you and cast you aside.

Only the ones who are following Christ can lay claim to the promise that God will work all things together for good. Those who trust and obey can rest in the assurance that everything (the good and the bad) fits together in the pattern He has laid out for them.

Lord, thank You for helping me bear my burdens and for keeping track of the things in my life. I know You are working all things for my good. In Jesus' name, amen.

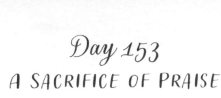

Day 153
A SACRIFICE OF PRAISE

*"Spread for me a banquet of praise, serve High God
a feast of kept promises, and call for help when you're
in trouble—I'll help you, and you'll honor me."*
PSALM 50:14–15 MSG

There are times in life when our faith wavers and we're not sure what we believe anymore. It's easy to trust God when everything in life is going well or when you've experienced a miracle. Maybe a loved one has been healed of a disease. Or maybe you've just witnessed the miracle of birth. Or had a mountaintop experience with God in His creation. It's easier to trust God when you can see the tangible evidence that He is working in your life.

But what about when life is dark? What about when a loved one isn't healed or financial burdens are wreaking havoc in your life? Is God still there?

In Hebrews 13:15 (NIV), God's Word tells us, "Through Jesus, therefore, let us continually offer to God a sacrifice of praise—the fruit of lips that openly profess his name." To sacrifice in worship means to have faith in God even when you don't feel like it. Even when you can't see Him anymore. The only way we can do that is through the power of Christ working in our lives in each moment. Because of the cross, we can rise above our circumstances and trust that the God of heaven has purpose for everything that comes our way. We are able to look at situations from God's perspective and trust Him no matter what.

*God, please increase my faith so that I can trust You
and worship You despite my circumstances. Amen.*

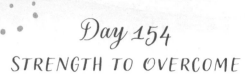

STRENGTH TO OVERCOME

*Then Hannah prayed and said: "My heart rejoices
in the LORD; in the LORD my horn is lifted high.
My mouth boasts over my enemies, for I delight in your
deliverance. There is no one holy like the LORD; there is
no one besides you; there is no Rock like our God."*

1 SAMUEL 2:1–2 NIV

Hannah was filled with sorrow because she could not have children;
and her husband's other wife taunted her because of this. Even though
Hannah was the favorite wife (her name means "favored"), she still
longed to be a mother. So she brought her suffering heart before God
in prayer, and God graciously answered. He gave her a son, whom she
named Samuel. He became one of the greatest judges and prophets
of the Old Testament. God did not stop there. He also gave her five
other children after Samuel. In the scripture passage above, the word
horn means "strength." Hannah acknowledges that Jehovah God is
her strength. In her deepest pain and overwhelming despair, she first
turned to God. His answer filled the longing in her heart and drew
her to a deeper worship of God. He is the only one who can give
strength to overcome the worries of this world. God calls His children
to seek deliverance from their burdens only in Him because any other
option is futile and fleeting.

*Rock of Ages, help Your children to rejoice in You as their
strength. Keep us from trusting in ourselves, and remind
us that You answer prayers, often in unexpected ways.*

Day 155
COMFORTED BY GOD

*Shout for joy, you heavens; rejoice, you earth; burst into
song, you mountains! For the LORD comforts his people
and will have compassion on his afflicted ones.*
ISAIAH 49:13 NIV

Comfort feels wonderful in a time of distress. It's like a warm blanket wrapped around a cold and lonely feeling. How do you comfort yourself? Perhaps you take a walk, bake a cake, or clean your house. Yet those things may fall short of your goal. Not to worry. For God is the best at helping you feel better. Second Corinthians 1:3 (NIV) calls Him the "God of all comfort."

David, the psalmist, considered God his Shepherd, writing, "Your rod and your staff, they comfort me" (Psalm 23:4 NIV). David, once a shepherd himself, used his rod to count his sheep, his staff to guide them. He knew those tools brought his sheep *comfort*, which means to strengthen, as the word *fort* in com*fort* implies.

And God doesn't just provide comfort. He is also the God of compassion, the Good Shepherd who never leaves one little lost lamb out in the cold night. In fact, He keeps a list of our tears (Psalm 56:8).

God's comfort for and compassion on the afflicted are a reason for praise. Creation joins in the song of joy. Will you worship along with the mountains today?

*God of all comfort, I am grateful for Your heart of compassion
for me. Strengthen me as I join in creation's song.*

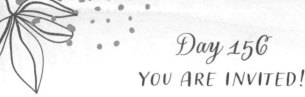

Day 156
YOU ARE INVITED!

*Let us then approach God's throne of grace
with confidence, so that we may receive mercy
and find grace to help us in our time of need.*
HEBREWS 4:16 NIV

It's always exciting to receive an invitation, whether it's for a party or a wedding or a graduation. It's nice to be welcomed to a happy event or opportunity.

With that in mind, you will be delighted to learn that God has given you an open invitation to approach His throne of grace with confidence. And not just on good days but especially when times get tough! You do not have to be afraid, for God states clearly you will receive both mercy and grace in your time of need.

God's throne room is a reception hall like no other. There you receive His infinite mercy and grace not because of anything you did but because you are in need. And with this mercy and grace comes peace. "Grace and peace be yours in abundance through the knowledge of God and of Jesus our Lord" (2 Peter 1:2 NIV).

How comforting to know God's mercy, grace, and peace come hand in hand. How will you RSVP to God's invitation to approach His throne of grace?

*Dear Lord, I thank You for Your grace, which works
through me to regenerate and sanctify me and inspires
me to persevere during good times and in bad.*

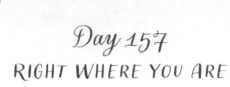

Day 157
RIGHT WHERE YOU ARE

*For consider your calling, brothers and sisters, that there were not
many wise according to the flesh, not many mighty, not many
noble; but God has chosen the foolish things of the world.*
1 CORINTHIANS 1:26–27 NASB

Once my life is running smoothly. . .
If I didn't have toddlers underfoot. . .
As soon as I get this anger problem under control. . .
When I get enough money. . .
*As soon as I (*fill in the blank*). . .then I can be used by God.*

We are *where* we are, *when* we are because our Father chose us for
such a time as this. Our steps are ordered by Him. Whether He has
called us to teach a Sunday school class, pray with other women, lead
a Bible study, or sing in the choir—we need not wait for the ideal time
and place to serve Him. The only "ideal" is where you are right now.

God delights in using His people—right in the middle of all that
appears crazy and wrong and hopeless. *Now* is the time to serve God,
not next week or next year or when things get better. He wants our
cheerful, obedient service right in the midst of—even in spite of—our
difficult circumstances.

*Father, help me see that there is no "ideal" place
or circumstance to serve You. You can, and will,
use me right where I am. Thank You that I do not
have to have it all together to be used by You.*

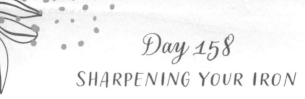

Day 158
SHARPENING YOUR IRON

As iron sharpens iron, so one person sharpens another.
PROVERBS 27:17 NIV

God never designed us to travel this journey of life alone. We need community. The book of Hebrews says we need to spur each other on to good works. We also need each other for accountability.

God uses other people to grow our character. Other people stretch us and challenge us. They point out our blind spots. They may make us uncomfortable at times.

Sometimes our churches are too big for us to develop true community, which is best done in smaller groups. Serving at church through various ministries or getting involved in a small group or Sunday school class is a good way to find community. Not every group will be a good fit, but don't give up. Pray and ask God to show you where you belong.

In a community group you can deepen your knowledge of worship and the Bible. You can reach out to your broader community and serve as a group. You can support each other with prayer and share each other's burdens. God will use these people to bring you closer to Him.

Dear Jesus, You prayed that we would be one as You and the Father are one. Help us to find the community You want us to be united with. Open our hearts to let others in, and make us willing to grow and let others speak into our lives. Show us how we can impact Your kingdom when we work with others. Amen.

Day 159

CONTINUAL CARE

*Immediately the [Holy] Spirit [from within] drove Him
out into the wilderness (desert), and He stayed in the
wilderness (desert) forty days, being tempted [all the while]
by Satan; and He was with the wild beasts, and the
angels ministered to Him [continually]. . . . Jesus said
to them, Come after Me and be My disciples.*
MARK 1:12–13, 17 AMPC

From the very beginning, God wanted us to be like Jesus, to follow
His example and walk in His way. And although that may be a huge
challenge, remember the tasks God gives you are also the tasks for
which He equips you (Hebrews 13:21). In other words, in all the challenges you face, you have a God who makes sure you have resources
on which to rely.

After Jesus was baptized and the Holy Spirit lit on Him like a
dove, that same Spirit drove Him into the wilderness where He was
surrounded by wild beasts. There He stayed for over a month, all the
while being teased and tempted by Satan. Talk about a challenge!

Yet Jesus remained unshaken. For not only was God the Spirit
with Him but God the Father had sent angels to take care of Him
continually!

The next time you feel you're out in the wilderness among the
beasts, surrounded by a myriad of temptations, don't crumble. Instead,
take courage. For God has already equipped you with the Spirit and
His caretaking angels.

*Thank You, Lord, for equipping me with
a calling as well as comforters! Amen.*

Day 160

PLAN NOT SUBJECT TO CHANGE

They plot injustice and say, "We have devised a perfect plan!"
Surely the human mind and heart are cunning. But God
will shoot them with his arrows; they will suddenly be struck
down. . . . The righteous will rejoice in the LORD and take
refuge in him; all the upright in heart will glory in him!
PSALM 64:6–7, 10 NIV

Plans change all the time. Because of things out of your control, carefully crafted days may need to be rescheduled, pushed back, or even canceled—even though they may have been extremely important or perhaps even reshaped your future.

Yet you can always find comfort that God's plans never change. His will isn't based on what happens in this world. When the Israelites disobeyed the Lord, He still allowed their descendants into the Promised Land. When others made plans to destroy David, they were shot down by God's own power. As the world became more and more corrupted, God made sure John the Baptist would still be in place so he could prepare the way for Jesus.

You can plan all you want, but life circumstances will get in the way sometimes. Yet you can trust God's got everything worked out for your good. Not because of who *you* are, but because of who *He* is. All His plans are good because He's good.

Dear God, thank You for goodness. Thank You for
always looking ahead and never changing Your plans.
Because of Your constancy, I can trust You.

Day 161
GOD'S LULLABY

He will not allow your foot to be moved; He who keeps you will not slumber. Behold, He who keeps Israel shall neither slumber nor sleep.
PSALM 121:3–4 NKJV

Suppose a homeowner or business owner decides to hire a security guard. How would either feel about an applicant with these qualifications? . . .

- Protects physical safety
- Doesn't fall asleep on the job, not even for a quick catnap
- Provides shelter from the elements
- Keeps a record of every entrance and exit
- Doesn't take a day off, ever

Sounds pretty impressive, doesn't it?

Suppose the same security guard offers to provide the service for free, no payment necessary, only a complete trust in his services and a recommendation to others in need.

That security guard's name would be GOD.

No wonder the psalmist said, "Where does my help come from? My help comes from the LORD!" (Psalm 121:1–2 NIV). Salvation guarantees the kind of security described above. God is with believers always, to the end of the age (see Matthew 28:20). Anyone can obtain that security: whosoever will may come (see Revelation 22:17).

When plodding through a morass of fear or depression, hum this psalm of God's love and protection. When sleep remains elusive, listen to His voice singing this lullaby.

That's where true freedom lies.

God, I rest in You. May I awake, refreshed, to move and act in the security of Your loving protection. Amen.

Day 162
PERFECT PRAYERS

Pray, therefore, like this: Our Father. . . .
Out of the depths have I cried to You, O Lord.
MATTHEW 6:9 AMPC; PSALM 130:1 AMPC

How many messages have you heard on prayer? Have you ever come away thinking, *Did you hear how eloquently they prayed? How spiritual they sounded? No wonder God answers their prayers!*

Sometimes we take the straightforward and uncomplicated idea of prayer—the simple give-and-take of talking with God—and turn it into something hard. How many times have we made it a mere religious exercise, performed best by the "holy elite," rather than what it really is—conversation with God our Father?

Just pour out your heart to God. Share how your day went. Tell Him your dreams. Ask Him to search you and reveal areas of compromise. Thank Him for your lunch. Plead for your family's and your friends' well-being. Complain about your car. . . . Just talk with Him. Don't worry how impressive (or unimpressive!) you sound.

Talk with God while doing dishes, driving the car, folding laundry, eating lunch, or kneeling by your bed. Whenever, wherever, whatever—tell Him. He cares!

Don't allow this day to slip away without talking to your Father. No perfection required.

Father God, what a privilege it is to unburden my
heart to You. Teach me the beauty and simplicity
of simply sharing my day with You.

Day 163
LAUGH TODAY!

*A happy heart makes the face cheerful,
but heartache crushes the spirit.*
PROVERBS 15:13 NIV

Some researchers say that a positive attitude can actually help you to live longer! Isn't that amazing? Did you know that laughter can do the same thing? Find something to laugh about today. Abraham's wife, Sarah, laughed when she discovered she was pregnant at an old age after longing for a baby for so many years. God surprised her when she had given up! Perhaps God has granted you an unexpected blessing. If so, laugh with joy today! If you have trouble with this, read the comics in the newspaper. Watch a humorous video of a dog or cat. Rent a movie that has some good, clean comedy. Read a few entries in a joke book. Do whatever it takes to find some humor in this day. Often, the greatest laughs come when we are free enough to laugh at ourselves. Have you done something really silly lately? Have you made a mistake that left you chuckling? Laughter is good for the soul. The book of Proverbs says that if your heart is happy, your face will show it. Are you going around with a long face? Do people look forward to seeing you or are you a "Debbie Downer"? If you find yourself complaining today, try replacing negative words with cheerful ones. Everyone enjoys being around someone who wears a smile.

*Father, grant me a happy heart today. Where there
is depression or bitterness within me, replace the
negativity with joy! Thank You, Father. Amen.*

Day 164
DON'T SWEAT IT

*I consider that our present sufferings are not worth
comparing with the glory that will be revealed in us.*
ROMANS 8:18 NIV

When a woman gives birth, the time she spends in pregnancy and labor can seem like an eternity. She's uncomfortable. She's nauseous. She's swollen. And it all leads up to hours, maybe even days, of painful labor and suffering.

But then she holds that beautiful son or daughter in her arms, and the memory of any pain fades so far to the background, it's not even worth considering. The joy of seeing the one she loves face-to-face fills up her heart and mind so completely, it wipes away any shadow of discomfort and suffering. Plus, the years of joy and fulfillment that child brings are much longer than the months of pregnancy or the hours of labor.

That's how heaven will be for us. Life is like pregnancy and labor. This life isn't the completion; it's the preparation! Our years here are just a moment compared to eternity. When life is difficult, don't sweat it. It won't last forever. One day we will leave it all behind to be flooded with His complete, perfect love and acceptance. All the pain of this life will be lost in comparison to the complete peace we'll experience, forever and ever.

*Dear Father, thank You for the promise of eternal
love and peace. Help me to keep life's hardships
in perspective of that eternity. Amen.*

Day 165
SERENITY

"They will be like a tree planted by the water that sends out its roots by the stream. It does not fear when heat comes; its leaves are always green. It has no worries in a year of drought and never fails to bear fruit."
JEREMIAH 17:8 NIV

Jeremiah paints a beautiful picture with his words. He describes what life is like for those whose trust is in the Lord, those who have full confidence in Him. This idyllic scene brings comfort and hope to the reader. It is a message of peace and serenity. A tree planted by water will never thirst; it will never fear excessive heat because it remains hydrated. No matter what, it will always bear fruit and thrive.

You will be like that tree if you trust in the Lord fully, knowing He will always care for you and meet your needs. Thus, you need not stress.

Psalm 1:3 (NIV) contains similar words to those of Jeremiah 17:8, saying that they who delight and meditate on God's law are "like a tree planted by streams of water, which yields its fruit in season and whose leaf does not wither—whatever they do prospers."

Fully trust in God, live in His Word, and then revel in His peace. Ah. . .that's better.

Dear Lord, take me to that place of peace where I trust in You with full confidence. With You, I have no reason to fear.

COURAGEOUS FAITH

*Just then a woman who had hemorrhaged for twelve years
slipped in from behind and lightly touched his robe. She was
thinking to herself, "If I can just put a finger on his robe,
I'll get well." Jesus turned—caught her at it. Then he reassured
her: "Courage, daughter. You took a risk of faith, and now
you're well." The woman was well from then on.*
MATTHEW 9:20–22 MSG

This woman mentioned in Matthew 9 had suffered from a health
issue for twelve long years. She had likely spent everything she had
on doctors who weren't able to heal her or even improve her bleeding
issue. We can imagine that she was most certainly desperate, maybe
on the verge of beyond hope.

But. . .Jesus. This woman's powerful combination of persistence
and courage led her to take action—and in the crowd that followed
Jesus, she reached out her arm to Him and touched His robe. In that
moment, she was healed from her bleeding issue.

When we know Jesus, we can *always* have a courageous faith. No
matter what we're in need of, all we need to do is reach out to Him.
And He will reassure us that all will be fine because He's there to see
us through. Praise Him!

*Father God, thank You for the courageous displays of faith
I can read about in Your Word. I'm done playing it safe.
Starting today. . .I will be courageous in my faith!*

Day 167
A BRUISED REED

"A bruised reed he will not break, and a
smoldering wick he will not snuff out.
In faithfulness he will bring forth justice."
ISAIAH 42:3 NIV

Jesus has walked this earth, experiencing both its joy and sorrow. He has suffered and cried and has a special understanding of the pain of heartbreak.

The bruised reed and the faintly burning wick mentioned in the verse above represent the person whose spirit is frail and crushed. If you feel weak and helpless, take comfort in the fact that Jesus is closer than your heartbeat. For "the LORD is close to the brokenhearted and saves those who are crushed in spirit" (Psalm 34:18 NIV).

Jesus is called "a man of suffering" (Isaiah 53:3 NIV). He understands grief and rejection. Who better to turn to when you're sad and hurting? Your Savior seeks out the broken for healing and relationship. He knows exactly where your wounds are and how to heal them. You may carry the scar, but His touch works miracles.

You need not keep score of hurts, grievances, or harm done you. Justice is Jesus' job. Let go of struggles to make things right for yourself. Let Jesus carry that burden for you. You get busy finding beauty in your day. Let gratitude and praise be your new song.

God, I trust in and praise Your healing touch in
my life. Though I sometimes feel bruised and broken,
I'm grateful Your loving presence will never leave me.

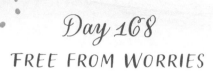

Day 168

FREE FROM WORRIES

*"So don't worry about tomorrow, for tomorrow will bring
its own worries. Today's trouble is enough for today."*
MATTHEW 6:34 NLT

What thoughts keep you up at night? Finances? Relationships? Work? Health or family concerns? We women are worriers by nature, but living in a constant state of dread isn't what God wants for us, His beloved daughters.

If we're honest with ourselves, we admit we sometimes hold on to our worries, thinking that keeping them close somehow keeps us in control of the situation. In reality, most of our worries concern things completely out of our hands.

Instead, Jesus offers us freedom from our chains of worry. "Trust Me instead of relying on yourself. Give Me the things that you fret over and stress about," He says. "How can you doubt that I'll take care of you when you mean so much to Me?"

Today, trust Jesus' assurance that He will take care of you. Ask Him to help you let go of your worrying nature and replace it with a spirit of praise and thanksgiving. It won't happen overnight, but soon you'll feel the true freedom from worry that only Jesus can supply.

*Jesus, You know the toll my worries take on my heart and mind.
I don't want to hold on to these negative thoughts, but it's hard to
let go of them! Help me to place all my concerns in Your capable
hands so that I can be free to praise You as You deserve!*

Day 169
LIVE FREE

*Now the Lord is the Spirit, and where the
Spirit of the Lord is, there is freedom.*
2 CORINTHIANS 3:17 NIV

The sun rises and sets daily, and no one attempts to alter its course. The waves of the ocean come and go on the sandy shore, too powerful to be deterred. So it is with the Spirit of the Lord. He is powerful and free. And with His power, He has set you free. This means you are not under the burden of striving. You can simply be who Christ made you to be. You are free to enjoy life without pressure to be who someone thinks you should be.

God loves you and has given you the freedom to live each day loving Him, yourself, and others. He's given you the freedom to make the best choices. You are not restricted to living in a small and painful world but have been set free to celebrate being alive.

Christ fulfilled the law so that you don't have to. You can eat the foods you prefer, sing the songs you choose, dress in your own style, read what interests you, and attend church where you like.

Ask yourself what Christ wants you to enjoy today. Listen for His Spirit's promptings. Be free to enjoy the day He created.

God, help me to truly enjoy my freedom and this day with You.

Day 170

THE BEST COUNSELOR

"Surely God does not reject one who is blameless or strengthen the hands of evildoers. He will yet fill your mouth with laughter and your lips with shouts of joy."
JOB 8:20–21 NIV

Job had lost *everything*—his sons and daughters, livelihood, even his health. He'd reached a point of desperation. Thinking he was offering sound advice, Bildad told his friend Job that he must have sinned or otherwise offended God. He insisted Job go to God and make things right so that laughter and joy could be restored.

There's a flaw in Bildad's logic! Psalm 103:8–10 (NIV) says, "The LORD is compassionate and gracious, slow to anger, abounding in love. He will not always accuse, nor will he harbor his anger forever; he does not treat us as our sins deserve or repay us according to our iniquities." God doesn't punish you for your deeds. He doesn't hold grudges.

What's more, deep in Job's heart, his faith remained. Though it was tested, he never renounced his beliefs nor blamed God.

Sometimes the advice of well-meaning friends can lead you in the wrong direction. When you need wise counsel, you would do better to follow your heart and keep your faith. God and His Word are the best advisors.

Dear God, it's so easy to get confused by the advice and ideas of others. Continually remind me that You are the best counselor, the only source of truth and light.

Day 171

THE TRUE STATUS OF YOUR HEART

*My dear Daughter—my people—broken, shattered,
and yet they put on Band-Aids, Saying, "It's not so bad.
You'll be just fine." But things are not "just fine"!*
JEREMIAH 8:11 MSG

"I'm fine." Isn't that how we all answer? Someone asks how we are doing, and we say, "I'm fine." We may be drowning in debt. "I'm fine." We may be fighting with our spouse. "I'm fine." We may be struggling with depression. "I'm fine." We may be trying hard not to give in to the same old temptation. "I'm fine."

The people of Jerusalem were in trouble. Deep trouble. God was not happy with their disobedience and idolatry. God still wanted to be their God, but they couldn't even see Him. Yet their leaders were acting as if all was well. Instead of being the voices for God to the people, they had become puppets of complacency. No one wanted to be the bearer of bad news. No one wanted to tell the truth. Or, perhaps, they couldn't even see what the truth was.

Don't be like those Israelites—keeping the peace up until the day of their destruction. Speak the truth, and let others speak the truth to you. You don't have to spill your guts to every person on the street. But have some accountability partners. Surround yourself with people you can trust to faithfully handle the true status of your heart.

Lord, help me be honest with others and with You. Amen.

Day 172
PEACE, BE STILL

GOD makes his people strong. GOD gives his people peace.
PSALM 29:11 MSG

At the center of life's storms, how do we find peace? If we're tossed about, struggling and hopeless, where is the peace? Don't worry—peace can be ours for the asking.

You see, *God* is our peace. He is ready to calm our storms when we call on Him. He will comfort and strengthen us each day.

The Bible tells of Peter and the other disciples, who were rowing their small boat against strong waves on the way to Capernaum. They knew Jesus was planning to join them, but they'd drifted out into the sea and left Him far behind. When they saw Jesus walking on the water, they were terrified—but He spoke and calmed their fears.

Impulsive Peter asked to meet Jesus on the water. He stepped out of the boat and, briefly, walked on the waves like his Lord. As long as Peter's eyes were on Jesus, he stayed atop the water—but the moment he looked away, he sank. Peter learned a valuable lesson.

The lesson works for believers today: Keep your eyes focused on the problems, and you'll have mayhem. Focus on Jesus, and you'll have peace.

Dear Lord, I thank You for Your protection.
Help me to keep my eyes on You. Please grant me peace.

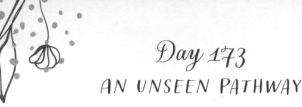

Day 173
AN UNSEEN PATHWAY

Your road led through the sea, your pathway through the mighty waters—a pathway no one knew was there!
PSALM 77:19 NLT

You have read the story. The Israelites, fleeing bondage in Egypt, arrive at the edge of the Red Sea with the Egyptians on their heels. At just the right moment, God parts the sea and every last Israelite passes through to the other side! And in the next instant, their pursuers are caught up in the raging waters, horses and chariots along with them.

Great story. Nice tale of long ago. Awesome movie clip. But wait. This is more than a fantasy. It really happened! And the miraculous part is that God still makes paths for you today.

When you find yourself between a rock and a hard place, cry out to God. When circumstances lead you to a dead end, lift your eyes toward heaven. God is the "great I Am," meaning that He is what you need in each moment. At times of anxiety or fear, you need the Prince of Peace. Other times, when filled with gratitude, you sing praises to the King of Glory.

Then there are Red Sea moments. At such crossroads, rely on Yahweh, the Lord who provides unseen pathways, who makes a way where there seems to be no way (see Isaiah 43:16–20)!

God, remind me that You are truly a God of miracles.
In my Red Sea moments, I trust You to make a way. Amen.

Day 174
MY BANNER AND MY SHIELD

For those who fear you, you have raised a banner to be unfurled against the bow. Save us and help us with your right hand, that those you love may be delivered.
PSALM 60:4–5 NIV

Who possesses a healthy regard for the Lord? Who has a firm hold on the divine shield in times of trouble? For times of trouble will surely come. The land will be shaken, fractured, and torn open. Indeed, the very ground under our feet will quake; the times will be desperate. But God has shown Himself to us. He has bequeathed to us His laws, ways, and awesome power. And the one who has built up in herself a strong regard for those things, for her, God will raise the banner against the bow. And again, she who has reflected well on her gifts from God will be shielded by Him in desperate times.

In the world itself there will be shows of power, demonstrations and strikes, petitions and drives of all sorts. But those are all nothing in comparison with the strength that comes from an alliance with God. For God loves you with a love far greater and far beyond the love of any human being. And God knows your needs. So the psalmist sings to Him to "save us and help us with your right hand."

Dear God, help us place our trust in You
in times of trouble and desperation. Amen.

Day 175
JUST THE PITS

But as for you, ye thought evil against me;
but God meant it unto good.
GENESIS 50:20 KJV

We can speak of ourselves as "being in the pits," which is symbolic of deep difficult experiences in life. Many times we are in the pits because of our mistakes, our wrongdoings. But sometimes there's no explanation. Sometimes it's an emotional pit—we are discouraged or depressed. And while in that pit, we can become comfortable. Either the pit makes us bitter, or we can let it make us better.

In Genesis, Joseph's brothers threw him into a pit to end his life. Instead, he was rescued and that life experience transformed him into a godly man. He experienced extremes in life: literally from rags to riches. Yet his character shone through because whether in the pits or the palace, his faithfulness to God never wavered. He defined his success as doing God's will. Then he was able to see the evil turned into good.

It might take some time to get to a mountaintop when we're in the valley, but we can struggle out of the murky depths with God's help. The Holy Spirit within can enable us to turn things around so we are at least on level ground.

Dear Lord, help me. I'm so down I don't know
which way is up. Please, Father, take me by the
hand and pull me from this pit. Amen.

Day 176

BREAKFAST OF CHAMPIONS

But He answered, "It is written: Man must not live on bread alone but on every word that comes from the mouth of God."
MATTHEW 4:4 HCSB

God has not created you then left you to fend for yourself.

Just as a good mother can never forget the baby who nurses at her breast (Isaiah 49:15), God will never forget you. Just as He remembered Noah and his family (Genesis 8:1), God remembers you and yours. Your Abba longs to be a part of your life, to build you up and keep you safe. And the best way He can do that is through His Word—the nourishment that will make your spirit strong and your soul sublime.

Today and every day, live on God's Word, all that comes from His mouth. Allow His voice—laced with encouragement, peace, strength, and light—to override thoughts of fear, anxiety, weakness, and darkness that swirl around in your mind. Then, in the evening, when you are lying upon your bed, present your petitions, remembering that God listens when you call to Him (Psalm 4:3). Afterward, as you begin to nod off, you can pray, "In peace I will both lie down and sleep, for You, Lord, alone make me dwell in safety and confident trust" (Psalm 4:8 AMPC).

Remind me each day, Lord, to feed on Your Word, eating the breakfast of champions. In Jesus' name I pray, amen.

Day 177

THE ANTIDOTE TO WORRY

*"So do not worry, saying, 'What shall we eat?' or
'What shall we drink?' or 'What shall we wear?'
For the pagans run after all these things, and your
heavenly Father knows that you need them."*
MATTHEW 6:31–32 NIV

What is weighing on your heart? It might be the burgeoning credit card bill from when the car's transmission failed unexpectedly last month. It might be a newly discovered lump—your palms sweaty as you wait for lab results. You might be wondering if your family is going to stay together or worrying about family members who don't love God. Worry can tangle a heart into fearful, anxious knots, cutting off its life.

Jesus tells us that the Creator who cares for the birds and the wildflowers knows our needs intimately (Matthew 6:26–30). The same God who keeps the earth perfectly tilted and spinning so that the seasons arrive at the right time also cares about medical bills, missing keys, and difficult family relationships.

The antidote to worry is prayer—telling our Father the things we lack, the things that hurt, the things that don't seem to have an answer—because He *listens*. He opens His hand to bless and fill us, to calm and heal us, to extend wisdom and peace. He invites us to seek Him wholly and to lean on His sure and faithful promise to provide for all our needs (Matthew 6:33).

Father God, I want to put You first in my heart. Help me to bring all my worries to You and to leave them at Your feet. Thank You for how You love me and promise to provide for me. Amen.

Day 178

HE'LL CARRY IT ALL

Give all your cares to the Lord and He will
give you strength. He will never let those
who are right with Him be shaken.
PSALM 55:22 NLV

The psalmist pours out his heart to his Creator, writing, "My heart is in pain within me. The fears of death have come upon me. I have begun shaking with fear. Fear has power over me. And I say, 'If only I had wings like a dove, I would fly away and be at rest'" (Psalm 55:4–6 NLV).

How many times have you, like this psalmist, wanted to run or fly away from your problems? Yet God knows that when we flee from problems, we aren't dealing with them the way He intended us to. For He knows that although we may be physically miles away from whatever issue is plaguing us, it still lingers in our minds, our hearts, and our souls. Holding on to such things can hurt us in the long run and maybe even lead us to hurt others.

Instead of avoiding your problems, run to God for strength and steadiness. With the biggest shoulders and the purest of hearts, God will carry all the shame, fear, anxiety, and stress that you try to bear alone. Simply align your heart with His, and He'll rush in to help carry your load.

Give me strength and peace, Lord, as I turn my cares over
to You. For only then will I find the calm I crave. Amen.

Day 179
AS PROMISED

The LORD kept his word and did for Sarah exactly what he had promised. She became pregnant, and she gave birth to a son for Abraham in his old age. This happened at just the time God had said it would.

GENESIS 21:1–2 NLT

Etch the words "The LORD kept his word and did. . .exactly what he had promised" on your mind. Write them on your heart. Store them so deeply inside you that when you are challenged, depressed, in trouble, doubting, harassed, distraught, and anxious, you can find your way out of it and into a place where you are assured, joyful, secure, certain, at peace, calm, and composed.

Steep yourself in God's promises when you feel the ground shaking beneath your feet. Allow His promises to give you firm footing. Begin with the ones that speak most to your heart, the ones that are medicine to your mind and a salve to your soul. Look up verses about His never-ending guidance, faithfulness, love, grace, blessings, wisdom, peace, joy, provision, power, etc. Then read the stories of the promises that God came through on in scripture.

Live your life knowing that God always keeps His word. That what He promised will come to fruition, in exactly the way He said it would. Doing so will change your life from one of pain to one of promise!

Lord of love, lead me to the promise You would have me claim as I read Your Word today. Amen.

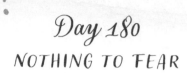

Day 180

NOTHING TO FEAR

"Be strong and courageous. Do not be afraid or discouraged
because of the king of Assyria and the vast army with him,
for there is a greater power with us than with him. With
him is only the arm of flesh, but with us is the LORD our God
to help us and to fight our battles." And the people gained
confidence from what Hezekiah the king of Judah said.
2 CHRONICLES 32:7–8 NIV

King Hezekiah and the nation of Judah were certainly up against it.
The powerful Assyrian army was closing in fast, set to invade, and
things looked bleak. While King Hezekiah instructed his army to
take precautions such as bolstering the city's walls and cutting off
water supply, he knew his biggest defense did not lie in his military
might. So he instructed his army to *not* be afraid, claiming there was a
greater power protecting them. His faith-filled words gave the people
confidence. In the end, God not only protected Judah but soundly
defeated the Assyrian army.

This dire situation helped an entire city learn to trust God, to have
faith that He'd always lead them down the right path. Have you ever
felt desperate, full of fear, convinced that you were facing defeat?
Consider the people of Judah and take a page from their book. The
Good Book. Know that with God, you've nothing to fear.

Dear God, with You leading me, I know I've
nothing to fear. I trust You will protect me.

Day 181
RECYCLING

*All praise to the God and Father of our Master, Jesus the
Messiah! . . . He comes alongside us when we go through
hard times, and before you know it, he brings us alongside
someone else who is going through hard times so that we
can be there for that person just as God was there for us.*
2 CORINTHIANS 1:3–4 MSG

Have you ever considered how much use the Lord can make out of
the garbage of our lives? As Christians, we can take the good and
bad events we've experienced and use them to witness to others of
the goodness of God. When we've walked a path and struggled with
a problem, and God has seen us through to the other side, we need
to reach out to a brother or sister. Ambassador Clare Boothe Luce
once stated, "There are no hopeless situations; there are only people
who have grown hopeless about them." That's when we might offer
encouragement.

God weaves a life tapestry for each of us; when we focus on the
knotted thread, we don't see any beauty. However, a fellow believer can
show us his tapestry made from similar knots, and we see the picture.
How precious of the Lord to allow us to share with one another. Never
underestimate the power of your testimony.

*Father, show me this day how You would have me
share what You have done in my life. Amen.*

Day 182

GOD—THINGS AND GOD—SONGS

I waited and waited and waited for GOD. At last
he looked; finally he listened. He lifted me out of the ditch,
pulled me from deep mud. He stood me up on a solid
rock to make sure I wouldn't slip. He taught me how to
sing the latest God-song, a praise-song to our God.
PSALM 40:1–3 MSG

When God alone teaches us how to worship, it is true and from the heart. Isaiah 30:20–21 (NLT) tells us that "though the Lord gave you adversity for food and suffering for drink, he will still be with you to teach you. You will see your teacher with your own eyes. Your own ears will hear him. Right behind you a voice will say, 'This is the way you should go,' whether to the right or to the left."

God Himself wants to rescue you and to teach you. He alone is your Savior. No human—as much as that person might try or intend to help you—can save you. If you allow Him, then the God of heaven and earth will lift you up out of your despair and striving and set you free. He will teach you how to praise Him, even in the midst of suffering and trials. Quiet yourself before God and He will teach you.

God, I want to hear from You. Forgive me for wanting
others to rescue me. That is only Yours to do. Please quiet
my heart so that I can learn from You. Amen.

Day 183

LEADING A LAMB TO SAFETY

But [God] led His own people forth like sheep and guided them [with a shepherd's care] like a flock in the wilderness. And He led them on safely and in confident trust, so that they feared not; but the sea overwhelmed their enemies.

PSALM 78:52–53 AMPC

Some days you may feel as if you are being squeezed, wrung out, hung out to dry. You mind is so scattered, your being so anxious, that no solutions come to mind. Any relief on the horizon appears distant, at best. It seems as if you have one problem coming from behind and nothing but a nameless dark out in front of you, keeping you from moving forward.

This is when it's good to remember God. How He led His people to safety over and over again. When you remember the plagues of Egypt, the parting of the Red Sea, the water gushing from a rock in the wilderness, the manna coming down from heaven, the water turned into wine, the waking and walking of the dead, the calming of a storm, then you realize you're safe in God's hands. You can move forward in confident trust. You can have the courage you need to let God shepherd you out of your wilderness and into His light.

I'm looking to You for all, Lord, my Shepherd, confidently trusting You to show me the way through this wilderness, to lead this lamb to safety.

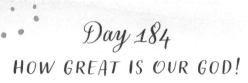

Day 184

HOW GREAT IS OUR GOD!

And I said, O Lord God of heaven, the great and terrible
God, Who keeps covenant, loving-kindness, and mercy for
those who love Him and keep His commandments.
NEHEMIAH 1:5 AMPC

When Dorothy finally met the wizard she had been searching for in *The Wonderful Wizard of Oz*, she was disappointed. The "Great and Terrible" magician, who had promoted himself as an all-powerful man with a short temper, turned out to be a normal person behind a curtain—albeit one who was good at special effects.

Rest assured, when we finally meet God, we won't have the same kind of letdown. The Bible notes God's inestimable qualities—unconditional love, unending mercy, unimaginable strength—with reverence. The New Testament authors also repeatedly wrote about God's mercy and compassion, lest we despair of ever coming near Him.

Of course, we need to fear the holy Creator and Maker of all things and strive to do His will; but as the one who formed us, God knows that we will fail (and loves us anyway). His love is why He sent Jesus to die on the cross.

Today, think about God's love, mercy, and strength as you go about your day. When you face problems, ask Him to solve them, instead of trying to fix them yourself. Repeatedly and reverently surrender to Him—because He is great, but He's certainly not terrible.

Creator, Maker, Redeemer God—You are wonderful.
Thank You for Your wisdom, strength, and love. Amen.

Day 185
I WILL CHOOSE
TO REMEMBER. . .

"Will the Lord reject forever? Will he never show his favor
again? Has his unfailing love vanished forever? Has his
promise failed for all time? Has God forgotten to be merciful?
Has he in anger withheld his compassion?" Then I thought,
"To this I will appeal: the years when the Most High
stretched out his right hand. I will remember the deeds of the
Lord; yes, I will remember your miracles of long ago."
PSALM 77:7–11 NIV

Today's verses give some insight into how the mind works. Thoughts
sometimes creep in suggesting God has rejected you, rescinded His
love, neglected to be merciful. But then another part of you, your
good angel, promptly remembers all the wonders and miracles He
has performed on behalf of you and other believers, reviving your
faith once more.

When doubts subtly worm their way into your thought processes,
think back to the promises God clearly states in His Word. You know,
where He says He will never leave nor forsake you. Consider all the
times you've felt and experienced His presence and power.

Consider writing down those times you've felt God's hand extended
into your life, so that when doubts rear their ugly heads, you'll know
and remember God is still in charge and still loves you dearly. Then
may hope rise up in your soul like sweet incense.

Lord, help me to remember, to never doubt
Your miracles and everlasting love for me.

Day 186

YOUR JOURNEY

*"I saw the Lord always before me, for he is at my right
hand that I may not be shaken; therefore my heart was glad,
and my tongue rejoiced; my flesh also will dwell in hope."*
ACTS 2:25–26 ESV

Queen Jezebel threatened the life of Elijah. Filled with fear, he ran for his life. Once he reached the wilderness, he journeyed for a day then sat under a broom tree and prayed that he would die, saying, "I have had enough, LORD. . . . Take my life, for I am no better than my ancestors who have already died" (1 Kings 19:4 NLT). He then fell asleep.

God sent an angel to wake Elijah and give him something to eat and drink. He slept again, and the angel came back and gave him more food and drink, saying, "Get up and eat, or the journey will be too much for you" (1 Kings 19:7 HCSB). On the strength gleaned from that angel food, Elijah journeyed for forty more days and nights, stopping when he got to the mountain of God. There God pointed out the error in Elijah's thoughts and sent him back from whence he'd come (1 Kings 19:13–18).

When you're soul weary, pour your heart out to God. When you do, He'll care for you, correct your thinking, and get you back on the right track.

*Lord, meet me where I am when I've had enough.
Then help me find the right road back.*

Day 187

NOTICING THE BLESSINGS

*So he brought his people out of Egypt with joy, his
chosen ones with rejoicing. He gave his people the lands
of pagan nations, and they harvested crops that others
had planted. All this happened so they would follow his
decrees and obey his instructions. Praise the LORD!*

PSALM 105:43–45 NLT

When you begin to notice the blessings God brings into your life, it
will turn your heart toward the Lord. The hardness in your spirit will
soften and become tender for Him.

So often we forget every good thing comes from Him. We keep
our eyes down as we plow through life, forgetting to look up and see
the beautiful things coming to fruition in our circumstances. And it
affects how we face the world.

The Lord has done amazing things for you, friend. Take time
today to think through the times He has intervened on your behalf
or restored something broken or met an unspoken need. And let it
be the fuel you need to glorify His name in all the world. Let it be
what drives you to share hope and love.

*Lord, open my eyes to see the ways You have brought beautiful
things into my life. Let those blessings penetrate any hardness
in my heart so I am freed up to live a life that glorifies Your
name. Let my life always point to You and Your goodness.*

THE IN–BETWEEN

For just as we share abundantly in the sufferings of
Christ, so also our comfort abounds through Christ.
2 CORINTHIANS 1:5 NIV

God never promised anyone a life without pain. Oh! What wretched depths of despair we descend into when we expect that life will be filled with only happiness because we know the Savior. We begin to think that we are unloved by Christ, or we believe He is mean, powerless, or passive—and our hope fails. We must remember that although God's plan for our lives includes pain—"In this world you will have trouble"—it also includes hope: "Take heart! I have overcome the world" (John 16:33 NIV).

Until Christ returns, we live in the in-between, where His glory has not been fully revealed and we suffer. We must remember that despite what happens to us, God is good and He loves us, and He will ultimately make things right. Until then, we share in the sufferings of Christ and we wait. And with the power that comes from the Holy Spirit, we choose gratitude over self-pity and complaining. We cast our broken hearts, broken lives, and cares at His feet because He cares for us (see 1 Peter 5:7). We give Him our burdens, and in exchange, we receive rest (see Matthew 11:28).

Living the abundant Christian life isn't about what happens to us. It's about how we respond to what happens to us.

Lord, thank You that even though life is
sometimes difficult, You have given me all I need
to be an overcomer through faith in You. Amen.

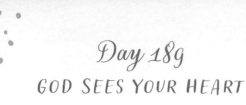

Day 189
GOD SEES YOUR HEART

God answered Solomon, "Because this was in your heart,
and you have not asked for possessions, wealth, honor,
or the life of those who hate you, and have not even asked
for long life, but have asked for wisdom and knowledge for
yourself that you may govern my people over whom I have
made you king, wisdom and knowledge are granted to you."
2 Chronicles 1:11–12 esv

This is such a beautiful story about the heart of Solomon. And it's the perfect example of the truth that God has the ability to see the depth of who we are.

Given the chance, what would you ask God for today? Maybe you need His provision. Maybe you need a change of heart. Maybe you need something broken to be restored. Maybe it's a fear that needs to be extinguished. Maybe you need hope or peace or the ability to love someone completely unlovable. Maybe you need the right words for a difficult conversation.

God will recognize and honor those requests made through faith. He will hear your heart through your prayers. So be thoughtful in what you ask for, and let it be an appeal that demonstrates your steadfast trust in the one you know can make a difference.

Lord, give me a pure heart like Solomon, and help me petition
You through unshakable faith in Your love and compassion.
Let my requests be examples of how much I trust in You.

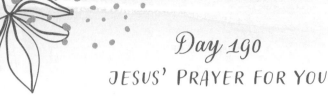

Day 190

JESUS' PRAYER FOR YOU

*Neither for these alone do I pray [it is not for their sake
only that I make this request], but also for all those who
will ever come to believe in (trust in, cling to, rely on)
Me through their word and teaching, that they all may
be one, [just] as You, Father, are in Me and I in You.*
JOHN 17:20–21 AMPC

If ever you have a day when you just can't drag your lower lip up off
the floor, remember how much Jesus loves you and how far His love
reaches across the ages. Most of all, remember how He prayed for
you—one of "all those who will ever come to believe"—thousands
of years ago.

Through the hearing of God's Word, the power of Jesus' prayer,
and the teachings of believers who walked the road you're now on,
you are one with other believers. So today, let go of all that discourages, disheartens, disturbs, and destroys. Tap into the power, prayers,
promises, and presence of God the Father, Jesus the Son, and the
Spirit of comfort. And acknowledge that the same love God had for
His one and only Son is the same love God has for you.

*Jesus, I'm honored that You prayed for me all those years ago and
that Your Father loves me just as He loves You. In the power
of that prayer I rise. In the power of that love I live. Amen.*

Day 191
GREAT EXPECTATIONS

Now there was a man in Jerusalem called Simeon,
who was righteous and devout. He was waiting for the
consolation of Israel, and the Holy Spirit was on him.
It had been revealed to him by the Holy Spirit that he
would not die before he had seen the Lord's Messiah.
LUKE 2:25–26 NIV

Simeon was an old man. He was righteous and devout. But surely there were other old men hanging around the temple who were righteous and devout. Of all the Pharisees and Sadducees nearby, of all the truly devoted, religious people of that day, why Simeon? Why did God choose this man to welcome His Son into the temple and proclaim His coming to all who would listen?

One key phrase offers a clue: "He was waiting for the consolation of Israel." In other words, Simeon knew God's promises, and he was looking for good things to happen.

What a lesson we can learn from this old saint! God has promised many good things to His people. But often, we mope around, stressed and anxious, worried that things won't go well for us. Why do we do that? Like Simeon, we should wake up each morning looking for God to do great things. We should greet each new day expecting God to work, to fulfill His promises.

Dear Father, thank You for Your promises. I know You
have good things in store. Help me to watch and wait,
expecting You to do great things each and every day. Amen.

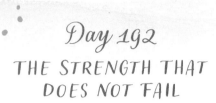

Day 192

THE STRENGTH THAT DOES NOT FAIL

But his bow remained strong and steady and rested in the Strength that does not fail him, for the arms of his hands were made strong and active by the hands of the Mighty God of Jacob, by the name of the Shepherd, the Rock of Israel.
GENESIS 49:24 AMPC

It's often easy to fight the battle on your own or try to fix things yourself, failing to remember that God stands ready to supply you with His strength. Whether the fight you face is physical or spiritual in nature, your rescue depends on your willingness to invite God to step in.

Joseph endured great adversity, starting with his older brothers selling him into slavery as a young boy. Each battle Joseph faced required courage and faith in God to rescue him and provide him with strength. Joseph's bow remained strong because he relied on God's strength. God's hands supported Joseph as he used his weapon against his enemies.

As you endure difficulties, burdens, and persecution, remember that you don't have to fight alone. God is with you and has provided you with the strength that does not fail.

God, remind me that I don't have to do things on my own.
Please give me the strength I need to face hardships.
I believe that as I follow You, I cannot fail. You will
fight for me. All I have to do is invite You in.

Day 193
FIND REST WITH JESUS

"Come to me, all you who are weary and burdened, and I will give you rest. Take my yoke upon you and learn from me, for I am gentle and humble in heart, and you will find rest for your souls. For my yoke is easy and my burden is light."
MATTHEW 11:28–30 NIV

Jesus says, "Come to me." Just as He invited the little children to come to Him, Jesus calls us to come to Him and bring all our burdens and lay them at His feet. He wants to help. He wants to relieve the load we're carrying.

A yoke is a harness placed over an animal or set of animals for the purpose of dragging something or carrying heavy equipment. Jesus liked to use visual imagery to get His meaning across. Can't you just picture all the burdens you are carrying right now strapped to your back like an ox plowing a field? Now imagine yourself unloading each one onto Jesus' shoulders instead. Take a deep breath.

Jesus tells us many times throughout the Gospels not to worry. Worrying about something will never help you. Worry makes things worse and burdens seem larger. Worry clutters up your soul. Jesus wants us to find rest in Him. Hear His gentle words rush over you—"Come to me." Find rest for your soul.

Jesus, thank You for taking my burdens. I give them fully to You. Help me not to take them back! I want the rest and peace that You are offering. Amen.

Day 194
A GOOD WORD

Anxiety in the heart of man causes depression,
but a good word makes it glad.
PROVERBS 12:25 NKJV

As most of us know, anxiety and depression are two sides of the same coin. According to this verse, keeping anxiety in our hearts causes depression. We are anxious about what might happen and we become depressed about what didn't. Anxiety and depression create a vicious cycle, keeping us bound to the past and paralyzed about the future.

But this proverb reminds us that "a good word makes [the heart] glad." Where can you get a good word? Philippians 4:8 (NLT) tells us to "fix [our] thoughts on what is true, and honorable, and right, and pure, and lovely, and admirable. Think about things that are excellent and worthy of praise." This is a good word! We know it to be true experientially, and studies prove that reading the Bible, singing praise songs, and hearing encouraging words from friends can literally change our brain's chemistry and lift a dark mood. These good words replace the anxiety and depression in our hearts with joy and peace in the Holy Spirit.

Father, my heart is sometimes weighed down by anxiety. I know what it feels like to be depressed. Thank You for Your Word and the reminder that I don't have to settle for these feelings. Thank You that I can trust You to bring joy back to my soul. Amen.

Day 195
GOD THE GUARDIAN

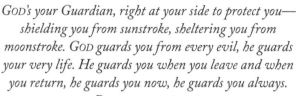

GOD's your Guardian, right at your side to protect you—
shielding you from sunstroke, sheltering you from
moonstroke. GOD guards you from every evil, he guards
your very life. He guards you when you leave and when
you return, he guards you now, he guards you always.
PSALM 121:5–8 MSG

When you find yourself stuck in a cycle of worry and anxiety, when you really need to change things up, to get your faith back in God's camp, ask yourself just one question: Where are you looking to for help? For strength?

Perhaps it's time to look up—not at the mountains but to God (Psalm 121:1–2). Because He's the one who made those mountains. He's the one who holds all the power and strength you need—emotionally, physically, mentally, and spiritually.

God is the one who guards you, stands at your side protecting you, shielding you, and sheltering you, keeping evil at bay. He sees and guards you as you're going out and coming in—and will do so always.

Go to God day and night for all the comfort, help, strength, and protection you need. Know He's never far. If you're worried, it's you who has moved, not Him. So snuggle up close, knowing God's on the job, ever awake and ever vigilant.

Thank You, Lord, for keeping such a close watch
over my coming and going. Help me stay attuned
to Your presence by my side, this day and always.

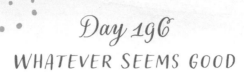

WHATEVER SEEMS GOOD

Then the king said to Zadok, "Take the ark of God back into the city. If I find favor in the LORD's eyes, he will bring me back and let me see it and his dwelling place again. But if he says, 'I am not pleased with you,' then I am ready; let him do to me whatever seems good to him."

2 SAMUEL 15:25–26 NIV

King David was in dire straits. The hearts of his people had been won by his son and usurper, Absalom. So David had to flee Jerusalem. The people in the countryside cried as the king and his retinue passed by. Even the Levites had followed him with the ark of God. But David told the priest Zadok to go back to the city with the ark. Not knowing what was going to happen, David determined to leave his life in the hands of God, ready for whatever would happen, satisfied God would do what He deemed best. This sentiment is echoed later by Jesus who would one day, while in a Jerusalem garden, pray to Father God, "Not My will but Yours."

When all looks hopeless, when your dreams have become nightmares, how wonderful to be calm and content, rather than complaining. Have no fear of whatever the future may hold, knowing all events are in God's hands.

Whatever You wish and will, Lord, I'm ready. I and my life are in Your hands, trusting You know best.

Day 197
CLIMBING MOUNTAINS

The LORD is my light and my salvation—
whom shall I fear? The LORD is the stronghold
of my life—of whom shall I be afraid?
PSALM 27:1 NIV

The Meteora in Greece is a complex of monastic structures high atop a mountain. Access to the structures was deliberately difficult. Some of these "hanging monasteries" were accessible only by baskets lowered by ropes and winches, and to take a trip there required a leap of faith. An old story associated with the monasteries said that the ropes were only replaced "when the Lord let them break."

While the vast majority of us will probably never scale the mountain to visit these monasteries, we often feel that we have many steep mountains of our own to climb. Maybe it's too much month at the end of the money. Or perhaps we are suffering with health or relationship troubles. Whatever the reason we are hurting, angry, or feeling despair or hopelessness, God is ready to help us, and we can place all our hope in Him who is faithful. We can do that because we are connected to Him and have seen His faithfulness in the past.

Lord, I will stay strong in You and will take courage. I can trust
and rest in You. Whatever I am feeling now, whatever emotions I
have, I give them to You, for You are my hope and salvation. You
are good all the time—of that I can be supremely confident. Amen.

THOUGHTS INFLUENCE ACTIONS

*They swore an oath to the LORD with a loud voice and with
shouting and with trumpets and with horns. And all Judah
rejoiced over the oath, for they had sworn with all their heart
and had sought him with their whole desire, and he was
found by them, and the LORD gave them rest all around.*

2 CHRONICLES 15:14–15 ESV

Notice the order in today's passage of scripture. They made a decision in their mind to commit themselves to the Lord, and then their voices erupted with rejoicing and praise. It's important to recognize how the mind influences actions.

If you focus your thoughts on the goodness of God, you will live in that belief. If you decide the Lord is for you, you will find patience to wait. If you choose to believe He's your provision, you'll live without worry. If you see God as your comfort, He will be your first stop when things get hard. In the same way, if you decide the Lord is weak and uninterested and unable, the struggles in life will eat you up.

Decide today to set your mind on God's sovereignty. Look through His Word for times He came through for those who believed. And ask for an extra measure of faith so your heart is full of expectation for His work in your life.

*Lord, help my mind stay steady on Your
magnificence so I live in Your resurrection power.*

Day 199

BE HAPPY DESPITE IT ALL

*A twinkle in the eye means joy in the heart,
and good news makes you feel fit as a fiddle.*
PROVERBS 15:30 MSG

The apostle Paul had much he could've grumbled about. He was beaten, jailed, shipwrecked, and nearly drowned; yet through it all, he discovered God was the source of his contentment. Paul understood God was in control of his life, even when he was in those overwhelming, tragic situations. Remember his songs of praise from the jail cell (Acts 16)?

Sometimes we find ourselves in hard places, and life isn't going the way we planned. This is the time when we have to look for the positive. We have to make the choice to "bloom where we're planted," and God will meet us there. In our songs of praise amid the difficulties, God will come. The Holy Spirit, the Comforter, will minister to our needs. The Lord has promised to never leave or forsake us, so if He is present, we should have no fear or worry. Without fear or worry, we can learn to be content. No fretting, no regretting, just trusting the Word is truth.

When we place our hope in Christ and He's our guide, He will give us the ability to walk satisfied, no matter our circumstances. He is our all in all.

*Lord, I give You thanks for all Your good gifts
but most of all for Your presence. Amen.*

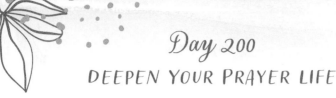

Day 200
DEEPEN YOUR PRAYER LIFE

Jesus told his disciples a parable to show them
that they should always pray and not give up.
LUKE 18:1 NIV

What is your prayer history? Most women find their prayer life jump-starts during affliction, darkness, and grief. Suffering can make God more real and intimate, or have the opposite effect—where we shake our fist instead of bend our knee. Therefore, we must fight despair with prayer. This spiritual battle requires discipline, like talking to God instead of listening to our self-talk, which can be deceptively untrue. When our minds do not have to concentrate on something, we can form the habit of turning our self-talk into "meditation moments" to nurture our relationship with God.

What if prayer is boring? We will minimize our need to pray if we forget to whom we are talking—our personal, loving Father *and* the awesome, almighty God. A practical suggestion is to use a 3x5 spiral card pack and write a scripture verse on each card. Select verses about God's character or names, about a temptation or struggle you face, or about encouragement to trust Him. Deliberately find times to pray these "battle verses"—God's words—back to Him. Try it while exercising or walking your dog, while waiting in line or riding as a passenger. You may think you could have battle verses on your phone instead, but that would tempt you to let your device steal your prayer time. Instead of texting a friend, take out your card pack and talk to your best friend forever.

My mind is a spiritual battlefield, Lord.
Help me make it the place for victories. Amen.

Day 201

THE BUILDING OF YOUR LIFE

The stone the builders rejected has become the cornerstone.
PSALM 118:22 NIV

Have you ever watched the process of an old building being deconstructed? Once the old structure is razed, the ground is prepared for the construction of a new building. And it begins with the assembly of a cornerstone on which the new building will stand. Slowly the progress spreads out from there, all resting on that strong, dependable, ever-reliable cornerstone that started it all.

In a similar way, you too have a cornerstone for the building of your life. You may have days when you feel the building is crumbling around you or perhaps some repairs are necessary. But if Jesus is your cornerstone, your building will *never* crumble. Sometimes a little renovation may be necessary to make your life the best it can be, but your base, your cornerstone, will remain forever constant.

No matter what challenges come your way, remember that God is the architect of a masterpiece. And that masterpiece is *you*.

Dear God, help me remember that You are the cornerstone upon which I can safely and confidently build my life, my world. It's comforting to know that, no matter what, my base cannot be shaken and that in You I can and will remain immovable when facing adversity. Thank You, Lord, for always holding me up.

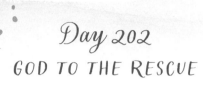

Day 202

GOD TO THE RESCUE

God's eye is on those who respect him, the ones who are looking for his love. He's ready to come to their rescue in bad times; in lean times he keeps body and soul together.
PSALM 33:18–19 MSG

You wake up, pray, get ready for the day, and at some point, see, hear, or read about what's going on in the world. The news isn't good. Before you know it, your happy-go-lucky attitude has gone right out the window and a bit of fear and anxiety has crept in.

Jesus knew this would happen. In fact, He tells you, "When reports come in of wars and rumored wars, keep your head and don't panic. This is routine history; this is no sign of the end" (Matthew 24:6 MSG). He encourages you, saying, "Staying with it—that's what God requires. Stay with it to the end. . . . You'll be saved. All during this time, the good news—the Message of the kingdom—will be preached all over the world" (Matthew 24:13–14 MSG).

So when world news ignites your panic, go to God in prayer. He'll keep you together—body and soul. With the realization that He's all you need, your fear will morph into joy (Psalm 33:20).

Love me, Lord, with all You've got—that's what I'm depending on [Psalm 33:22 MSG]. Help me focus on Your good news. Bring me to Your place of joy.

Day 203
FEARLESS

God is love. Whoever lives in love lives in God, and God in them. . . . There is no fear in love. But perfect love drives out fear, because fear has to do with punishment. The one who fears is not made perfect in love.
1 JOHN 4:16, 18 NIV

First John 5:3 says that if we love God, we will do what He commands. It sounds simple enough, but fear can creep in when we consider what it means to show Him complete devotion. Putting Him first in our lives might cost us more than we expect—in our relationships, in our jobs, in how we spend our money or time. We might worry about what others might think of us or fear that we can't accomplish what God calls us to do.

God's unconditional love frees us from fear—the fear of punishment, failure, or harsh judgment from our fellow men and women—because His opinion of us matters most. Through everything, He has promised to be with us and strengthen us. We may feel ashamed of our fear, but God is not angry. Instead, He gives us exactly what we need to strengthen our faith, whether it's the sign of a damp sheepskin (Gideon, Judges 6) or inviting us to touch His wounds (Jesus to Thomas, John 20:24–29).

Do not fear. Christ shows us the vastness of His love to drive out our worries and anxieties. When we rely on Him, we can accomplish *anything* He asks of us.

Father God, I want to step out in faith and do what You command. Banish my fears by showing me how perfectly You love me. Amen.

Day 204
FAITH IS THE VICTORY

For we live by faith, not by sight.
2 CORINTHIANS 5:7 NIV

When we find ourselves in the dark, our first response is to find a flashlight. We like to see where we are stepping. . .in the backyard as well as in life. We prefer knowing which direction, how fast, and how long the journey will take at every turn. We are, however, called to walk by faith, which usually means "lights out." Yet when confusion and uncertainty cause darkness, we try to regain control, a wild scramble to stop the pain of walking in the dark.

Uncertainty is uncomfortable. Yet in these situations, we are to remember that faith is the victory, not the outcome. God is responsible for the results. Our job is the faith.

Trusting that God will take care of the outcome is a muscle that gets stronger each time you practice it. Instead of worrying over the test results, the job interview, or the bill payment, tell God you trust Him to take care of you. Tell Him that over and over until both your mind and heart believe it. Know that no matter how the details play out at the end, God is most assuredly in control and working for your best.

God, thank You that You are responsible for all outcomes.
Help me to trust You today, to walk by faith, not by sight.

Day 205
LAID LOW

*I am laid low in the dust; preserve my life according
to your word. . . . My soul is weary with sorrow;
strengthen me according to your word.*
PSALM 119:25, 28 NIV

We all have bad days, times when we feel beaten down, defeated. To feel lowly and unworthy, "laid low in the dust," is a sad feeling indeed.

How can we rise up from the dust? The answer is God's Word. Isaiah 40:8 (NIV) says, "The grass withers and the flowers fall, but the word of our God endures forever." If ever there was energy for our soul, it is the Word of God. It can bring strength to the weak, comfort to those in need, and peace to those who believe and seek His grace.

When you feel like you are surrounded by darkness, when you feel as if you can fall no further, when your soul and heart are weary with sorrow, when you can barely catch your breath, reach out for the Word of God. Its light will illuminate your path and direct your feet, leading you back up from the dust, giving you the strength to rise up, a new woman.

*Dear God, many are the times I have been laid low,
sad and lonely, weary and despondent. I thank You for
Your Word that pulls me up from the depths. May Your
light be my strength, my guide, my life preserver.*

GOD OF YOUR UPS AND DOWNS

*Hallelujah! You who serve GOD, praise GOD! Just to speak
his name is praise! Just to remember GOD is a blessing—
now and tomorrow and always. From east to west, from
dawn to dusk, keep lifting all your praises to GOD!*
PSALM 113:1–3 MSG

As you read through the psalms, you gain a glimpse of the highs and
lows from the writer's soul. In the lowest points of his life journey,
he pours out his heart, hopeless and distressed, maybe even feeling
disconnected from God, thirsting for His presence.

Yet, through prayer, the writer finds comfort in God for his brokenness and pain. He reminds himself of God's faithfulness and
unfailing love and how it refreshes his spirit. Then he pulls himself up,
encourages himself in the Lord, and becomes determined to experience
the joy that only God can give. He rises again through faith in God,
climbing ever higher with praise and thanksgiving.

Like the psalmist, you too can trust God with your ups and downs.
Allow Him to go with you to the mountaintops and back down into
the valleys. Wherever you are in your journey, you can safely and freely
bare your soul to the God who listens and knows you like no other.

*God, You are always with me. You faithfully walk with
me no matter what situation I face. I will rejoice in
You at all times because I know I can count on You.*

Day 207
HOLD ON

"Listen now, you who know right from wrong, you who hold my teaching inside you: Pay no attention to insults, and when mocked don't let it get you down. Those insults and mockeries are moth-eaten, from brains that are termite-ridden, but my setting-things-right lasts, my salvation goes on and on and on."
ISAIAH 51:7–8 MSG

Isaiah provided words of comfort to God's people that they would be taken care of. His encouragement was to hold on to the teachings of God. To focus on God and to not pay attention to the challenging things going on around them. God was their source of peace and comfort, even in the most tumultuous of times.

These same words spoken thousands of years ago can be ones that you hold on to today. When you feel uptight, when everything looks and feels like a mess, remember that God is holding on to you. Because you have been reading God's Word, you know right from wrong, you know His truths. So hold them inside you, allowing them to guide your thoughts and heart. Let your outward actions demonstrate that you're secure in Jesus Christ, forever!

Lord, help me to hold on to You and Your Word. I want my life to be an example of what it means to be passionate about reading the Bible and taking the words written seriously.

TWENTY–TWENTY VISION

*[Elisha] answered, Fear not; for those with us are more
than those with them. Then Elisha prayed, Lord, I pray
You, open his eyes that he may see. And the Lord opened
the young man's eyes, and he saw, and behold, the mountain
was full of horses and chariots of fire round about Elisha.*
2 KINGS 6:16–17 AMPC

One morning Elisha and his servant were surrounded by an enemy army with its horses and chariots. Having seen the odds against them, his servant man, who apparently had only earthly vision, freaked out, asking Elisha, "What will we do?"

The prophet seems rather calm with his reply of "Don't worry. Our army is bigger than theirs." But then he prayed that God would open the servant's eyes so that he could see how well protected he and the prophet were. So God honored Elisha's request—and the scales from the servant's spiritual eyes fell away, revealing a mountain full of charioted cavalry.

When women of the Way open their eyes of faith, the shadows of this world shrink away and fear abates. The more they understand the absolute and awesome power of their God, the better their twenty-twenty vision and the less terror this world holds for them. And with the fading of the darkness of worry, dread, and anxiety comes the Son's brilliant light of peace, faith, and serenity.

*Lord, help me to throw open the shades and let the "Sonlight" in.
Give me the eyes of faith so that I have twenty-twenty vision.*

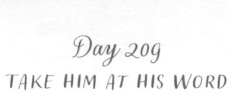

Day 209
TAKE HIM AT HIS WORD

The royal official said, "Sir, come down before my child dies."
JOHN 4:49 NIV

While people from Jesus' hometown were reluctant to believe Him, elsewhere people who had heard He performed miracles were desperate to have Him meet their needs.

One such desperate man was a royal official who asked Jesus to heal his sick son. But the way he did it reveals how often we limit our view of Jesus. The man told Jesus, "Go heal my sick son," because in his mind the only way his son could be healed was if Jesus went there to heal him.

Are we like that? We are limited in what we think God can do. Or we think He can act only in a certain way or only within the realm of our imagination. The official thought Jesus had to lay His hands on the boy to heal him. But Jesus only had to speak a word.

The man does show a capacity for growing his faith. When Jesus tells him to go home, that his son is healed, the man takes Jesus at His word and goes home. There is a lesson in that act of faith for us. When Jesus tells us to do something, we need to do it without arguing, complaining, or asking for an explanation. We need to trust that He works beyond our expectations.

*Lord Jesus, we ask for forgiveness for the times we
don't obey immediately or take You at Your word.
Help us to have the courage to step out in faith and to
trust You to work in unexpected ways. Amen.*

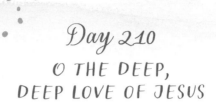

Day 210

O THE DEEP, DEEP LOVE OF JESUS

I pray that out of his glorious riches he may strengthen you with power through his Spirit in your inner being, so that Christ may dwell in your hearts through faith. And I pray that you, being rooted and established in love, may have power, together with all the Lord's holy people, to grasp how wide and long and high and deep is the love of Christ.
EPHESIANS 3:16–18 NIV

The apostle Paul encouraged the people in Ephesus with his words in an effort to explain how far-reaching God's love was. Immeasurable. Unfathomable.

In the late 1800s, the lyricist Samuel Trevor Francis entertained the idea of ending his own life. In the midst of despair, he felt God reach out to him, and he wrote a stirring hymn echoing Paul's words: "O the deep, deep love of Jesus, vast, unmeasured, boundless, free! Rolling as a mighty ocean in its fullness over me! Underneath me, all around me, is the current of Thy love, leading onward, leading homeward to Thy glorious rest above!"

What an amazing picture. That He should care for us in such a way is almost incomprehensible. Despite our shortcomings, our sin, He loves us. It takes a measure of faith to believe in His love. When we feel a nagging thought of unworthiness, of being unlovable, let's trust in the Word and sing a new song. For His love is deep and wide.

Lord, thank You for loving me, even when I'm unlovable. Amen.

Day 211

YOUR CHOICE

But the Lord answered her, "Martha, Martha,
you are anxious and troubled about many things,
but one thing is necessary. Mary has chosen the good
portion, which will not be taken away from her."
LUKE 10:41–42 ESV

Every human being on earth has a choice. Either believe in God, loving and obeying Him, or don't. Moses outlined that choice for God's people on the plains of Moab. He said, "Today I have given you the choice between life and death, between blessings and curses. . . . Oh, that you would choose life, so that you and your descendants might live!" (Deuteronomy 30:19 NLT).

Over a thousand years later, Jesus addressed another choice for believers on a visit to His friends Mary, Martha, and Lazarus. While Martha hurried around serving her guests, Mary hunkered down at Jesus' feet. But in response to Martha's request—"Tell her to help!"— Jesus replied, "Martha, Martha. . ." He knew what would help Martha more than an extra pair of hands. Mary's choice to worship her Lord and to soak up His teaching was "the good portion," an investment in her soul.

Moses longed for Israel to choose life. Can you hear the longing in Jesus' words also? Oh, that we would choose the good portion and see what a difference it makes!

Lord, You deserve my full attention. And as I spend time with
You, You work in me. So I choose life. I choose You every day.

Day 212
STRENGTHENING YOURSELF IN HIM

*David was greatly distressed, for the men spoke of stoning
him because the souls of them all were bitterly grieved,
each man for his sons and daughters. But David encouraged
and strengthened himself in the Lord his God.*
1 SAMUEL 30:6 AMPC

Upon their return from battle, not only had David's family been kidnapped, but also the families of his men. In their grief, they blamed David and plotted his death. He had no one to help him process his own sorrow. Except God.

Have you ever navigated a tough situation alone? There are times we have to walk through the valley without anyone by our side. No one there to encourage us or share hard-won wisdom. No one available to hold our hand through the hard parts. No one around to give us a hug or sit and listen as we talk it out. Sometimes it's just us. Going solo.

Like David, it's vital we know how to strengthen ourselves in the Lord. It might consist of desperate conversations with Him. It might entail reading His Word or speaking out scriptures that remind us who He is. It might be listening to worship music or figuratively crawling into our Daddy's lap and crying.

Remember, you have everything you need to encourage and strengthen yourself in God as you walk out this hard season.

*Lord, help me learn to strengthen myself when no one is
around. I'm so thankful that You always make a way.*

Day 213
FULLY BELIEVE

"Blessed is she who has believed that the
Lord would fulfill his promises to her!"
LUKE 1:45 NIV

The first day of spring bodes a promise for many people. It is the start of warmer weather, more sunlight, and longer days. Nature is given a brand-new fresh start that springs up all around us.

With great expectations, we look forward to the changing of the seasons. The winter may be long and cold, but we know that spring will come, and with that truth we trudge onward. Oh, if we only believed God's promises like we believe in the promise of spring! For then we would find ourselves rejoicing every day.

Today's verse from Luke doesn't say Mary is blessed because the Lord fulfilled His promises to her or that the Lord fulfilled His promises because she was already blessed. Mary was considered blessed the moment she fully believed that the Lord would keep His promises to her. The belief in her heavenly Father is what took away her fear, uncertainty, and confusion and replaced it with His powerful peace and joy—even as Mary waited with great expectation for God to come through for her.

When we believe in our hearts that a long-awaited blessing will come as we faithfully wait upon Him, we can and will find ourselves already blessed.

Heavenly Father, thank You for the blessings
found in the waiting. Amen.

Day 214

BLESSED BELIEVER

*That Sunday evening the disciples were meeting behind locked
doors because they were afraid. . . . Suddenly, Jesus was standing
there among them! "Peace be with you," he said. . . . Eight days
later the disciples were together again, and this time Thomas
was with them. The doors were locked; but suddenly, as before,
Jesus was standing among them. "Peace be with you," he said.*
JOHN 20:19, 26 NLT

No matter where you are, Jesus can reach you. No matter what barriers, locked doors, or walls are surrounding you, Jesus can get through, stand beside you, show you His face, His hands, His feet, His love, His Spirit. No doors can shut out His presence.

And where Jesus gains entrance, His peace follows. He blesses you with peace with God, with your own conscience, and with others. His presence stills the storms of your life, the waves of anxiety, the eddies of troubles. He not only gives you His peace but asks you to carry it with you.

Although you have not yet met Jesus physically face-to-face, nor put your hands on His wounds, Jesus favors you because of your trust in Him, saying, "Blessed and happy and to be envied are those who have never seen Me and yet have believed and adhered to and trusted and relied on Me" (John 20:29 AMPC).

"Peace be with you."

*Lord, nothing can keep You from me! Thank You
for the calming peace Your presence provides.*

Day 215
NO ROOM FOR GUILT

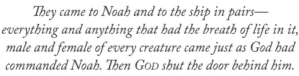

*They came to Noah and to the ship in pairs—
everything and anything that had the breath of life in it,
male and female of every creature came just as God had
commanded Noah. Then GOD shut the door behind him.*
GENESIS 7:16 MSG

Can you imagine the weight that must have immediately lifted off Noah's shoulders when it was God who closed the ark's door behind him? There was no opportunity for him to second-guess himself, wondering if he should have done more. He didn't have to worry about offering space to his neighbors or others as the waters began to rise. Noah didn't have to battle any anxiety about closing the door too early, wondering if others would have been saved too had he given it five more minutes.

There was room for every kind of male and female animal. There was room for Noah and his family. But God made sure there was no room for guilt.

What role does guilt play in your life? Sometimes guilt is the Holy Spirit's conviction to help us make better choices, but other times guilt is nothing more than condemnation from the enemy. It's the kind of guilt that leaves you feeling horrible, and it isn't from God.

You don't have to live in guilt any longer. With God's help, you can live in freedom with a God-given grace to embrace your imperfections.

*Lord, help me remember there's no room for
condemnation in my life. What a gift!*

Day 216

BEAUTY FOR ASHES

*To appoint unto them that mourn in Zion, to give unto them
beauty for ashes, the oil of joy for mourning, the garment of
praise for the spirit of heaviness; that they might be called trees of
righteousness, the planting of the LORD, that he might be glorified.*
ISAIAH 61:3 KJV

Repentance calls believers to mourn for their sin. This mourning requires Christians to recognize their sin and to feel remorse for their actions that offended God. God will use this humility and love of Him to give His children freedom and joy. Ashes were a sign of death and mourning—of being overcome by grief. However, God takes away death and the destruction of sin and instead gives the beauty of His presence. He molds the hearts of Christians to be more like the beautiful heart of Jesus. The second gift mentioned in the verse, oil, was an important medicine of antiquity; when Christians mourn their sin, God gives the medicine of joy by reminding His children that He cleanses them of the darkness in their hearts. When they are burdened by the cares of this world, He removes the spirit of heaviness and depression and clothes His people with praise and blessings. God then makes His children stand tall and firm like trees; they have inherited the righteousness of Christ because they realize they have no righteousness of their own. The great gardener does this work of healing and reconciliation because He is good.

*Jehovah, let us glorify Your name for all Your
gifts and trust only in You for lasting joy.*

Day 217
STAYING CLOSE

"Be strong and courageous. Do not be afraid; do not be discouraged,
for the LORD your God will be with you wherever you go."
JOSHUA 1:9 NIV

It's easy to tell others not to worry. It's easy to remind our friends that God is with them and He's got everything under control. And it's easy to remind ourselves of that when everything's going smoothly.

But when life sails us into rough waters, our natural instinct is to be afraid. We worry and fret. We cry out, not knowing how we will pay the bills or how we will face the cancer or how we will deal with whatever stormy waves crash around us. When life is scary, we get scared.

And believe it or not, that's a good thing. Because when we are afraid, when we are overwhelmed, when we realize that our circumstances are bigger than we are, that's when we're in the perfect place for God to pour out His comfort and assurance on us.

He never leaves us, but sometimes when life is good, we get distracted by other things and don't enjoy His presence as we should. When we feel afraid, we are drawn back to our heavenly Father's arms. And right in His arms is exactly where He wants us to be.

Dear Father, thank You for staying with me and giving me courage.
Help me to stay close to You, in good times and bad. Amen.

Day 218

FREE FROM DISTRACTIONS

*[Jesus] came near the path down the Mount of Olives,
and the whole crowd of the disciples began to praise God
joyfully with a loud voice for all the miracles they had seen:
The King who comes in the name of the Lord is the blessed
One. Peace in heaven and glory in the highest heaven!*
LUKE 19:37–38 HCSB

What occupies your mind throughout the day? Are you able to stay focused on what truly matters? Or do your thoughts dart from worry to worry? Is your heart centered on the Savior—or on the world's distractions?

When Jesus came on the scene, as described in these verses from the book of Luke, the crowd was wholly focused on Him. They had nothing but Jesus and praise on their minds. Their words and actions showed their honor and love for Jesus. Certainly, the people in the crowd had problems of their own—maybe a sick family member, possibly a difficult relationship, or perhaps tight finances. Regardless, they didn't let their human problems stand in the way of celebrating and praising Jesus. Their focus on the one who matters most kept them free from life's distractions.

Today, keep your heart and mind focused on Jesus. What are you praising Him for today? When your focus is heavenward, your soul will overflow with thanksgiving!

*Father God, I praise You for all You have done in my life.
Thank You for saving me, for blessing me. I love You! Amen.*

Day 219

CAN YOU HEAR ME NOW?

*"Call to me and I will answer you and tell you
great and unsearchable things you do not know."*
JEREMIAH 33:3 NIV

Although Jeremiah was imprisoned in a courtyard of King Zedekiah of Judah, God never abandoned him. His message of comfort and hope came to Jeremiah at a time when he needed it. Imprisoned and alone, he was still relaying God's messages to the unreceptive ears of the people he was trying to help.

Did you ever feel all alone while facing a daunting task or a bleak outlook? Remember, there is someone there at your side to hear your pleas. God is clear in His message to Jeremiah and to all of us: We need only call on God and trust in Him. He will fill us with awe and comfort.

Psalm 50:15 (NIV) has a similar message of hope from God: "And call on me in the day of trouble; I will deliver you, and you will honor me."

Call on God. He will answer you. He will support you, comfort you, and direct you. You have but to make that toll-free call. No telephone—neither cell nor landline—needed.

*Dear Lord, help me to come to You in times of trouble.
Help me to remember that You will answer me and tell me
great and wonderful things. Help me also reach out to You in
times of bounty and give You thanks for the joy it brings.*

Day 220
BROAD PLACES

"But those who suffer he delivers in their suffering;
he speaks to them in their affliction. He is wooing you from
the jaws of distress to a spacious place free from restriction,
to the comfort of your table laden with choice food."
JOB 36:15–16 NIV

When we are in distress or affliction, we may feel consumed by the sadness or anxiety that the crisis brings. It seems as if our circumstances will never change. Our imagination convinces us that the current torment will continue forever, that it will eat us up. Yet that is not the truth.

God has ways and means that we cannot understand. He is better to us than we can imagine. He is more merciful and more powerful than we can comprehend. God may use the pain of our circumstances to get our attention. Then, coaxing us like reluctant sheep, He leads us away from the gaping jaws of an all-consuming anxiety and into a wide-open space, "to a place free from distress" (Job 36:16 NLT).

Ask God to open your heart to any truths He would like to teach you. Be transformed by the painful circumstance you find yourself in. Trust that God will rescue you and lavish you with things for your heart to enjoy. What would you like to ask God for today?

God, please lead me into a broad and
peaceful place. I trust You with the journey.

Day 221

A BEAUTIFUL WAY TO LIVE

Steadfast love and faithfulness meet; righteousness and peace kiss each other. Faithfulness springs up from the ground, and righteousness looks down from the sky. Yes, the LORD will give what is good, and our land will yield its increase.
PSALM 85:10–12 ESV

This passage in Psalms is one of the most beautiful in the Bible, offering us by far the loveliest way to live. How wonderful to know that the Lord wants to give us what is good and that "our land will yield its increase." But for that glorious living to happen, steadfast love and faithfulness should meet up with one another in our hearts. And peace will then follow so closely behind righteousness that it will almost seem that they are kissing.

That deep trust in God is so pleasing to Him, He looks down from the heavens and calls it righteousness. Just as He did in the days of Abraham. Ahhh, yes.

May we be swept away from the old way of living, and may this beautiful way of life be ours.

Lord, I want to trust in You fully. Please push away my old habits that are trapping me in a way of life that is neither healthy nor positive nor victorious. Help me to live a new way—Your way. Amen.

Day 222

LINKING HEARTS WITH GOD

"You will receive power when the Holy Spirit comes on you;
and you will be my witnesses. . .to the ends of the earth."
ACTS 1:8 NIV

God knows our hearts. He knows what we need to make it through a day. So in His kindness, He gave us a gift in the form of the Holy Spirit. As a counselor, a comforter, and a friend, the Holy Spirit acts as our inner compass. He upholds us when times are hard and helps us hear God's directions. When the path of obedience grows dark, the Spirit floods it with light. What revelation! He lives within us. Therefore, our prayers are lifted to the Father, to the very throne of God. Whatever petitions we have, we may rest assured they are heard.

We can rejoice in the fact that God cared enough to bless our lives with the Spirit to direct our paths. God loves the praises of His people, and these praises revive the spirit within you. If you are weary or burdened, allow the Holy Spirit to minister to you. Seek the Holy Spirit and His wisdom, and ask Him to revive and refresh your inner woman. Place your hope in God and trust the Spirit's guidance, and He will never let you down.

Father God, how blessed I am to come into Your presence.
Help me, Father, when I am weak. Guide me this day. Amen.

Day 223
A MATTER OF TRUST

It is better to take refuge in the LORD than to trust in humans.
It is better to take refuge in the LORD than to trust in princes.
PSALM 118:8–9 NIV

These days, it's becoming increasingly difficult to know what information sources to trust. News outlets and political parties seem to have vastly different takes on the issues of the day. Medical science has different suggestions for keeping optimum health. And they all seem to be prefacing their advice with the same words: "Trust me."

So who can we trust? God. Trust in the one true source. No matter the status or position of the people seeking your trust, He is the only one that is steadfast and reliable. According to Isaiah 12:2 (NIV), "Surely God is my salvation; I will trust and not be afraid. The LORD, the LORD himself, is my strength and my defense; he has become my salvation."

It's easy to become disheartened by being led in so many different directions these days by human entities and talking heads. So do yourself a favor and seek your answers in God's Word and through prayer. Soak yourself in His teachings and His love for you. Take refuge in Him alone, and He will guide you down the right road in the right way.

Dear God, these days it is easy to feel lost or alone. Please lead me down the path that is right, down a road paved with Your love. Guide me in these difficult times, and bring me peace.

Day 224
WHY PRAISE GOD?

Though he slay me, yet will I trust in him.
JOB 13:15 KJV

One woman asked an honest question: "How can I praise God when everything in my life is falling apart?" Who hasn't pondered that question in moments of defeat, despair, or grief?

In the book of Acts, Paul and Silas, under Roman law, were publicly stripped and severely beaten for their faith. Afterward, they were jailed. Yet with bloody backs and shackled feet, they sat in a dirty cell undefeated. Rather than question God's intentions or apparent lack of protection, around midnight "Paul and Silas were praying and singing hymns to God" (Acts 16:25 NIV).

The power of prayer and praise resulted in complete deliverance. The prison doors flew open, and their chains fell off. What's more, the jailer and his family accepted Christ, and these ardent believers were able to witness to other inmates.

It's difficult to praise God when problems press in harder than a crowd exiting a burning building. But that's the time to praise Him the most. We wait for our circumstances to change, while God desires to change us despite them. Praise coupled with prayer in our darkest moments is what moves the mighty hand of God to work in our hearts and lives.

How can we pray to and praise God when everything goes wrong? The bigger question might be this: How can we not?

*Jesus, help me to pray to and praise
You despite my circumstances. Amen.*

Day 225
LIVING GRATEFULLY
EVERY DAY

True godliness with contentment is itself great wealth.
After all, we brought nothing with us when we came into the
world, and we can't take anything with us when we leave it.
1 TIMOTHY 6:6–7 NLT

As children, we learn the difference between *needs* and *wants*. We need food and clothes and shelter and love. Wants? Well, wants can be anything and often *everything*. Our wants can balloon into an Amazon wish list a mile long, just waiting for the day we swipe "buy now." Because those things will make us feel better, right?

After the initial jolt of dopamine that comes with the thrill of a purchase, we realize *things* don't bring peace or lasting happiness. What brings real peace and joy is contentment. The importance of this spiritual discipline can't be overlooked. For contentment coupled with godliness equals "great wealth." Why? Because when we live in a state of gratitude, trusting God will supply all we need, we realize just how immensely blessed we are. Paul writes, "Teach those who are rich in this world not to be proud and not to trust in their money, which is so unreliable. Their trust should be in God, who richly gives us all we need for our enjoyment" (1 Timothy 6:17 NLT).

Do you feel anxious, always striving for the next thing, for more? Pause. Rest, relying on God's unending strength and love.

Father, calm my heart and help me to live every day
grateful for Your surpassing goodness to me.

TRUE INNER PEACE

Great peace have those who love your law,
and nothing can make them stumble.
PSALM 119:165 NIV

There certainly are a lot of resources for self-help in the world today. At the bookstore, the self-help section is brimming with topics from Acrophobia to Zoophobia and everything in between. There are self-diagnosing websites and toll-free numbers you can call. There are television shows and podcasts on virtually every self-help topic, which seemingly provide a myriad of solutions to eradicate every possible stumbling block. But, according to today's verse, the road to true inner peace is loving God's Word.

The word used in today's scripture for "peace" is the Hebrew *shalom*, which translates to wholeness, tranquility, prosperity, and safety. The psalmist is telling you that you will not stumble once you realize loving God's law is the key to opening the door of inner peace.

If you feel locked out or isolated from the calm and cool that God promises, turn to His Word. Love His instructions. Walk as He would have you walk. And you'll not only find yourself sure-footed but possessing great peace.

Dear God, I long for shalom, for the peace only You can
provide, the true peace that comes from loving Your
laws and from believing in You with all my heart.

Day 227
PERFECTLY PEACEFUL

You will keep in perfect peace those whose minds are steadfast,
because they trust in you. Trust in the LORD forever,
for the LORD, the LORD himself, is the Rock eternal.
ISAIAH 26:3–4 NIV

When Jesus was in a small boat whipped about by fierce winds and enormous waves, He trusted God and was at peace. He was fully human and completely capable of feeling fear and anxiety, but He chose peace. You too can choose peace. You need not be at the mercy of your thoughts and feelings, for you can "take captive every thought to make it obedient to Christ" (2 Corinthians 10:5 NIV). That means not letting your thoughts land where they please but deciding instead what you will think about.

God gives you a clear picture of where to place your troubled thoughts. The Lord is "the Rock eternal." He's powerful and able to hold whatever worries you. He can stop the storm, but sometimes He chooses to hold you through it. He's also everlasting and constant. God doesn't falter and disappear when you need Him most. He's always present.

What concerns do you wrestle with today? Take them to God. Tell Him you trust Him. Proclaim aloud, "There is no Rock like our God" (1 Samuel 2:2 NIV). Peace will fill you as your mind is stayed on Him.

God, there's no rock like You. Remind me of Your faithfulness
and power today. I choose to put my trust in You.

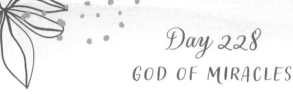

Day 228

GOD OF MIRACLES

He listened to Paul as he was speaking. Paul looked directly at him, saw that he had faith to be healed and called out, "Stand up on your feet!" At that, the man jumped up and began to walk.
ACTS 14:9–10 NIV

Paul and Barnabas were traveling around, sharing the gospel message. They preached it boldly. Many accepted, while others rejected their message. When they were in Lystra, Paul was given power by the Lord to heal a lame man, a man who had never walked—until now! Through the power of the Holy Spirit, Paul healed him, and scripture reveals to us why this man was selected: when Paul looked at the man, he could see "that he had faith to be healed."

Do you believe as this man did? Do you wake up each day expecting the Lord to do great things? Or have you given up and laid to rest a big dream in your life?

You serve a God who is powerful enough to make a lame man stand up and walk! Believe in Jesus. He's above and beyond all you can imagine. He can bring beauty from ashes in your life. He can make dry bones live again.

God, give me hope again where I am hopeless. You are a God who still works miracles in Your children's lives. Help me to believe. Help me to stand up on my feet again! Amen.

Day 229
A NEW SONG

Hallelujah! Sing to the Lord a new song, His praise in the assembly of the godly. Let Israel celebrate its Maker; let the children of Zion rejoice in their King. Let them praise His name with dancing and make music to Him with tambourine and lyre.
PSALM 149:1–3 HCSB

According to the psalmist, there was much to rejoice about. Although God's people had endured much, they were committed to singing a new song to the Lord. They focused their thoughts, heart, and actions toward their Creator. They danced and made music! Their praises flowed from inside of them, outwardly toward God.

God-followers like Job, Abraham, Sarah, Elijah, Ruth, Naomi, Hannah, Esther, the disciples, Mary Magdalene, and the apostle Paul endured so much for their Creator. Yet they still knew how to shift their mind, heart, and actions toward praising and thanking God.

You too have a new song that you can sing to the Lord. Look back over your life and recount the times God pulled through for you. Consider your present circumstances. Is there anything worth praising God for? Of course there is! So sing, dance, make music to the Lord. Then watch how it changes your perspective from the inside out.

Abba Father, help me to choose to focus on the joy and peace that only comes from You! Today, I lift my voice in a new song of praise to You!

Day 230
BE STRONG

Be not grieved and depressed, for the joy of
the Lord is your strength and stronghold.
NEHEMIAH 8:10 AMPC

Nehemiah, Ezra, and other religious and civil leaders of their day had been given the job of leading the Jews back to Jerusalem after seventy years of exile. It hadn't been easy work for those who had made the long journey. Solomon's beautiful temple had been destroyed, and the attempts to rebuild it had resulted in something very inferior to what they remembered. Rebuilding the walls and reestablishing their homes were tasks made more difficult when they only had one hand with which to build. They held weapons in their other hand in order to defend their right to live in the land. At one point the work of rebuilding was stopped after their enemies wrote a letter to the Persian king pointing out the unsuitability of the Jews to live out from under the immediate control of their captors.

Now the work was done, and the people wanted to hear what the law of God said so they could avoid making the same mistakes again. All the Jews in the land came to Jerusalem and listened as Ezra read from the Law and Levites explained what they were hearing. The renewed understanding of God's Word caused them to weep. Finally, Nehemiah stood before the people he now governed and begged them not to be grieved and depressed. God was pleased with their desire to do what He commanded. It was a day for rejoicing, for they were back in the land.

Father, joy gives us strength to do Your will.
Let us find our joy in You today.

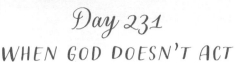

Day 231
WHEN GOD DOESN'T ACT

LORD, you have seen this; do not be silent. Do not be far
from me, Lord. Awake, and rise to my defense!
PSALM 35:22–23 NIV

David's cry is as ancient as Job's, as modern as the Holocaust and beyond: "Awake, and rise to my defense!"

"Abba Daddy, wake up! I need help."

Things were beyond bad for David. Although he'd done nothing wrong, others gloated over him, hated him without cause, and accused him falsely.

After unburdening his heart, David returned to an attitude of praise. Placing full confidence in God's trust, he says, "My tongue will proclaim your righteousness. . .all day long" (Psalm 35:28 NIV).

Centuries later, the Son of David, Jesus Christ, reached the hour planned since before time began. Feeling overwhelmed, lonelier than at any point in all eternity, He begged God, "Let this cup pass from Me" (Matthew 26:39 NKJV).

Like David, Jesus circled back to trusting faith. "Nevertheless, not as I will, but as You will" (Matthew 26:39 NKJV). His absolute surrender is an example of trust carried to the extreme.

You may not be called to such extreme tests. But whenever it seems God is taking a break, voice your fears and requests—then fall back to trust God to do what's best.

Whenever Your silence adds confusion to the attacks of
the enemy, thank You for accepting my complaints and cries.
Let praise and trust rise up in me before I see You in action.

Day 232
FINDING CALM

But I have calmed and quieted myself, I am like a weaned child with its mother; like a weaned child I am content.

PSALM 131:2 NIV

There are a couple of apps you can purchase on a smartphone that promise calm. They include soft music, white noise and rain sounds, meditation and breathing exercises. The makers of these apps know what a lot of the women in this world need—a chance to escape, to relax and recharge, to find contentment. Although you may not be able to control your circumstances, you can try to get a rein on your emotions.

Like an anxious child who only wants her mother, your heart longs for a place of comfort, peace, and contentment. Although you know there are some things in this world that can give you momentary peace and comfort, where can you go for something long lasting?

Go to God. He yearns to be that source of long-lasting calm you need. He wants you to come into His presence for comfort, peace, and contentment. This type of calm is unshakable and immovable because it comes straight from God. It will never fade away or falter.

To obtain that kind of calm, all you need to do is put your faith and trust in the Lord. Because when you trust that God is working in your now, you aren't anxious for your future.

Lord, thank You for the everlasting calm
You provide when I'm anxious. Amen.

Day 233
A JOY FOCUS

For the joy set before him he endured the cross. . . . Consider
him who endured such opposition from sinners, so that
you will not grow weary and lose heart.
HEBREWS 12:2–3 NIV

We cannot sustain emotional health without hope—something good to anticipate. Believers in Christ have a hopeful future even when our prognosis is death, because we will forever be with the Lord (see 2 Corinthians 5:8). Nonetheless, during trials, it takes determination and spiritual power to meditate on the joys set before us, like Jesus did.

One way to keep a joyful focus is found in Psalm 68:19–20 (NIV): "Praise be to the Lord, to God our Savior, who daily bears our burdens. Our God is a God who saves; from the Sovereign LORD comes escape from death." In the margin by these verses, I have listed the "escapes from death" God has mercifully granted our family—fifteen times so far we have been delivered from life-threatening accidents or potentially fatal illnesses. (What names and dates can you list in your Bible?)

What if God does not deliver *from* a trial? Then He will sustain us *through* the trial by bearing our burdens with us every day.

When we grow weary and find ourselves losing heart, let's focus on God our Savior, our Sovereign Lord, our burden bearer. If the joy of the Lord is our focus, it will also be our strength (see Nehemiah 8:10).

God of my salvation, I look forward to spending eternity
with You. Until then, thank You for bearing my
burdens and giving me escapes from death. Help me
stay joyful because I'm focused on You. Amen.

Day 234
PRECIOUS TO GOD

*She is more precious than rubies: and all the things thou
canst desire are not to be compared unto her. Length of
days is in her right hand; and in her left hand riches and
honour. Her ways are ways of pleasantness, and all her
paths are peace. She is a tree of life to them that lay hold
upon her: and happy is every one that retaineth her.*
<small>PROVERBS 3:15–18 KJV</small>

Solomon described what life would be like for those who sought
Wisdom. She would lead the way to honor and a fruitful life. When
trouble came, they wouldn't stumble or fall.

You are a precious child of God. You are His daughter. He loves
you and sent His Son to die for you. He wants you to live a full and
abundant life filled with blessings and goodness. And all through that
life, amid good times and bad, God wants you to seek Him for wisdom.

Precious daughter of God, take some time to let that sink in. No
matter who you are, what you've suffered or endured, rich or poor,
plain or fancy, God adores you! And when you seek after Him and
His wisdom, He won't fail you!

*Lord, thank You for loving me unconditionally, for always
looking out for me, for answering my call, for being such a
wonderful Father and guide. Linger with me here as I let
that sink in. Then fill me with Your love and wisdom.*

Day 235
TRUST IN THE LORD

Those who trust in themselves are fools,
but those who walk in wisdom are kept safe.
PROVERBS 28:26 NIV

Repeatedly in scripture, we find admonitions to trust in God. And today's scripture makes it clear only a fool trusts in herself.

An earlier verse in Proverbs states: "In their hearts humans plan their course, but the LORD establishes their steps" (16:9 NIV). This tells us that it's good to plan for the future. Certainly, we're not meant to just stagger into each day haphazardly. But God clearly reminds His children that, ultimately, we must pray for His will. He knows what's best.

When your plans regarding work or relationships seem to fall apart, resist the urge to panic. Trust not in those plans you had carefully laid for yourself. Trust in God. Later on, even if it's years down the road, when you look back, you'll see that what seemed to be a disaster at the time was, in fact, a blessing. God makes no mistakes!

The Lord assures us that when we seek wisdom, we'll find it (James 1:5). So seek God's will for your life, make plans, and then consistently lay those plans at the feet of the Almighty. Ask Him to open and close doors in your life as He sees fit. You'll be amazed at the peace that follows.

Sovereign God, please help me to walk in wisdom
according to Your will all the days of my life. Amen.

DO THIS INSTEAD OF WORRYING

*Fear not, little flock; for it is your Father's
good pleasure to give you the kingdom.*
LUKE 12:32 KJV

Your heart is beating fast. Your mind won't settle. Your breaths barely reach your lungs. You're anxious, worried about this or that. Truth is, there's a lot you can choose to be anxious about—family, work, money, health, war, weather, the future. . . . But this is also true: you can't change anything with anxious thoughts. Even before there was cyberbullying, nuclear weapons, and pages-long to-do lists, Jesus anticipated your tendency to worry. He told His disciples, "And which of you by being anxious can add a single hour to his span of life? If then you are not able to do as small a thing as that, why are you anxious about the rest?" (Luke 12:25–26 ESV).

Since worry achieves nothing but more worry, what should you do instead? "Seek the Kingdom of God above all else, and he will give you everything you need" (Luke 12:31 NLT). Your God—the one who fills the bellies of the birds and clothes the lilies like royalty—knows your needs, and He is capable and faithful to satisfy them. More than that, it is His *pleasure* to care for you. So turn every anxious thought into a chance to focus on your Father. With eyes fixed on Him, the kingdom itself is yours.

*Father, use this anxiety to draw me toward
You. I can be calm because You care.*

Day 237

YOUR DAY TO CHOOSE

And [Jesus] said to His disciples, Therefore I tell you, do not be anxious and troubled [with cares] about your life, as to what you will [have to] eat; or about your body, as to what you will [have to] wear. For life is more than food, and the body [more] than clothes.

LUKE 12:22–23 AMPC

Do you often find yourself anxious, overwrought, and worried? If so, Jesus offers you a cure.

In His Word, Jesus makes it clear you're not to be troubled about anything in your life, neither as to what you'll eat nor as to what you'll wear. Instead, you're to trust God to provide for you, just as the birds trust Him for their food. Besides, Jesus says, your worrying will get you nowhere. It only subtracts, not adds, to your life.

Yet not worrying can be difficult if you were raised with the conviction that you need to be able to take care of yourself. Thus, it can take some time to let go so that you can let God. But it can be done. How? By choosing to seek the Lord and His kingdom above all things and before all people. That means looking to God and His Word in the beginning of the day, before your feet even touch the ground.

Lord, above all other things and people in my life, I choose to trust and seek You. I know that as I do, You will supply all I need.

Day 238

BEATITUDE ATTITUDE

*"Blessed are you when people hate you, when they
exclude you and insult you and reject your name
as evil, because of the Son of Man."*
LUKE 6:22 NIV

Jesus preached a series of blessings known as the beatitudes. These blessings provided perspective to those in the faith, a viewpoint on how to live in such a way that the challenges and cruelties of this world would not taint a relationship with God.

This life isn't easy. There may be times when you want to throw in the towel. Yet your faith can be a catalyst to break through and create change in your life or in the lives of others, if you are able to endure some of the curveballs that come your way.

Sometimes you might experience seasons of being financially deprived. Sometimes you might know what it's like to not have enough to eat. Sometimes circumstances may figuratively or literally bring you to tears. Sometimes you might experience a cold shoulder because of who and what you believe in. If—or when—these things happen, look to God. Remember the beatitude attitude He desires you to have. Know He will see you through whatever your circumstances are and will bless you because of it. That's His promise!

*Lord, when my attitude gets the best of me, help me to remember
the blessings You have in mind for me. Help me look up to You
instead of down and to rest in Your promises all around.*

Day 239
FIXED AND FOCUSED

I trusted in, relied on, and was confident
in You, O Lord; I said, You are my God.
PSALM 31:14 AMPC

Trusting God might sometimes seem attainable. Other times, not so much. Factoring in things like your background, your upbringing, your childhood, and the relationships you have experienced throughout life, trust might be a very difficult thing to do.

If trusting God seems like it's nearly impossible, you might be tempted to put your faith and hope into things and people. This is because they might seem to be able to provide a quick fix or instant gratification. Yet the paradox is that as you abide in Jesus, all you need is to trust *Him* with things and people.

In Psalm 31, David petitions for God to shower His grace and mercy on him, for help and protection in regard to his enemies. He cries out to God in desperation for the challenges in this life, looking for—and expecting—God to fight for him.

Can you relate to David's pleas when you consider the stories and struggles both you and your fellow brothers and sisters face? No matter what's happening, know that God is able. Have mustard seed faith to trust in, rely on, and be confident in His faithfulness, and He will lead you to victory.

Jesus, I trust You in the good and hard times. Holy Spirit,
please fill me with the ability to stay fixed and focused on You.

Day 240

NIGHTTIME INSTRUCTION

I will bless the LORD who guides me; even at night my heart instructs me. I know the LORD is always with me. I will not be shaken, for he is right beside me.
PSALM 16:7–8 NLT

Ah, finally! You're all tucked in, the lights are off, and you're free to just relax. There, in that peaceful, quiet place, the Lord begins to whisper to your heart. He tickles your ear with His still, small voice and gives insight about the problems you're facing. Or perhaps He speaks to you through a dream, giving you ideas about how to handle a situation you're walking through.

Why do you suppose God often speaks in the night like this? You didn't deliberately set out to encounter Him in this way, after all! But when your mind is finally free from the cares of the day, you're able to hear His voice. You aren't distracted by money worries or relationship squabbles or the roar of the television. You're finally free to just be. And the Lord sees this as the perfect time to give you instructions for the tasks ahead.

"I will not be shaken, for he is right beside me." This is true, you know. . .even when you sleep. So, whatever you're wrestling with during the daylight hours, sleep in peace, knowing God is still on the job, even when your eyes are closed.

Lord, thank You for speaking to me in the night. Even then, my heart instructs me as I hear Your still, small voice. Amen.

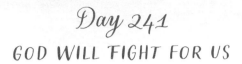

Day 241

GOD WILL FIGHT FOR US

*When all our enemies heard about this, all the surrounding
nations were afraid and lost their self-confidence, because they
realized that this work had been done with the help of our God.*
NEHEMIAH 6:16 NIV

The Israelites faced much opposition when rebuilding the wall of
Jerusalem—insults, threats, weariness, and hardships. But they knew
that their God would fight for them. And He was indeed faithful.

We may not be building a city wall, but we will face any number
of hardships in our lives. Perhaps a wayward teenage daughter will
come home pregnant. Or you will face the sudden disloyalty within a
lifelong friendship. Maybe you will suffer the bullying of a boss or the
tremendous challenges and disappointments in a career you thought
was tailor-made by God. Perhaps the painful issues will be health or
marriage related, or you may have bouts of poverty or depression or
experience ridicule because of your faith in Christ. Life can be brutal
at times, but God *will* fight for us, for you.

Stay close to God and ask Him to come alongside you. The Lord
is willing and waiting, and He is full of love and mercy.

*Dearest Lord, in this troubled world, please be my stronghold and
my courage. In Jesus' powerful and holy name I pray, amen.*

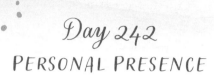

Day 242

PERSONAL PRESENCE

*There I will meet with the Israelites, and the Tent of Meeting
shall be sanctified by My glory [the Shekinah, God's visible
presence]. . . . I will dwell among the Israelites and be their
God. And they shall know [from personal experience] that
I am the Lord their God, Who brought them forth out of
the land of Egypt that I might dwell among them.*
EXODUS 29:43, 45–46 AMPC

With God in our lives, we can be unshakable believers. Yet to maintain
and replenish that unwavering confidence in our Lord God, we need
to spend time in God's presence.

In the days of Exodus, God made His presence known visibly.
His people could see Him as the Shekinah, the visible presence in
the Tent of Meeting. He had also appeared "before them by day in
a pillar of cloud to lead them along the way and by night in a pillar
of fire to give them light, that they might travel by day and by night"
(Exodus 13:21 AMPC). God actually dwelled amid His people so that
they could know Him from personal experience.

Today, God's presence is within His people. Thus, to "see" Him or
spend time with Him, all it takes is some quiet. Some silence. Some
prayer. Some peace.

Find time each day to meet with your Lord, to personally experience His presence. And He will bring you forth.

*I come before You, Lord, seeking Your face. Make Your
presence known to me. Let's get personal. Amen.*

Day 243

LOVE'S CURRENT

*The grace of our Lord was poured out on me abundantly,
along with the faith and love that are in Christ Jesus.*
1 TIMOTHY 1:14 NIV

Giving a gift to a loved one often gives us great pleasure. We shop in anticipation of the recipient's excitement in our purchases. When we love that person, our joy can be even greater. So it is with God's love for us. He gave us His Son, a pure and perfect gift, because He loves us in vast measure.

No matter what our attitude may be toward God, we can never forget His precious gift of Jesus Christ. Even if we reflect despair or anger, He loves us. Scripture states grace and love are given abundantly, which means bountifully, plenteously, generously. How can we miss God's love when He is so gracious?

The famous theologian Charles Spurgeon put it this way: "Our God never ceases to shine upon his children with beams of love. Like a river, his lovingkindness is always flowing, with a fullness inexhaustible as his own nature."

This day, rise with the expectation of God's great grace and love. Let your life reflect that love, and feel His pleasure. Plunge into the river of His love and feel Him carry you on its current. Relax in His arms in the knowledge that He cares for you.

*Lord, carry me along in the current of Your
love's stream. I love You extravagantly. Amen.*

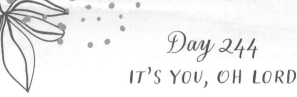

Day 244
IT'S YOU, OH LORD

When I said, "My foot is slipping," your unfailing love, LORD, supported me. When anxiety was great within me, your consolation brought me joy.
PSALM 94:18–19 NIV

If you've ever walked through a particularly difficult period, you know what it's like to feel deflated. Perhaps there were moments when you wondered if you would make it through, when you felt like giving up. Isn't it remarkable to know that God was right there, even in the midst of your pain? He never left you. He never quit on you. And He never will.

When you hit your jumping-off point, He's right there, catching you midleap. When your feet are stuck in clay, He reaches down and plucks you up again. When the stresses are weighing you down, bringing nothing but tears and despair, He consoles and brings joy.

God cares deeply about your situation, and He longs to be your all in all. Don't give up on Him. He will never give up on you.

I needed that reminder, Lord, that You will never give up on me. I've given up on myself more times than I can count. But You, oh Lord, go on supporting me. You go on consoling. You continue to give joy. So many times, my feet have slipped out from under me, but I can count on You not to let me go, Father. I'm so very grateful for that. Amen.

Day 245
A GENERATIONAL BLESSING

*"And you, Solomon my son, know the God of your father
and serve him with a whole heart and with a willing mind,
for the LORD searches all hearts and understands every
plan and thought. If you seek him, he will be found by you,
but if you forsake him, he will cast you off forever."*
1 CHRONICLES 28:9 ESV

Do you recognize the generational blessing in today's scripture? The fact that Solomon knew his father's God proves the authenticity of King David's faith. And that Solomon chose to serve the Lord shows the faith he grew up watching and learning about became real and true in his own heart.

Let this be encouragement that how you live your life matters because others are watching. They're looking to see how you handle both joyful times and difficult ones. They're watching how God manifests in your mess and how you respond. They are looking at the ways you manage stress and anxiety and fear.

Solomon didn't see perfection in his father's faith but instead saw a man who lived with purpose and passion for God. He recognized the strong connection between his father's thought life and actions. And it helped secure his own faith in God, which is a blessing we all hope to pass down to the next generation.

*Lord, let me live my faith out loud in honest and transparent
ways. And let it positively affect the hearts of others for You.*

Day 246

CALM, COMFORT, AND CHEER

*The Lord knows the thoughts of man, that they are
vain (empty and futile—only a breath). Blessed
(happy, fortunate, to be envied) is the man whom You
discipline and instruct, O Lord, and teach out of Your law.*
PSALM 94:11–12 AMPC

It's difficult to admit that, compared to God's thoughts, ours are so fleeting and futile. Yet when we read through God's Word and compare our thoughts with His, we cannot help but concede it's true!

Fortunately, we can learn about God, learn to think what He thinks, by studying His Word and following it. When we do so, a strange and wonderful thing happens: God gives us the power to keep ourselves "calm in the days of adversity" (Psalm 94:13 AMPC).

By soaking our minds in God's Word and following His will and way, we can find the calm we need to face anything that comes. But that's not all! We also begin to recognize our thoughts. When we think we're slipping, we can tap into His steadfast love and stay upright (verse 18). When we're filled with anxiety and turn to Him, we can be sure His comfort will cheer us (verse 19). And when we're joyful in Him, we'll find He's delighted in us!

*You, Lord, are my refuge, my stronghold,
and my rock—my calm, comfort, and cheer!*

Day 247
SECURITY FROM NEGATIVE THOUGHTS

*"They will fight against you like an attacking army,
but I will make you as secure as a fortified wall of
bronze. They will not conquer you, for I am with you
to protect and rescue you. I, the LORD, have spoken!"*
JEREMIAH 15:20 NLT

We may think that our spiritual enemies attack us from the outside—but sometimes, our own thoughts can be like a destructive army, pulling us down spiritually. When anxiety and fear beset us, when our thoughts are crowded with frustration or resentment, or when guilt and self-doubt make us question ourselves, our thoughts and emotions can rob us of the strength we need to live with love and courage. But God understands—after all, He created our human nature—and He promises to help us. His Spirit can act as a "wall" between our thoughts and our true and deepest identities. With God on our side, we don't have to be defeated by our own thoughts.

*Protect me from my obsessive thoughts, Lord.
Rescue me from my overwhelming emotions.
May Your presence surround my heart and mind.*

Day 248

HELP ME BELIEVE!

Lord, I believe! [Constantly] help my weakness of faith!
MARK 9:24 AMPC

A man's young son had issues. He would go into convulsions, foam at the mouth, grind his teeth, and then fall into a stupor. The danger was that the boy would be thrown into fire *and* water. The loving yet desperate father said to Jesus, "If You can do anything, do have pity on us and help us" (Mark 9:22 AMPC).

Jesus replied, "[You say to Me], If You can do anything? [Why,] all things can be (are possible) to him who believes!" (Mark 9:23 AMPC). That's when the father asked Jesus to constantly help him with his weakness of faith. Moments later, Jesus healed the boy of his affliction.

Jesus has one request when you ask for help with your own issues: Take the *if* out of the equation when it comes to believing in His power. Have faith that *He can do* anything in your life, that for Him *nothing is impossible*.

But when (and *if*) you do fall short in faith, know that the Lord will constantly help you, pouring on you more than a sufficient amount of grace, enabling Him to work even through your weakness.

No matter what your level of faith, constantly call on Jesus. He will come, grip your hand, and lift you up into a life of seemingly impossible miracles.

Jesus, everything is possible with You in my heart.
Help me to believe this more and more each day.

Day 249
GOD SENT

"Don't be upset, and don't be angry with yourselves for selling me to this place. It was God who sent me here ahead of you to preserve your lives. . . . God has sent me ahead of you to keep you and your families alive and to preserve many survivors. So it was God who sent me here, not you!"
GENESIS 45:5, 7–8 NLT

Sometimes we may find ourselves in hard places because of the manipulations or machinations of those who wish us ill. Yet while we are going through such difficulties, we can be assured that we're still in God's hands. That He's the sovereign ruler over all. That He'll make sure to use whatever happens to us for good.

To stay on the right track, we must trust not only that God knows what He's doing, even when we can in no way fathom how, but (1) He will ever find a way to make good come of our situation or (2) He will get us out, around, or through it.

So when the hard times come, when others plot against you, when it seems as if there is only darkness and despair surrounding you, when through no fault of your own you are in a mess, remain firm in both faith and hope, remembering God has a plan and all will someday be well.

I'm trusting myself to You, Lord, for You are my light and hope.

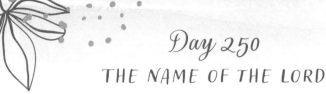

Day 250

THE NAME OF THE LORD

*The name of the Lord is a strong tower; the [consistently]
righteous man [upright and in right standing with God]
runs into it and is safe, high [above evil] and strong.*
PROVERBS 18:10 AMPC

The "name of the Lord" is the expression for the entire character of
God, the person He has revealed Himself to be. That's why His name
is a strong tower, a place of safety, high above this world of humankind.

When you're afraid, you can run to the Lord, your rock of refuge.
When you're in want, run to the Lord who will provide. When you're
alone, run to the Lord that heals. When you need guidance and
protection, run to the Lord my Shepherd. When you're anxious, run
to the Lord who is peace. When you feel ignored or invisible, run to
the Lord who who sees or watches over me. When you need wisdom
and calm, go to the Wonderful Counselor and Prince of Peace. When
you need a path to understanding, head to the teacher.

When you have a particular need, run to and pray in the name
of that aspect of God you require. You will find all you need in the
name of the Lord.

*Strong Tower, I run to You when I am troubled in mind,
hurting in heart, out of sync in spirit. Reveal Yourself
to me in all Your many aspects. You are all I need.*

Day 251
GOOD SHEPHERD

Then we your people, the sheep of your pasture,
will praise you forever; from generation to
generation we will proclaim your praise.
PSALM 79:13 NIV

Although not the smartest animals, sheep can easily distinguish their own shepherd's voice from all others. That may not cause sheep to rank higher than other creatures on the IQ scale, but it shows they have their priorities straight!

Oftentimes, you may stumble through life a lot like a ewe. You go astray. You wander from the fold. You encounter dangers and snares. But your Good Shepherd remains faithful. He knows the sheep of His pasture. He watches over you. He guides you back toward home.

What a blessing it is that you can know you belong to God! Listen for the still, small voice of your Good Shepherd. He may be calling you to pursue a dream you think is unattainable, a reminder that nothing is impossible with God. He may be asking you to reach out to another woman or a child who desperately needs a word of encouragement or a bit of help. This too is a reminder that He will not call you to that which you cannot accomplish in His name.

Praise your heavenly Father today. Thank Him for being such a loving Shepherd. He will never lose sight of His own. May your ears always be fine-tuned to His voice.

Good Shepherd, lead me today in Your everlasting ways. Amen.

Day 252
TAKE HEART

"I have told you all this so that you may have peace in me.
Here on earth you will have many trials and sorrows.
But take heart, because I have overcome the world."
JOHN 16:33 NLT

When you read the words "take heart," what image comes to mind? Do you see your broken heart cradled in your hands, being massaged back to life? Do you envision a frown turning into a smile, anguish replaced with peace? Perhaps you see yourself drawing in a deep breath and putting one foot in front of the other, determined you can make it the rest of the way if you just have faith.

When Jesus says to "*take* heart," He's implying that somewhere along the way you may have *lost* heart. But not to worry. As God transforms your life, He will gift you with His courage and peace, hope and confidence, joy and patience. For He works to replace your fearful, discouraged, worry-filled, and broken heart with His. When you yield yourself to the Master's ministrations, you'll experience His supernatural ability to overcome any circumstance that might come your way. What an amazing heart swap that would be!

Father, how grateful I am that You have overcome the world!
I would despair, otherwise. Thank You for the reminder that You're
my courage giver, my peace, my overcomer. Without You, I would
surely fail, Lord. With You, I can face any obstacle. Amen.

Day 253
JONAH'S PRAYER

*"When my life was ebbing away, I remembered you,
Lord, and my prayer rose to you, to your holy temple."*
JONAH 2:7 NIV

Jonah ran from God. He knew where God had directed him to go, but he refused. He thought he knew better than God. He trusted in his own ways over God's. Where did it get him? He ended up in the belly of a great fish for three days. This was not a punishment but rather a forced retreat! Jonah needed time to think and pray. He came to the end of himself and remembered his sovereign God. He describes the depths to which he was cast. This was not just physical but emotional as well. Jonah had been in a deep struggle between God's call and his own will.

In his great prayer from the belly of the fish, we read these words: "But you, Lord my God, brought my life up from the pit" (Jonah 2:6 NIV). When Jonah reached a point of desperation, he realized that God was his only hope. Have you been there? Not in the belly of a great fish, but in a place where you are made keenly aware that it is time to turn back to God? God loves His children and always stands ready to receive us when we need a second chance.

*Father, like Jonah I sometimes think my own ways
are better than Yours. Help me to be mindful that
Your ways are always good and right. Amen.*

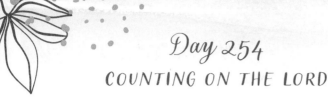

Day 254

COUNTING ON THE LORD

*I am counting on the LORD; yes, I am counting on him. I have put
my hope in his word. I long for the Lord more than sentries long
for the dawn, yes, more than sentries long for the dawn. O Israel,
hope in the LORD; for with the LORD there is unfailing love.*

PSALM 130:5–7 NLT

When you find yourself in the depths of despair, do as this psalmist
did. Call upon God for help.

Step 1: Ask Him to hear your cry, to pay attention to your prayer.

Step 2: Remind yourself that your God is a loving and forgiving
God. That He is the one you can count on. He is the one in whose
Word you can hope.

Step 3: Hope. And do so with a sense of expectation. Make it a
firm fact in your mind that God *will* do something. He *will* forgive
and help you. He *will* enfold you within His everlasting arms. He
will provide what you lack. He *will* see you through this—no matter
what "this" may be.

Step 4: Wait. Look for Him around every corner, behind every
word in His Book. Know that He holds for you the love that never
fails, the mercy that lasts forever.

And lastly, Step 5: Believe.

*Lord of my life, thank You for hearing my prayer. For loving
me and forgiving me. You are my hope, my love, my light. For
You alone I wait and live, knowing You will see me through.*

Day 255
SEEKING GOD

I sought the LORD, and he answered me and delivered me from all my fears. . . . The angel of the LORD encamps around those who fear him. . . . Those who seek the LORD lack no good thing. . . . Seek peace and pursue it. . . . The LORD is near to the brokenhearted and saves the crushed in spirit.
PSALM 34:4, 7, 10, 14, 18 ESV

Anything you need can be found by applying to God. For He is the one listening, the one who will answer your cries and turn your fears into faith. When your courage is faltering, God will *thunk* down a wall of protection, surrounding you, keeping you from harm.

You see, God is looking to meet the eyes of those seeking His. And once that connection is made, there is nothing He will not do to bless you.

Your task is to simply do good things. To look for peace, embrace it. And on those days when your heart breaks, when you feel as if your spirit has been pounded down to the ground, He will be so close to you that you will feel His breath warm your neck. Feeling His presence so close, your spirit will immediately be lifted and embraced by His.

You are my all in all, Lord. As I seek You, as I turn away from evil, as I look for Your peace, Lord, be ever so close to me.

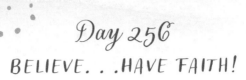

Day 256

BELIEVE. . .HAVE FAITH!

"If you follow my decrees and are careful to obey my commands. . .
I will grant peace in the land, and you will lie down and no
one will make you afraid. I will remove wild beasts from the
land, and the sword will not pass through your country."
LEVITICUS 26:3, 6 NIV

Did you ever wake up in the middle of the night, filled with fear for an unknown reason? Perhaps you had a nightmare. Maybe you heard a noise. Whatever the reason, the fear was real in the darkness of night.

In Leviticus 26, God reminds you that He will keep you safe and will grant you peace in exchange for your faithfulness to Him and your observance of His commandments. In verse 2 (NIV), He states, "I am the LORD." What a wonderful assurance of His sovereignty and His ability to protect you!

God offers the same assurance to you. You can lie down and trust that you will have peace and protection from all fears. Believe. Have faith in God. It is such a small ask on your part for security and tranquility in your life!

Dear Lord, help me to adhere to Your observances and
commandments. Help me to do what is right in Your eyes
and to be able to enjoy Your peace and Your assurance so that
I will be unafraid. Help me to face each day in peace.

Day 257

MOMENTARILY TONGUE—TIED

Then a cloud appeared and covered them, and a voice came from the cloud: "This is my Son, whom I love. Listen to him!"
MARK 9:7 NIV

During the transfiguration, Elijah and Moses appeared on the mountaintop with Jesus. When His clothes became "dazzling white," Peter, James, and John were momentarily dumbstruck. Very confused and astonished at this incredible sight, Peter, not really sure what to say, offered to build three shelters for Elijah, Moses, and Jesus. Then, suddenly, a voice from above made it all clear. God spoke, saying, "This is my Son, whom I love. Listen to him!" And suddenly, the three men saw no one but Jesus.

Jesus talks to all believers, including you, although sometimes it may be hard to hear Him. Although His voice may sometimes get lost in the clutter of life, He is most definitely there, waiting for you to turn your mind to Him.

Listen for Jesus' words in your heart. Dive into the Gospels, in which you can see His words and their intent. Allow them to guide your actions. Pray for direction, knowing that with Jesus the Word in your heart, you will find peace of mind and clarity of thought.

Dear God, I thank You for the gift of Your perfect Son.
Help me to listen to Him and to follow His word and teachings.
For then I will find direction, wisdom, peace, and clarity.

Day 258
CASTING CARES

Cast all your anxiety on him because he cares for you.
1 PETER 5:7 NIV

Do you have tiresome work that beckons, follows, and awaits you? No matter how demanding it is, the way you handle that work can reflect God.

Do you have relationship challenges with a husband, parent, friend, or child? The way you handle those challenges can be a bright spot for everyone involved.

Are you fearful about the future, either for yourself or for your children? The way you handle that fear can be a blessing into eternity.

Are there health issues that you or a loved one face? What you do with those can speak to the lives of many.

Do your friends, neighbors, or coworkers have things they are deeply struggling with that they have asked you to talk about with them or pray for? Listening and praying can make a world of difference for them in so many ways.

Does it seem that there are too many burdens, people, problems, and things to pray for? Give them all to God. He wants to take care of every one.

Lord God, thank You for being the sovereign Almighty who can handle all of the cares we have. Amen.

Day 259
MORNING BLESSING

"The LORD bless you and keep you; the LORD
make his face shine on you and be gracious to you;
the LORD turn his face toward you and give you peace."
NUMBERS 6:24–26 NIV

As you head out the door in the morning, remember this blessing given by God to Moses for the Israelites. What wonderful words to begin any journey in your day, be it a commute to work, a drive to the supermarket, a ride to school, or wherever you're heading today. Imagine the joy the Israelites must have felt, to know that God blessed them with a reminder and reassurance of His protection, favor, kindness, approval, and peace.

You too can be confident in God and empowered by all His blessings, such as this one related by God to you through Jeremiah: "For I know the thoughts and plans that I have for you. . .thoughts and plans for welfare and peace and not for evil, to give you hope in your final outcome" (Jeremiah 29:11 AMPC).

Woman of God, the Lord knows your future and gives you peace and hope, even when you cannot see where your life may be heading. What better gift could there be to keep yourself standing tall and unshaken?

Dear God, I thank You for the wonderful blessings You
have given me. I pray Your gift of peace would be with me,
giving me strength and courage to begin each day's journey.

Day 260
THE LORD'S PRAYER

Deliver me from my enemies, O God;
be my fortress against those who are attacking me.
PSALM 59:1 NIV

The Lord's Prayer is likely the most recognized prayer in the Christian world. And it continues to be learned early in the lives of Christians. Jesus used it to teach people how to pray. Part of the Lord's Prayer includes the words "And lead us not into temptation, but deliver us from the evil one" (Matthew 6:13 NIV). Sound familiar?

In Psalm 59:1, David wrote very similar words when Saul sent men to watch David's house in order to kill him. God heard David's prayer and protected him.

Although David needed deliverance from a physical attacker, enemies can take many forms. Perhaps you're battling illness or experiencing difficult times. Whatever or whoever your enemy might be, raise your voice to God and He will deliver you.

Reciting the Lord's Prayer can bring peace to your mind and calm to your soul. Give it a try. Based on Matthew 6:9–13 and Luke 11:2–4, here's the full prayer:

Our Father, who art in heaven, hallowed be Thy name;
Thy kingdom come; Thy will be done on earth as it is in heaven.
Give us this day our daily bread. And forgive us our trespasses,
as we forgive those who trespass against us. And lead us not
into temptation; but deliver us from evil. For Thine is the
kingdom, the power, and the glory, forever and ever.

Day 261
REST

Joshua fought against these kings for a long time.
Not one town made peace with the People of Israel,
with the one exception of the Hivites who lived in
Gibeon. Israel fought and took all the rest.
JOSHUA 11:18–19 MSG

After Joshua, as God had instructed, took control of the land and split the inheritance between the tribes, "Israel had rest from war" (Joshua 11:23 MSG). The Word doesn't say the war was over. It doesn't say this was the ending wrapped up in a bow. It says Joshua and the tribes had rest. They were able to breathe, look around at this land that had been promised to them, and *rest*.

While God may call you to many things in this life, and it may feel as if you're fighting battles, remember that God allows times of rest for His children. This isn't just a good night's sleep or a day to treat yourself. This rest is meant to refill your spirit with the Lord's presence so you can continue doing God's work in your life. It's a time meant for worship and praise.

When you find it hard to slow down or take a break because of all that needs to be done, know that God asks you to spend time with Him for the unshakable strength and power to continue on.

Father, please refill me with Your Spirit and Your
strength. In this time of rest, my eyes are on You.

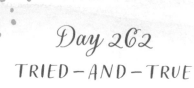

Day 262
TRIED–AND–TRUE

"This promise is to you, to your children, and to those far away—all who have been called by the Lord our God."
ACTS 2:39 NLT

When Peter preached a sermon at Pentecost, he drew from the scriptures, which had stood the test of time. Peter quoted David's inspired words: "I saw the Lord always before me. Because he is at my right hand, I will not be shaken. Therefore my heart is glad and my tongue rejoices; my body also will rest in hope, because you will not abandon me to the realm of the dead. . . . You will fill me with joy in your presence" (Acts 2:25–28 NIV). People were yearning for stability, for peace, hope, and joy. David was a king who had seen much trouble in his life, some self-inflicted, some not. Yet he was a man who loved God despite the trouble. And he was a child of God—God, who had held him through the trouble. Because God was near, David would not be shaken.

God's promise of a restored relationship with Him was not for David alone. It is to everyone He calls to Himself. He wants to be ever before us, ever at our side, so that we will not be shaken. That's a promise that stands the test of time.

God, sometimes I depend on temporary things to provide stability. Open my eyes to see You—my eternal rock—before me.

Day 263

WHERE ARE YOU TODAY?

My God, my God, why have You forsaken me?
Far from my help are the words of my groaning.
PSALM 22:1 NASB

Have you ever cried out to God with such despairing utterances as these? I have. Amid the deep black void of a moonless night, my loneliness threatened to pull me into a swirling, spiraling eddy of emptiness. The sound of my own raspy voice screamed out from my inmost being: "God, if You really exist, show me how to find You! I don't know where You are!" Church hadn't met my needs. People who promised love only provided pain. While my clenched fists beat against my bedroom wall, twelve years' worth of tears, a maelstrom of anger, hurt, and frustration, flowed freely.

He showed me the cross. The year was 1973. I left my knapsack of grief on the bloodstained ground beneath His wooden cross. And I never looked back. He has met my every need in surprising, miraculous, and incredible ways.

Jesus, separated from the Father because of our sin, reached the ear of God with His own desperation. He experienced for us this ultimate terror. . .so that we would never be forsaken or walk alone the road that leads to Calvary.

Where are you today? On the road, walking toward Him? Sitting down, too bewildered to even formulate questions? Or are you kneeling, as I did, right at His bleeding feet?

Lord, no matter what hazards are down the road, You've got
a signpost ready to hang on whatever misleading marker is
already in the ground. And the Son is shining ahead!

Day 264
THE ANSWER

Seek the Lord and His strength; yearn for and seek His face and to be in His presence continually! [Earnestly] remember the marvelous deeds which He has done, His miracles, and the judgments He uttered [as in Egypt]. . . . Honor and majesty are [found] in His presence; strength and joy are [found] in His sanctuary.
1 CHRONICLES 16:11–12, 27 AMPC

Feeling directionless, weak, alone? Beginning to doubt? Thinking that the magic you once felt in your relationship with God has diminished? Are you a bit down in the mouth—and heart?

God has the answer for you, the remedy to what ails you. It's a solution He shared with David and that David then shared with his peeps. It's the remedy that the chronicling scribe then left in writing for you.

The answer to all your ailments is to simply and heartfully thank God for all He's done. Call on Him. Sing to Him. Rejoice in Him. And most importantly, seek His face and strength. Long to be in His presence—not just during your prayer and praise time, but *all. . . the. . .time*! Remember who He is, everything He has done for His people—including you! Then you will find strength and joy and peace in the presence of your God—the God of all gods!

You, Lord, are my answer. I yearn to seek Your face, to spend time in Your presence. In You I find unshakable hope, strength, joy, power, and peace. Amen.

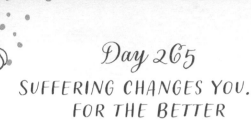

Day 265

SUFFERING CHANGES YOU. . . FOR THE BETTER

After you have suffered a little while,
[God] will himself restore you.
1 PETER 5:10 NIV

Before the Civil War, women avoided "improper" environments, including hospitals and battlegrounds. But as men faced death, women stepped into a new role.

Susie King Taylor was a laundress, teacher, and nurse for the Union Army. She said, "It seems strange how our aversion to seeing suffering is overcome in war,—how we are able to see the most sickening sights, such as men with their limbs blown off and mangled by the deadly shells, without a shudder, and instead of turning away, how we hurry to assist in alleviating their pain, bind up their wounds, and press the cool water to their parched lips."

Susie went from a woman of self-protection to a woman of compassion. Her actions reflected the nature of Christ, the suffering servant, who brought us living water (see John 7:38) and who bound up our wounds (see Psalm 147:3).

Don't despair in the dark places of suffering, but rather consider the ways God has used it to enrich your character. As the apostle Paul explained, "We also glory in tribulations, knowing that tribulation produces perseverance; and perseverance, character; and character, hope. Now hope does not disappoint" (Romans 5:3–5 NKJV).

In times of travail, watch as the Lord conforms you to His image, and consider yourself blessed.

Jesus, show me the value of my suffering, and make
me more like You through it all. Amen.

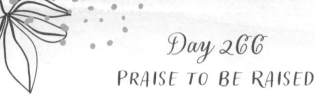

Day 266

PRAISE TO BE RAISED

*My God, I cry out by day, but you do not answer, by night,
but I find no rest. . . . To you they cried out and were
saved; in you they trusted and were not put to shame.*

PSALM 22:2, 5 NIV

Life isn't easy. We've heard many platitudes meant to encourage us. Being a complainer is not attractive. You need to find the silver lining in every cloud. If life gives you lemons, make lemonade. Smile even when it hurts.

Most of us try to begin our day by thanking God for our blessings before we face our challenges. But when we feel despair, is it acceptable to complain or do we need to bury those emotions? The Bible recounts times when people cried out to the Lord, times when they voiced their complaints. In Psalm 22, we're told that Christ poured out His soul to His heavenly Father throughout His sufferings. If we follow Christ's example, we can take our complaints to God in prayer as long as we, like Christ, also acknowledge our love for and trust in God.

If we just complain to others, we won't solve our problems. If we praise God and trust Him to stand with us during our trials, He will raise us up to handle our problems. Maybe we need to replace those old platitudes with this one: complain and remain, or praise to be raised.

*Lord, thank You for listening to my complaints and
saving me from my sins. Even during my struggles I
will praise You as my God and Savior. Amen.*

Day 267

GOD HAS NOT FORGOTTEN

Then said he unto me, Fear not, Daniel: for from the
first day that thou didst set thine heart to understand,
and to chasten thyself before thy God, thy words
were heard, and I am come for thy words.
DANIEL 10:12 KJV

Sometimes it seems God is silent. When you pray and ask God to intervene in a situation or help you with a difficulty and you don't hear back right away, there is a temptation to interpret that as God is inactive. The truth is He is never too busy to hear you.

Daniel had great concern for his people. He spent weeks fasting and praying, and he desperately wanted direction—an answer for his people. Imagine being fervently on your knees for three weeks, fasting and praying, and *nothing*! Some would have given up and maybe even assumed that God had forgotten. Three weeks pass and an angel comes to let Daniel know that God heard his prayer and went to work the very hour he spoke it.

What are you on your knees before God about? What have you asked Him to do on your behalf? Know that God has not forgotten you. He is working behind the scenes to bring about good in your life. He has the answer you need. Hold on to Him, and believe He will come through for you.

Lord, help me hold on to You, believing
that my answer is on the way. Amen.

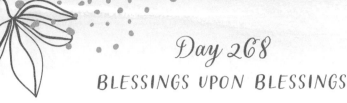

Day 268

BLESSINGS UPON BLESSINGS

For to everyone who has will more be given,
and he will be furnished richly so that he will have
an abundance; but from the one who does not have,
even what he does have will be taken away.
MATTHEW 25:29 AMPC

This verse above doesn't seem quite fair, at least not when we think about it within the context of worldly possessions; it sounds as though God takes from the poor and gives to the rich. But once again, the Bible wants us to understand the connection between our inner thoughts and our outer reality.

When we focus on our blessings, our thoughts dwelling on them, we'll not only adopt a grateful and positive attitude but find more and more blessings coming into our lives. On the other hand, if we focus only on what we lack, we not only are going to become discouraged and develop a hopeless outlook but will find more and more reasons to be discontent. Our perceptions shape our realities and attitudes.

Jesus, help me to look at life with Your eyes. Teach me to
see the many blessings You have given me, so that my
eyes will be open to all You have in store for me.

Day 269
PRAISE THE LORD!

*Great is our Lord and of great power; His understanding
is inexhaustible and boundless. The Lord lifts up the
humble and downtrodden; He casts the wicked down
to the ground. Sing to the Lord with thanksgiving;
sing praises with the harp or the lyre to our God!*
PSALM 147:5–7 AMPC

God heals those whose hearts are broken, those wounded by pain or sorrow. When you're looking for understanding, He's the guy to go to. When you're humbled and downtrodden, He's the one who will lift you up.

Yet that's not all. God calls out the stars, each of which He has named. He controls the weather. He feeds the animals and birds. And He takes great pleasure in those who worship Him, those who hope in His mercy and loving-kindness.

Yes, God has indeed done wonderful things and is worthy of praise.

Of course, we, like the apostle Paul, may endure many hardships. Yet if we have faith in our God, we, like Paul, will be willing to go to great lengths to do what He calls us to do.

No matter what challenges or blessings you have in your life right now, take a minute to praise the Lord aloud or in writing. Call a friend to pray with. He is your God and wants to hear from you.

*Lord, I take this time to shift my thoughts toward Your goodness.
Whether my heart is happy or down, I will praise You.*

Day 270

A REFUGE FROM OUR DESPAIR

Hear my cry, God; give Your attention to my prayer.
From the end of the earth I call to You when my heart is faint;
lead me to the rock that is higher than I. For You have been a refuge
for me, a tower of strength against the enemy. Let me dwell in
Your tent forever; let me take refuge in the shelter of Your wings.
PSALM 61:1–4 NASB

King David, writer of this psalm, composed it as a song, acknowledging God as his rock. He clung with tenacity to the fact that no matter how desperate his situation appeared, God was as immovable as a huge rock or boulder. Although David's trials may differ from yours, you too can use strong coping mechanisms.

First, David acknowledged that God remained all-powerful, despite life circumstances. And second, David looked back at God's past rescues: "My soul is in despair within me; therefore I remember You from the land of the Jordan and the peaks of Hermon, from Mount Mizar. Deep calls to deep at the sound of Your waterfalls; all Your breakers and Your waves have passed over me. The LORD will send His goodness in the daytime; and His song will be with me in the night, a prayer to the God of my life" (Psalm 42:6–8 NASB).

Lord, I search for a way through the torrents of despair.
How precious is the knowledge that You hear and care.

Day 271
KEEP ASKING

You shall have charge over my house, and all my people shall be governed according to your word [with reverence, submission, and obedience]. Only in matters of the throne will I be greater than you are.
GENESIS 41:40 AMPC

And just like that, Joseph went from a prisoner to second-in-command in Egypt. Talk about an immediate promotion! One minute he was in jail for a crime he didn't commit, and the next Joseph is interpreting a dream for the king and is elevated to Pharaoh's number one. For years Joseph had been praying and hoping for his situation to change, and when God's plan called for a move. . .a move happened.

Let this encourage you! Sometimes it's hard to continue praying for God's intervention over and over and over again. Our perseverance peters out. We worry He may grow tired of our request, or we give up altogether because we think His answer is a firm *no*. But the truth is that it's not yet time for the next right step.

It's hard to understand God's timing, so we have to choose to trust it because God is God and we are not. Yet we need not grow weary of asking, for we won't wear God out. And we'll have peace if we live our lives knowing that when it *is* the right time, God's answers *will* come.

Lord, I want Your timing over mine any day. Please give me perseverance to keep asking and patience to wait for Your perfectly timed answer!

Day 272
BREATH OF LIFE

He heals the brokenhearted and binds up their
wounds [curing their pains and their sorrows].
PSALM 147:3 AMPC

As a result of sin, every person on the earth is born into a fallen world. The sinful condition brings hurt and heartache to all men—those who serve the Lord and those who don't. The good news is, as a child of God, you have a hope and eternal future in Christ. Jesus said, "I have told you all this so that you may have peace in me. Here on earth you will have many trials and sorrows. But take heart, because I have overcome the world" (John 16:33 NLT).

When your life brings disappointment, hurt, and pain that are almost unbearable, remember that you serve the one who heals hearts. He knows you best and loves you most. When the wind is knocked out of you and you feel like there is no oxygen left in the room, let God provide you with the air you need to breathe. Breathe out a prayer to Him and breathe in His peace and comfort today.

Lord, be my breath of life, today and always. Amen.

Day 273
LIGHT WILL RETURN

*I waited patiently for the LORD to help me, and he turned
to me and heard my cry. He lifted me out of the pit of
despair, out of the mud and the mire. He set my feet on solid
ground and steadied me as I walked along. He has given
me a new song to sing, a hymn of praise to our God.*
PSALM 40:1–3 NLT

Following Jesus doesn't mean we have a magic get-out-of-trouble
guarantee. Christians are as likely to encounter uncertain times as
anyone else, and they may also experience times of depression and
hopelessness. Again, the psalmist reminds us that God never condemns
us for our emotions.

Even during our bleakest times, we can hold on to the promise
of God's presence with us. We can be confident that light will return
to our lives and we will once more be filled with the joy of His love.
All we have to do is wait.

*Teach me patience, Lord. Remind me that Your sense of
timing is not the same as mine—but that, ultimately,
You will work out all the details of my life. When I can't
see You either inside my heart or in the world outside, help
me rest in the assurance that a new song is on its way.*

Day 274
SIDE BY SIDE

*Have no fear of sudden disaster or of the ruin that
overtakes the wicked, for the LORD will be at your
side and will keep your foot from being snared.*
PROVERBS 3:25–26 NIV

Our world today is crammed with grim news. Television and internet reports blast us with every detail of a disaster, often filling our hearts with dread. From the pulpit we hear "perfect love casts out fear." However, we frequently remain apprehensive. There are things of which we must be aware, but we do not need to become overtaken with fear and worry. For the Lord our God has given us a promise in His Word. He is at our side.

The Lord sees the concerns and fears of His children and has surrounded us with His love. When we gaze into His face and seek His presence, the light of His love will flood any dark corners, dispelling the anxious thoughts and scary shadows. His hand is there to hold us close, allowing us to feel His heartbeat.

As a boat casts off its tether from the dock, we need to cast off the ties to fear and worry and drift upon the sea of peace offered by our heavenly Father. He is at our side and will keep us safe, for He is true love.

*Father, this day I surrender my cares to You,
for I know You love me. Amen.*

Day 275

THE PRISON OF PARANOIA

*But Benjamin, Joseph's [full] brother, Jacob did not
send with his brothers; for he said, Lest perhaps
some harm or injury should befall him.*

GENESIS 42:4 AMPC

Dad was scared to send his youngest to Egypt with the older brothers. Benjamin was the baby of the family and loved by all. And after the supposed death of his favorite son, Joseph, Jacob was too paranoid something might happen to Benjamin as well. He knew his aging heart just couldn't handle the loss of his beloved Rachel's second son, so he kept Ben home safe with him.

Too often, we live our lives like this—afraid that bad events will happen. That mindset keeps us from branching out and trying new things. It makes us second-guess our plans or cancel them altogether. It breeds distrust in relationships, prompting us to obsess over all that could go wrong. Fear traps us and robs us of joy and peace.

While it's wise to be aware, it's foolish to let worry take control, because it will always point to horrible outcomes and endings. It will point to the worst-case scenario. And if you choose to live here, your life will be wasted on what-ifs.

Give your fears to God. Ask Him to replace them with faith.

*Lord, living in a place of fear is a dead-end street and one
road I don't want to travel. Will You give me courage and
confidence to trust You instead? Help me be brave!*

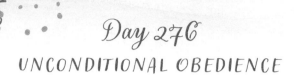

Day 276

UNCONDITIONAL OBEDIENCE

*"Whether it is favorable or unfavorable, we will obey the
LORD our God, to whom we are sending you, so that it will
go well with us, for we will obey the LORD our God."*
JEREMIAH 42:6 NIV

Desperate times call for desperate measures. In the aftermath of the invasions by Babylonian forces, the surviving Israelites sought out Jeremiah's help. Desperate, they realized the only path available to them was to heed God's instructions through Jeremiah, His messenger. They were finally resigned to the fact that they must obey God's words, whether or not they liked what He had to say.

Sometimes the right course in your life may seem counterintuitive. That's when you need to let go and let God. Once you renounce what you feel you should do and do what you realize God wants you to do, your situation will improve, and peace will be restored to your soul. Within God's plan lies your correct course. Although His course may appear difficult, in the end your pledge of obedience will be the best choice you can make to lay the foundation for the best course you can take.

*Dear Lord, I ask that You help me to be Your obedient servant,
to trust in Your supreme plan for me, and to rest assured that Your
will is the best course for me. Though I may not be happy with the
path You have laid out for me, Lord, Your will, not mine, be done.*

Day 277
PROMISED PEACE

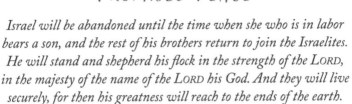

Israel will be abandoned until the time when she who is in labor bears a son, and the rest of his brothers return to join the Israelites. He will stand and shepherd his flock in the strength of the LORD, in the majesty of the name of the LORD his God. And they will live securely, for then his greatness will reach to the ends of the earth.
MICAH 5:3–4 NIV

This is one of the many predictions of the coming Messiah, the King, who would rule and reign over His chosen people. While there would be great turmoil during the time of His birth, Jesus would bring peace in the midst of it. His birth would be the beginning of a time of advancement and protection for those who believed in Him. Unlike the kings who had come and gone before Him, the Messiah would rule differently.

Your life right now might be filled with many challenges. Though it might be different from those who had waited for and needed Jesus thousands of years ago, your need for a Messiah and the promised peace that comes with Him is just as important.

Open up your hands and heart to Jesus today. Tell Him what is troubling you. Invite Him, your Lord and miracle worker, to be your promised peace.

Jesus, I need Your deliverance right now. Thank You for filling me with Your Holy Spirit's provision of power and peace.

*Jesus came, though they were behind closed doors,
and stood among them and said, Peace to you! . . .
Jesus said to him, Because you have seen Me,
Thomas, do you now believe (trust, have faith)?*
JOHN 20:26, 29 AMPC

By the time the disciples were hiding behind closed doors, Jesus had already been crucified, had died, was buried, and had risen again. He'd already been seen by Mary Magdalene, as well as some of the other male and female disciples. The only one who had yet to encounter Him was Thomas. That's when Jesus appeared in the disciples' upper room, blessing them with His peace and convincing Thomas that He was alive! Then, Jesus blessed *you*, saying, "Blessed and happy and to be envied are those who have never seen Me and yet have believed and adhered to and trusted and relied on Me" (John 20:29 AMPC).

Before His ascension, Jesus showed up once more in an unexpected time and place. It happened when the disciples went fishing. All night they'd caught nothing. Then a stranger (who was actually Jesus) from the shore told them to "Cast the net on the right side of the boat and you will find [some]. So they cast the net, and now they were not able to haul it in for such a big catch (mass, quantity) of fish [was in it]" (John 21:6 AMPC).

Expect Jesus where and when you least expect Him.

*Lord, I live in expectation of Your presence
in my life! Come, Jesus! Come!*

Day 279
JOY IN TRIALS

Consider it pure joy, my brothers and sisters, whenever you face trials of many kinds, because you know that the testing of your faith produces perseverance. Let perseverance finish its work so that you may be mature and complete, not lacking anything.
JAMES 1:2–4 NIV

James begins his letter by encouraging his brothers and sisters in Christ to find joy in their trials. The word *consider* tells us to move this discussion about trials out of our emotions and into our heads.

Stop and think about this for a minute. Trials are going to come. That is a fact of this life. We can't waste our time trying to avoid them. So instead, let's remember we have the ultimate victory in Christ. Nothing that happens on earth will take away our heavenly reward and the joy we will have in heaven.

With Christ, the fruit of our trials can be growth, maturity, peace, and the fruit of the Spirit instead of despondency, discouragement, depression, and hopelessness. Ask God for wisdom for the next step. Draw close to Him. Let perseverance finish its work to increase your maturity. Take real steps of obedience and faith, because the key to joy is obedience.

Lord, as hard as it is, help us to find joy in the difficult things that come our way, because we know You have given us the ultimate victory. And in the process, we can become more like You. Amen.

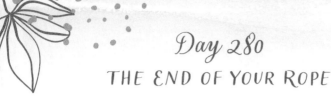

Day 280

THE END OF YOUR ROPE

*Do not be far from me, for trouble is
near and there is no one to help.*
PSALM 22:11 NIV

You can feel the desperation in David's prayer as you read Psalm 22. He feels utterly rejected and alone as he cries out to God.

Have you been there? Have you ever felt so alone and helpless that you are sure no one is there for you? Jesus meets us in those dark places of hopelessness. He calls to us and says, "Don't let your hearts be troubled. Do not be afraid" (see John 14:27). "I will never leave you or forsake you" (see Hebrews 13:5). You are never alone.

The late youth evangelist Dave Busby said, "The end of your rope is God's permanent address." Jesus reaches down and wraps you in His loving arms when you call to Him for help. The Bible tells us that He is close to the brokenhearted (Psalm 34:18).

We may not have the answers we are looking for here in this life, but be sure of this: God sees your pain and loves you desperately. Call to Him in times of trouble. If you feel that you're at the end of your rope, look up! His mighty hand is reaching toward you.

*Heavenly Father, I feel alone and afraid.
Surround me with Your love and give me peace. Amen.*

Day 281
NEW THINGS

"See, I am doing a new thing! Now it springs up;
do you not perceive it? I am making a way in the
wilderness and streams in the wasteland."
ISAIAH 43:19 NIV

God is not limited as you are. He makes new paths for you where you see none. He provides refreshing streams where there were none. When your way seems blocked and circumstances distressing, look for God to surprise you with an unexpected solution. God is constantly moving you forward in life. New things will appear on the horizon.

Do you struggle with change? Do transitions leave you anxious? Trust that God's plans for you are good and that His heart is loving. God will not give you more than you can handle.

Do not focus on previous years or past hurts. Be available for what God has for you today. Look attentively for what may seem like a small trickle. Be ready for that trickle to turn into a spring and then a river. Prepare to get wet as you wade into your future personally designed by God with you in mind. He knows you better than you know yourself. Celebrate new life in abundance without looking back to the solid shore of your past. Go have your adventure with God at your side.

God, let my heart trust You today as You
prepare a "new thing" for my future.

Day 282
STRONG HANDS

"Do not fear. . .let not your hands be weak. The LORD your God in your midst, the Mighty One, will save; He will rejoice over you with gladness, He will quiet you with His love, He will rejoice over you with singing."
ZEPHANIAH 3:16–17 NKJV

Sometimes we may find ourselves heading in the wrong direction. This can happen because we've given in to a particular sin one time too many. Or we've stopped connecting with the Lord. Or we're listening to what He says but not obeying Him. Whatever the cause, the result is always the same. We become fearful, anxious, worried. And before we know it, our hands are lying listless in our laps. That's when we need to let God get ahold of us again. Remember, He is in our midst and doing amazing things. He is the one who will bring us back to Him, saving us from whatever is leading us away. And then He'll rejoice over our return! He'll calm our worries with His amazing love and light. And before we know it, we'll once again have the courage we so desperately need to live this life to which He has called us. Our hands will once again be strong, lifted up in prayer and praise. We'll be singing in harmony with our Lord.

I'm running back into Your open arms, Lord. I'm reveling in Your Sonshine, feeling Your breath upon my face. Only You can quiet my fears with Your love. Only You can strengthen my hands. In You, I find the song of my life. To You, I lift my hands and voice in praise! Amen!

Day 283
JOY IN JESUS

I saw the Lord constantly before me, for He is at my right hand that I may not be shaken or overthrown or cast down [from my secure and happy state]. . . . You have made known to me the ways of life; You will enrapture me [diffusing my soul with joy] with and in Your presence.
ACTS 2:25, 28 AMPC

Death is no match for the God to whom you belong, to the Son of God you serve. And because you believe in God, death is no match for you either. But the good news does not end there.

If you keep God constantly before you, keeping Him close, right by your side, you will never be shaken up. Nothing can defeat you or bring you down. Then, all that's left for you to do is rejoice! You can say, "I'm glad from the inside out, ecstatic; I've pitched my tent in the land of hope. I know you'll never dump me in Hades; I'll never even smell the stench of death. You've got my feet on the life-path, with your face shining sun-joy all around" (Acts 2:26–28 MSG).

Today, stay close to Jesus. When you do, He'll stay close to you. And with Him constantly before you, beside you, and within you, you too will find the joy He alone can bring today and forevermore.

With You right beside me, Lord, my joy, peace, and contentment know no bounds!

Day 284

CRY OUT TO GOD

GOD, you're my last chance of the day.
I spend the night on my knees before you.
PSALM 88:1 MSG

The psalmist was in misery and cried out to God. He felt as though he were near death. Been there?

In one form or another, every woman experiences extreme despair in her life. It may be due to loss of a loved one. You may find yourself abandoned by a family member, dealing with a chronic illness, or desperate over a prodigal child who makes one bad choice after another.

Whatever the cause of your heartache, if you have not yet been in the depths of despair, at some point in your life you will be. Human existence brings with it times that are simply unbearable on your own.

During such times, you must rely on God. You may not feel Him or sense His presence, but His Word declares that He will never leave you nor forsake you.

Talk to God first thing in the morning and just before your head hits the pillow at night. He is your refuge and your strong tower in times of trouble. A brighter day will come. Joy comes in the morning. Hold on tight to God. Find strength in knowing you are never ever alone.

God, I find comfort in knowing You are always with me and
will always see me through to the other side of sorrow. Amen.

Day 285

JESUS NEVER FORSAKES

Be satisfied with your present [circumstances and with what you have]; for He [God] Himself has said, I will not in any way fail you nor give you up nor leave you without support. [I will] not, [I will] not, [I will] not in any degree leave you helpless nor forsake nor let [you] down (relax My hold on you)! [Assuredly not!] So we take comfort and are encouraged and confidently and boldly say, The Lord is my Helper; I will not be seized with alarm [I will not fear or dread or be terrified].

HEBREWS 13:5–6 AMPC

Count the negatives in these verses. Nine times—including four *I will nots*—God assures His people He has everything under control. What a wonderful "comfort" verse, filled with the promise of God's protection, help, and provision. Because of what God does, we have no reason to be dissatisfied with anything God allows into our lives—either good or bad.

Study the book of Job. Listen to Job's statements of faith throughout the book. But none are so convincing as his statements in chapters one and two, refusing to sin against God with his words. Even after his wife—his closest companion here on earth—urged him to curse God and die, Job refused to comply. He acknowledged that God had the right to give and to take away. And he blessed the Lord throughout, accepting that God never revealed the whys to him.

Father, I don't need to know the whys. You are in control no matter what happens. Thank You for this promise.

Day 286

PROMISE FULFILLER

"God is not human, that he should lie, not a human being, that he should change his mind. Does he speak and then not act? Does he promise and not fulfill?"

NUMBERS 23:19 NIV

Our opinions of God are often shaped by our experiences with people. When we've been hurt, we see God as hurtful. When people lie to us, we subconsciously think of God as a liar. After all, if humans are created in His image, it only stands to reason that God would be like the people in our lives. Right?

Well, no. Yes, we were created in God's image. But we humans are a fallen, broken race. We're sinful. God is without sin.

Humans lie. God doesn't.

Humans go back on their word. God doesn't.

Humans can be mean and hurtful. God is love, and He only acts in love.

God promised good things to those who love Him, those who live and act according to His will. That doesn't mean others won't hurt us or that we won't experience the effects of living in a sin-infested world. But where there's pain, we have a healer. Where there's brokenness, we have a comforter. And where we feel alone, we know we have a friend.

And one day we'll experience the perfect fulfillment of all His promises without the burdens of this world to weigh us down.

Now that's something to look forward to.

Dear Father, thank You for Your promises. When I feel discouraged, help me to remember those promises. Amen.

Day 287
WHAT WE CANNOT SEE

*Now faith is confidence in what we hope for
and assurance about what we do not see.*
HEBREWS 11:1 NIV

Faith is mentioned so many times in God's Word, but did you ever stop to think about exactly what the word *faith* means? You've only to read this verse to understand it. Faith is confidence. It is the firm belief that you can completely rely on someone or something that may not yet be in existence.

Faith is also described as the assurance of that which we cannot see. It is full trust that God, even in the darkness, will be holding our hand and leading us to the light. *You* may not fully understand what comes your way, but you can certainly have confidence that *He* does. What a wonderful feeling, to have full assurance and confidence in God! This faith isn't blind but rather comes from the knowledge we have in the Word of God through His scriptures and the teachings through His Son, Jesus Christ.

So, woman of Christ, have confidence in your hopes. Have assurance and peace about what has not yet been made visible to you. Fully trust in God with all.

*Dear Lord, how wonderful it is to know that I can be
completely confident in You and Your promises, that I can
live each day in peace, knowing I can have assurance of those
things I cannot see but that You have declared to be true.*

Day 288

THE CURE

Is anyone among you suffering? Let him pray.
Is anyone cheerful? Let him sing praise.
JAMES 5:13 ESV

God's formula for powering through rough times doesn't always make sense, does it? Take a look at today's verse. When you're suffering, pray. When you're cheerful, bump it up a notch and sing a song of praise. In other words, never be content to stay where you are. Always shoot for the next highest level and keep going.

We're not usually wired that way. When we're suffering, we tend to pull inward. And when we're happy, we don't always make a big deal about it. But when we step out of our comfort zone, we see there's a bigger God-way to deal with life's circumstances, and it requires something more of us than what we're used to giving.

It's not good to grovel in the pain, so bump it up to prayer. And when things do resolve, don't be content to just be happy about it—begin to shout a praise to the Lord at the top of your voice. In other words, keep going, even when you don't feel like putting one foot in front of the other. When you stay in perpetual motion, you're acting in faith.

Lord, I'll keep going. The cure is in perpetual motion
forward. So I'll pray. I'll sing. I'll keep taking
steps of faith, and I won't quit. Amen.

Day 289
A LIFE ON FIRM FOOTING

Friends, confirm God's invitation to you, his choice of you.
Don't put it off; do it now. Do this, and you'll have your life on
a firm footing, the streets paved and the way wide open into
the eternal kingdom of our Master and Savior, Jesus Christ.
2 PETER 1:10–11 MSG

Have you accepted the Savior's invitation? Or have you been putting it off—waiting for just the "right time"?

The truth? . . . No matter what decision you might be considering, there will likely never be the perfect time. Life is messy. . .and without Jesus, it will likely get messier with each passing day. And, as this scripture from 2 Peter says, there's no better time than right now! So don't put it off!

Sure, you can wait one more day, but one more day without Jesus means one less day of comfort and assurance, one less day of knowing what the future holds for you. Wouldn't you rather have a lifetime of joy with Jesus rather than years of insecurity and doubt?

The invitation is right there. . . . God's waiting for you to accept Him. And with your acceptance comes the promise of "firm footing"—and a sure path to eternal life.

Thank You for this invitation, Lord. I accept! Please
come into my life and give me the assurance that only
You can provide. . .a certain, firm footing as I approach
each new day with a heavenly perspective. Amen.

Day 290
LIVING WATER

*"For the Lamb at the center of the throne will be their
shepherd; 'he will lead them to springs of living water.'
'And God will wipe away every tear from their eyes.'"*
REVELATION 7:17 NIV

The book of Revelation contains a lot of imagery, and the precise meaning of what John saw is debated by many. However, what is *not* debatable are the words of today's verse.

Jesus, the Lamb of God, is at the center of His heavenly throne. He is the shepherd of the survivors of the end days, the ones God deemed worthy. And as their shepherd, Jesus will lead believers to the springs of living water. And God will wipe away their tears and quell their fears.

Are you craving for Jesus to quench your thirst? If so, remember Jesus' words: "Whoever believes in me, as Scripture has said, rivers of living water will flow from within them" (John 7:38 NIV). And allow the Lord your shepherd to make you lie down in green meadows and to lead you beside the quiet waters (Psalm 23:1–2). Visualize the abundant water, flowing and calm, and the fact that God will truly wipe every tear from your eyes, bringing you the peace and comfort you're longing for.

*Dear Lord, I pray there is a place for me at Your
springs of living water. Guide me and console me,
that I may live in Your kingdom forever.*

Day 291
BEAUTIFUL BEGINNINGS

God made my life complete when I placed all the pieces before him. When I got my act together, he gave me a fresh start. Now I'm alert to God's ways; I don't take God for granted. Every day I review the ways he works; I try not to miss a trick. I feel put back together, and I'm watching my step. God rewrote the text of my life when I opened the book of my heart to his eyes.
<small>Psalm 18:20–24 msg</small>

Think about where you are in your life story. . . . Are the chapters before you met Jesus overflowing with one hot mess after another? Bad choices? Jumbled thoughts? Unclear direction? If so, what about *after*?

While life with Jesus certainly isn't all sunshine, rainbows, and unicorns, this new way of living does have its perks. With God in the lead, you always have a guide to help you navigate the messiness of life. You have someone by your side to help you make sense of the madness, to turn your chaos into peace.

Truth is, God's story for you is so much better than anything you could ever write on your own. So don't attempt to write it all by yourself. Make sure you hand over the pen to the heavenly author Himself. He'll see to it that your story of transformation has a beautiful, eternal theme of hope and security.

Father, thank You for rewriting my life story!

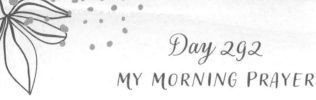

Day 292
MY MORNING PRAYER

Let me hear Your faithfulness in the morning,
for I trust in You; teach me the way in which
I should walk; for to You I lift up my soul.
PSALM 143:8 NASB

Do mornings excite or depress you? "Good morning, Lord!" or "Good Lord, it's morning!" When David wrote Psalm 143, he probably dreaded the sun coming up because that meant his enemies could continue pursuing him and persecuting his soul. "The enemy. . .has crushed my life to the ground" (verse 3 NASB). "My spirit feels weak within me; my heart is appalled" (verse 4 NASB).

What did David do when he didn't know which way to turn? He turned to the Lord. He stayed in prayer contact with God and meditated on God's faithfulness and righteousness (verse 1), God's past work in his life (verse 5), and His loyal love (verses 8, 12). He also took refuge in God (verse 9) and continued serving Him (verse 12).

No matter what our day holds, we can face it confidently by practicing verse 8. Let's look for God's loving-kindness and keep trusting Him no matter what. Ask Him to teach and lead us in the way He wants us to go. We have the privilege of offering up our souls (thoughts, emotions, and will) to Him anew each morning. Have a good day.

Good morning, Lord. You are my loving Father, secure refuge,
and trustworthy God. Deliver me from my enemies and show
me Your loving heart as I trust in You. Help me to please
You today in my decisions and goals, in my attitudes toward
circumstances, and in the way I respond to people around me.

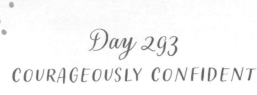

Day 293

COURAGEOUSLY CONFIDENT

Though an army besiege me, my heart will not fear;
though war break out against me, even then I will be confident.
PSALM 27:3 NIV

Some changes can turn your world upside down. It happened to the Israelites. They'd been slaves in Egypt for four hundred years. Then God called Moses to lead them to freedom. Ten plagues later, the Israelites were walking out of Egypt with all the goods they could carry.

But then God's people found themselves trapped between Pharaoh's army and the Red Sea. Driven by fear, they cried to Moses, "Why did you lead us here? It'd be better to be slaves in Egypt than to die here in the wilderness!" Moses answered their complaint, saying, "Do not be afraid. Stand firm and you will see the deliverance the LORD will bring you today. The Egyptians you see today you will never see again. The LORD will fight for you; you need only to be still" (Exodus 14:13–14 NIV). The Red Sea was parted, the Egyptian army was destroyed, and God's people began their journey toward the Promised Land with God leading them in front and protecting them from behind.

God is with you. So don't wrestle with change—or Him. Just stand still, courageously confident He's clearing a new path—just for you! As you do so, He'll transform your panic to peace.

Lord, I'm courageously confident You're with me,
paving a new path ahead, leading me to promised ground.

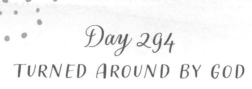

Day 294

TURNED AROUND BY GOD

*You have turned my mourning into joyful dancing. You have
taken away my clothes of mourning and clothed me with joy,
that I might sing praises to you and not be silent.*

PSALM 30:11–12 NLT

Jesus told us we'd encounter trouble in this life (John 16:33). But along with that trouble He promised that in Him we'd have peace.

Thus, when you encounter misfortune, when you lose someone you love, your job, your health, your trust in someone you counted on, call on God. Cry out to Him for help (Psalm 30:2). Beg Him to give you His comfort, a new perspective, His love, His balm of healing, His promise of hope, His strength to get through the next moment, hour, day, week. And little by little, or perhaps quite suddenly, you will find God has lifted your head, given you the courage and strength to look up to Him, filled your heart with song, and turned your mourning into joy.

Be assured that your God is a God of transformation. He alone is able to give you exactly what you need when you need it, prompting you to sing your praises to Him.

*Thank You, Lord, for turning me around, for showing me the Son.
With You in my life, I cannot help but dance and sing praises as
You continue to bless me beyond all I can expect or imagine.*

Day 295
KINGDOM COME

Give the king Your judgments, O God,
and Your righteousness to the king's Son.
PSALM 72:1 NKJV

Psalm 72 is a coronation psalm asking God's favor for the reign of Solomon, who became king of Israel following his father, David. Although no New Testament writers use the psalm to describe Jesus, Psalm 72 also anticipates a future time when the King of kings will reign. Here are just a few glimpses of what His kingdom will be like:

> *He will bring justice to the poor of the people; He will*
> *save the children of the needy, and will break in pieces*
> *the oppressor. . . . He shall come down like rain upon*
> *the grass before mowing, like showers that water the*
> *earth. In His days the righteous shall flourish, and*
> *abundance of peace, until the moon is no more. He*
> *shall have dominion also from sea to sea, and from the*
> *River to the ends of the earth. . . . Yes, all kings shall*
> *fall down before Him; all nations shall serve Him.*
> PSALM 72:4, 6–8, 11 NKJV

If life today discourages you, train your eyes on Jesus. One day, maybe this very day, He will return, and when He moves in He'll renovate this old world. He'll reign over every inch and every being, and with His reign there will be justice, blessing, and peace.

> *Lord, You already reign in my heart—*
> *I can't wait for You to reign here on earth!*

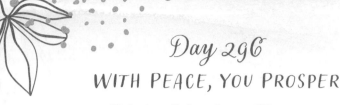

Day 296
WITH PEACE, YOU PROSPER

"Submit to God, and you will have peace;
then things will go well for you. Listen to his
instructions, and store them in your heart."
Job 22:21–22 nlt

Different Bible versions use different words for *submit* in the verses above, words such as *acquaint* or *agree* or *give in*. But they all mean the same thing. When you know God, trust Him, yield to Him, allowing Him to have full sway over you, then and only then will you have the peace you crave. And when you have that peace, "[you shall prosper and great] good shall come to you" (Job 22:21 ampc).

Part of that yielding, that surrendering, involves listening to God's Word, instructions, and wisdom and storing all those things up in your heart so that when you need them you'll know how to respond in thought, word, and deed in every situation.

Begin today. Consider the areas of your life where you've not given God full rein. Think about what situations are contentious, who gives you anxiety, or where you feel angst. Then ask God to help you submit to Him, His instructions, His wisdom, whatever He has in mind. Before you know it, not only will you have more peace, but much good will come from your efforts. God can do amazing things when you yield yourself to Him.

Show me where I need to yield to You,
Lord, for I so crave Your gift of peace.

Day 297

KEEP HIS COMMANDS AND LIVE

My son, keep my words, and treasure my commands within you. Keep my commands and live, and my law as the apple of your eye. Bind them on your fingers; write them on the tablet of your heart. Say to wisdom, "You are my sister," and call understanding your nearest kin.
PROVERBS 7:1–4 NKJV

Many people believe that God's commands are restrictive, that He wants to somehow stop people from having a good time in life. Nothing could be further from the truth! His commands bring life, joy, and peace, and they ultimately help His children remain healthy and strong.

Don't you just love the image painted in verse 3 above? "Bind them on your fingers; write them on the tablet of your heart." What an awesome way to say, "Learn the scriptures. Keep them close by because you're going to need them."

You may not be good at memorizing scripture verses. But in God's will, you'll find a way. Today, choose several of your favorites. Write them down and post them in places around your house where you're sure to see them every day—on your bathroom mirror, refrigerator door, nightstand, and so on. The more you see the Word, the more you'll remember it. . .and that's a good thing.

Father, I want to immerse myself in Your Word, to bind Your commands on my fingers and keep them close to my heart. May Your words flow out of me, in good times and in bad. Amen.

THE SPIRIT OF TRUTH

*"If you love me, keep my commands. And I will ask the Father,
and he will give you another advocate to help you and be
with you forever—the Spirit of truth. The world cannot
accept him, because it neither sees him nor knows him. But
you know him, for he lives with you and will be in you."*
JOHN 14:15–17 NIV

Turn the other cheek. Love your enemies. Do good to those who hurt you. Give generously. Don't be anxious. Store up treasures in heaven. In the Sermon on the Mount (Matthew 5–6), Jesus presents a perspective on living that must have confused many of His listeners.

For those who don't know or recognize the Holy Spirit, Jesus' teachings don't make any sense. They are countercultural and go against the grain of natural instinct. When Christians are able to forgive those who have hurt them, give generously, or refuse to follow the latest trends and fashions, the world gets confused. To those who don't have the Holy Spirit, these seemingly extraordinary actions must seem unreal, impossible even. Knowing the Holy Spirit makes all the difference. When the Holy Spirit lives in us, we can finally see truth. We have the advocacy and the help we need to follow Jesus' commands—and they make all the sense in the world.

*Jesus, thank You for the gift of the Holy Spirit. My life
would be so meaningless and confusing without this precious
comforter, advocate, and friend. Help me to follow Your
commands and shine Your light to a watching world. Amen.*

Day 299
QUIET DAWN

"A new day will dawn on us from above because our God is loving and merciful. He will give light to those who live in the dark and in death's shadow. He will guide us into the way of peace."

LUKE 1:78–79 GW

Today's scripture comes from Zechariah's prophecy about his son, John, who would prepare Israel for the dawning of "a new day," the Messiah—Jesus, who would liberate Israel from "the dark" and "death's shadow." The Light of the World dawned to bring humanity peace with God.

Perhaps your story of meeting Jesus was like a slow sunrise: His light spread over the landscape of your heart, the blazing warmth of His love overtaking where death and sin had formerly reigned. Because God's kingdom is both "here and not yet"—Jesus is victorious over sin and death but all things have not yet been "made new"—there are still places in your heart where you need His restoring light, whether it's to drive out icy fears, stormy anger, or the fog of nagging sins. In your times of confession, invite Jesus into those places. He will not condemn or criticize but heal you and illuminate the path to His ways of peace. Though the process of change can be long and tough, you can trust Jesus to shed His light, His truth, where you need it most.

Jesus, You know where I need Your light today.
Thank You for patiently teaching me Your ways.

Day 300
ENTRUST AND REMEMBER

Jesus cried out in a loud voice, "Father, into your hands I entrust my spirit." . . . Then the women remembered what Jesus had told them.
LUKE 23:46; 24:8 GW

Jesus knew how His life was going to play out. He'd already told His followers how He'd fulfill the prophecies. And now, during His most extreme trial, hanging upon the cross, He publicly entrusted His Father with His human spirit.

Afterward, His grief-stricken female followers embarked upon the societal routine prompted by the death of a loved one. "The women who had come with Jesus from Galilee. . .observed the tomb and how his body was laid in it. Then they went back to the city and prepared spices and perfumes. But on the day of rest—a holy day, they rested according to the commandment" (Luke 23:55–56 GW). The next day they went back to the tomb to complete the burial ritual, but instead of finding Jesus, they stumbled upon two angels. Terrified, they bowed down and heard the angels say their Savior had risen, just as He said He would. Then they remembered His words and ran to tell the others.

What would your life be like if every morning you entrusted your spirit to God? What would happen if, amid panic—or preferably before you got to that point—you remembered God's words of comfort, prophecy, hope, and peace?

Lord, today, I entrust my spirit, putting it into Your hands, remembering Your words of comfort, prophecy, hope, and peace.

Day 301

LEAN BACK UPON JESUS

The disciples kept looking at one another, puzzled as to whom He could mean. One of His disciples, whom Jesus loved [whom He esteemed and delighted in], was reclining [next to Him] on Jesus' bosom. . . . Then leaning back against Jesus' breast, he asked Him, Lord, who is it?
JOHN 13:22–23, 25 AMPC

Some days can be confusing. We're a bit puzzled, unsure of what God's telling us. We look for answers in the world and people around us. But the true source of wisdom is found in the one who loves us—Jesus. It's to Him we can address our questions, in Him we'll find the truth. It's His answer we can trust.

To clear the confusion, come to a quiet place. Lean back upon Jesus' breast. Absorb His love and light. Bathe in the intimacy of His presence. Whisper the questions you want to ask. Then patiently and peacefully wait for His answer, for it will surely come.

Jesus isn't some god so far removed from you that you cannot reach Him. He's all around you, waiting for you to lean upon Him, ask Him questions, abide in His love. So, go to Him now, knowing He'll provide you with all the knowledge you need. Trust that you can rely on both Him and His Word.

Lord, I'm leaning back on You, ready to whisper in Your ear, bathing in the intimacy of our love.

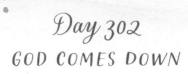

Day 302

GOD COMES DOWN

When Solomon finished praying, a bolt of lightning out of heaven struck the Whole-Burnt-Offering and sacrifices and the Glory of GOD filled The Temple. The Glory was so dense that the priests couldn't get in—GOD so filled The Temple that there was no room for the priests!

2 CHRONICLES 7:1–2 MSG

It is often in those silent moments, when you're taking in God's creation, that you feel close to Him. The sand, the beach, the rushing sound of the ocean coming in to kiss the shore—it stirs something deep within your soul. Taking in an evening sunset on the beach or a slow walk down to the water's edge somehow compels you to connect with the one who created all this for you. Even the sound of rushing waves, no matter how loud, can serve as a calming roar and settle every stressor weighing on you.

Times like that, it often feels that God comes down and you can experience His presence in a tangible way. Life's busyness fades away and all of who He is envelops you like a waterfall, washing away the stress.

Take time today to step back from the traffic, the turmoil, the loud shouts of life, and into the calm of His creation. Embrace the silence and step into the peace right now.

Savior, You are welcome in this place.
My body is Your temple. Come and visit me today.
Wash over me and fill me with Your peace.

Day 303
LIGHT OF LIFE

" 'God has delivered me from going down to the pit, and I
shall live to enjoy the light of life.' God does all these things
to a person—twice, even three times—to turn them back
from the pit, that the light of life may shine on them."
JOB 33:28–30 NIV

How wonderful it is to know that we are pursued by God every day. That we are continually sought by God, whose heart wants the best for us. Although He would like to save us from trips to a miserable pit, sometimes we must be rescued repeatedly.

We are designed to walk with God in beautiful light. Sometimes, though, the light is not apparent. We feel like we're living in the shadows. In these times, it's important to remember that God is close. And that dark times do not mean God has abandoned us or is unhappy with us.

We can trust that God desires to speak to us and to lead us. We do not need to linger in confusion. God may speak to us in scripture or in the words of a song or sermon, drawing us back to Him and away from the darkness. At times, God leads us away with a sense of peace.

Listen for and trust God to speak. His desire is to redeem your soul through salvation and to restore light and joy to your life.

God, thank You that Your plan for me is
to walk in the light with You.

Day 304
CONSIDER GOD

They have harps and lyres at their banquets, pipes and timbrels and wine, but they have no regard for the deeds of the LORD, no respect for the work of his hands. Therefore my people will go into exile for lack of understanding; those of high rank will die of hunger and the common people will be parched with thirst.
ISAIAH 5:12–13 NIV

God pursues you and knows you. He follows hard after you. In fact, "the eyes of the LORD search the whole earth in order to strengthen those whose hearts are fully committed to him" (2 Chronicles 16:9 NLT). And just as God pursues you, He knows you. He knows your name, your thoughts, and the things that bring you sadness or joy. He wants you to know Him as well as He knows you.

Acknowledge God in your day today. Recognize the unique beauty around you and praise the Creator. Did He bless you with sunlight, food, breath for your lungs? Reflect on how He has worked in your life. Has He provided health, safety, work, family, or friends? As you read the scriptures, ask God to reveal Himself to you in truth. Get to know Him as a savior, a provider, a pursuer, a healer, and a friend. Peace and joy will be your reward.

God, let me know You in spirit and in truth.
Remind me to look for Your works today and to praise You.

Day 305
"YES" IN JESUS

For no matter how many promises God has made,
they are "Yes" in Christ. And so through him the
"Amen" is spoken by us to the glory of God.
2 CORINTHIANS 1:20 NIV

God has made you over 5,000 promises. It is encouraging to know He will provide and fight for you, give you strength, grant you wisdom, go before you, and never leave or forsake you (see Exodus 4:14; Isaiah 40:29; James 1:5; Deuteronomy 31:8). These promises are grounded in the ultimate proof of love displayed in Christ Jesus—the undeniable love of God for humanity. With His promises God says, "Yes! I love you." And in them, we grasp hold of the truth of His unfaltering affection and confidently respond with "Amen."

What does our expression of an "Amen" look like? An open heart. A willingness to let go of control. An attitude of hope. A trust that does not falter in the face of adversity.

You can trust that God will fulfill every commitment He has made to you. Take courage in your loving God. Let His words strengthen your heart and give peace to your mind. God is more than capable of helping you today. Amen to that!

God, please help me to comprehend Your great love for me.
Help me to stand firm in Your glorious promises. Amen!

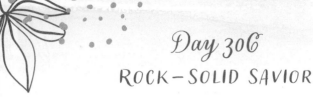

Day 306
ROCK—SOLID SAVIOR

Because of the Truth which lives and stays on in our
hearts and will be with us forever: Grace (spiritual
blessing), mercy, and [soul] peace will be with us, from
God the Father and from Jesus Christ (the Messiah),
the Father's Son, in all sincerity (truth) and love.
2 JOHN 2–3 AMPC

How many times have you reached rock bottom only to find Jesus right there, the rock at the bottom? Throughout scripture Jesus is referred to as "the rock of your salvation." His truth is what lives in your heart and provides freedom to live your life with an eternal perspective.

Your relationship with Jesus is the only thing that really offers you safety and stability while you navigate the violent maelstroms life often brings. When you can't depend on others, and maybe don't even trust yourself, you have a trustworthy, rock-solid Savior. He's the one you can always depend on forever. He faithfully points you in the way you should go. When life spins out of control, He stops the merry-go-round with His truth, helping you to focus.

Are you experiencing challenges that make you feel unstable right now? Ask Jesus to bring balance and stability today.

Jesus, You are my stability. You are my strength.
I depend on Your truth to keep me in balance.
Thank You, Lord, for anchoring my soul today.

Day 307
PERSISTENT BELIEF

Jesus, replying, said to them, Have faith in God [constantly].
MARK 11:22 AMPC

This faith thing isn't a once-and-done deal, nor is it something to be thrown away at the first sign of trouble or forgotten when all is well. It's a persistent, dogged, determined belief in God.

This faith is the constant belief that a beneficent force, one that sustains and propels everything around you—from the tiniest of ant colonies to the farthest of planets—is blessing, guarding, watching, and keeping you; smiling down, bursting to favor you with gifts galore; looking you in the face and giving "you peace (tranquility of heart and life *continually*)" (Numbers 6:26 AMPC, emphasis added).

Your only part is to be constant in your faith. And the only way to do that is to spend lots of time with God. When you do, His part is to be continually giving you peace—within and without—no matter what is going on in your life.

God has created you to be with Him, so abide in Him. He has given you His Son, Jesus, to guide you in all things, so follow Him. He has left behind His Spirit to comfort you, so cling to Him. This faith is fed and fueled by your actively spending time with the greatest of beings—Father, Son, and Spirit. Do your part (He is already doing His), and you will have a constant, living faith and a continual, abiding peace.

Here I am, God. Let's talk.

Day 308
LIFE JEWELS

Choose my instruction instead of silver, knowledge rather than choice gold, for wisdom is more precious than rubies, and nothing you desire can compare with her.
<small>PROVERBS 8:10–11 NIV</small>

Imagine a treasure chest full of sparkling red rubies, radiant gold coins, and gleaming silver candlesticks. Could anything be more spectacular?

Well, yes. *Far* more spectacular are these:

- instruction—learning;
- knowledge—understanding what you have learned;
- and wisdom—practicing that understanding in your life.

Wisdom will add a special radiance and beauty to all the daily dilemmas it touches. So sprinkle God's wisdom into each aspect of your life and watch for blooms to appear where once there was barrenness. For wisdom directs you to make the best financial choices, strengthens your relationships, and helps you find balance and peace in a fast-paced life.

Wisdom is the *real* jewel of life, and God is the abundant supplier. Yet how do you gain wisdom? You can download it into your brain via wise counsel, Christian messages, and spiritual songs. But the *best* method is to consume God's Word like a slice of pie, taking small bites and slowly savoring and swallowing. Then pondering how those small pieces of truth might be applied to your personal circumstances.

Choose instruction, knowledge, and wisdom—and you will have all the treasure you can imagine.

God, I love the richness of Your Word. Show me how to apply Your wisdom to my life. Amen.

Day 309
BELOVED SHEEP

"I myself will gather the remnant of my flock out of all the countries where I have driven them and will bring them back to their pasture, where they will be fruitful and increase in number. I will place shepherds over them who will tend them, and they will no longer be afraid or terrified, nor will any be missing."
JEREMIAH 23:3–4 NIV

If you ever have an identity crisis, here is a beautiful reality to fall back on. You are God's beloved sheep. This truth is enough to outshine everything the world tells you that you are *not*. You can be confident that God has set you securely in His fold. He has elaborate plans to care for you, make you successful, and eradicate your fear and dismay.

Because your trustworthy Shepherd loves each member of His flock, you can trust Him to care for those you love as well as yourself.

Being God's sheep means that you (or *ewe*) can reside in a peaceful pasture, green with peace and gladness at any time or place. When you feel a little beat up by life outside the pasture, you can remember that your Good Shepherd understands. He promises not to lose even one of His fold. He keeps a careful head count and goes in search of those who wander off.

Thank You, Good Shepherd, for providing what I need in a pasture. I trust You to care for us all. Amen.

Day 310

MOVING IN GOD'S STRENGTH

*I am full of power by the Spirit of the LORD. . . . In God I have
put my trust; I will not be afraid. . . . I am for peace. . . . My help
comes from the LORD, who made heaven and earth. . . . Because
You have been my help, therefore in the shadow of Your wings I
will rejoice. . . . Now therefore, O God, strengthen my hands.*
MICAH 3:8; PSALM 56:11; 120:7; 121:2; 63:7; NEHEMIAH 6:9 NKJV

At times, when a task lies before us, we begin to doubt our ability.
Writers hesitate, their hands hovering above the keyboard. Mothers
look at their to-do lists, the words blurring before them as overwhelmed
feelings creep in. Businesswomen consider the meeting they will soon
be leading, not sure of the words to say. Unfocused, unsure, untethered
around the tasks before us, we flounder.

Let God take over. Tap into His power and claim it for yourself.
Put all your trust in the God who vanquishes fear, who can help you
do all He has called you to do. He's done so in the past, and He will
definitely do so in the present. Rejoice in His presence, and allow Him
to work through you as your hands begin moving in His strength.

*Lord, truly I am full of power by Your Spirit. Trusting
You, I will not be afraid but be at peace because You are my
help. As I rejoice in You, I feel Your energy move through
me, Your strength moving my hands. And I begin. . . .*

Day 311
REVEALING AND HEALING

"Call to Me, and I will answer you, and show you great and mighty things, which you do not know. . . . I will bring [them] health and healing; I will heal them and reveal to them the abundance of peace and truth."
JEREMIAH 33:3, 6 NKJV

God again beckons His people to put Him to the test. He wants His daughters to call to Him so that He can answer them. He longs to show them great and mighty things. One of these great and mighty things is healing—both physical and spiritual. Part of healing includes an abundant knowledge and experience of God's peace and truth.

In Jeremiah 33, God told the prophet His plans to restore Jerusalem, to bring the people back from captivity in Babylon and to forgive their rebelliousness. He promised mercy and the coming of a descendant of King David who would be called the Branch of Righteousness and who would rule in joy. Chapter 33 bursts with the beauty of God's grace as it points forward to the great plan of rescue, not just for the Jewish people captured by the Babylonian King Nebuchadnezzar during Jeremiah's time, but also to the salvation of creation through Messiah Jesus. God accomplished in Jesus the mightiest of deeds, a plan for redemption that we could never imagine. Through Jesus, God revealed to us, daughters of Eve, peace and truth since He is the Prince of Peace and the Way of truth.

Lord of our righteousness, thank You for the beautiful picture of healing in Jeremiah 33 and for its fulfillment in Jesus. Keep healing! Amen.

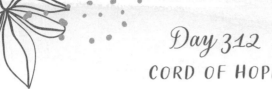

Day 312
CORD OF HOPE

By faith the harlot Rahab did not perish with those who did
not believe, when she had received the spies with peace.
HEBREWS 11:31 NKJV

The life of Rahab is beautiful. She was a harlot. Hardly worth noticing. Yet the writer of Hebrews pointed to her as a woman of faith. And even more astonishing, she is highlighted in Jesus' family tree.

You may know the story. Joshua sent spies to Jericho to scope out the land. They went to Rahab's house, which was probably an inn situated on the city wall. She, along with everyone in the town, knew about the strength of Israel and realized their victories came from "the Lord your God" (see Joshua 2:11).

Rahab hid the spies on her roof when soldiers came searching for them, and sent the soldiers off on a wild-goose chase. Later, she asked the spies to spare her family when Israel attacked Jericho. She proved her faith by helping them escape; she lowered them on a scarlet cord from her window. Because of her assistance, they told her to mark her home with the scarlet cord in her window when they came to conquer the town.

The word translated in Joshua 2:18 as *cord* can also mean *hope*. So, Rahab tied a cord in the window as a sign of hope that she and her family would be saved. Her life may have been marked by a scarlet cord, but her heart was golden to the Lord.

Heavenly Father, show me that You don't keep track
of my past mistakes. Let my life reflect Your mercy.
You are my hope for the future. Amen.

Day 313

LAUGHING AT THE DAYS TO COME

She is clothed with strength and dignity;
she can laugh at the days to come.
PROVERBS 31:25 NIV

You mean a woman of God can laugh at the days to come? Really? Wow. Most of the world wakes up each morning under a black cloud of regret and a debilitating fear of the future. That sounds more realistic, right? To laugh at the future is hard to imagine. To see hope instead of futility? Promise in the pain? What would that kind of woman look like? Sound like?

Perhaps a woman of God as described in Proverbs 31 doesn't necessarily have a lot of confidence in herself, but rather in God. Perhaps she trusts so implicitly in His divine plan and goodness that she can sleep deeply. She can wake up refreshed each morning.

And this woman of God knows some truths: That God will indeed work everything for good in her life. That He is watching over her comings and goings, and nothing will befall her that He can't handle. She knows that this earthly life is temporary. That heaven is not only for real but forever. Knowing these truths all the way to her soul gives her peace and joy, and it shows in her countenance. Yes, and even in her laugh.

Jesus, help me trust in You every hour of every day, and let me be
so full of peace that I too can laugh at the days to come. Amen.

Day 314

A LITTLE SUFFERING FOR A WHOLE LOT OF FAITH

Resist him, standing firm in the faith, because you know that the family of believers throughout the world is undergoing the same kind of sufferings. And the God of all grace, who called you to his eternal glory in Christ, after you have suffered a little while, will himself restore you and make you strong, firm and steadfast.

1 PETER 5:9–10 NIV

Why does God allow suffering? It is the question asked by both believers and non-Christians. God doesn't want His children to suffer. Enmity toward God produces suffering. And resisting Satan means going through lots of pain because we are fighting against the sinful nature around and in us. Gold is only refined through fire, and so Christians can only grow to be more like Jesus if they die to themselves increasingly each day. That is painful. However, the outcome is stronger, bolder, and kinder women who shine like gold because they radiate the light of Christ. God brings about this restoration and renewal. The follower of Jesus is also encouraged that she is never alone in her suffering. Jesus experienced the ultimate suffering by bearing the sins of humankind, and His followers throughout the ages suffer for teaching a rebellious world to return to God. He knows how hard it is, and He is right there beside His daughter giving her greater hope and peace.

God of all grace, help Your daughters stand firm in their love of You. Enable us to remain strong and steadfast so that we can have faith as great as a mustard seed, which can move mountains.

Day 315
OPT FOR A SMALL DEAL

Each one should test their own actions.
Then they can take pride in themselves alone,
without comparing themselves to someone else.
GALATIANS 6:4 NIV

Do you have a tendency to overreact to life's challenges? Do you make a big deal out of things? If so, it's time to accept a challenge. For a full week, make up your mind to make a small deal out of your challenges. When you're tempted to panic, take a deep breath, count to ten, and make the smallest possible scenario out of it that you can. Will this be difficult? Absolutely. Is it possible? Definitely.

When you decide to create big deals out of everyday situations, you find yourself facing relationship strains, high blood pressure, and other woes. These things morph and grow to crazy proportions when you overreact. When you choose small deals, you will experience forgiveness, peace, and the ability to bounce back without holding bitterness. It's your choice!

When you opt to make a small deal out of things, you will also have the satisfaction of knowing that you are pleasing your heavenly Father's heart. Now, that's a very big deal!

Lord, I don't want to be seen as someone who overreacts
to things. I acknowledge that I've done this at times.
Please remove this tendency from me so that I can live at
peace with others. I want to please Your heart, Father.

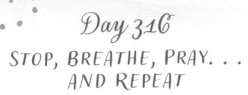

Day 316

STOP, BREATHE, PRAY. . . AND REPEAT

Do not be anxious about anything, but in every situation,
by prayer and petition, with thanksgiving, present your requests
to God. And the peace of God, which transcends all understanding,
will guard your hearts and your minds in Christ Jesus.
PHILIPPIANS 4:6–7 NIV

Being a woman in these times is challenging. Many of us are working demanding jobs, managing our homes and crazy schedules, and taking care of children or aging parents. Often, we feel we don't have enough time to get everything done, let alone take care of ourselves properly. All of this creates stress and anxiety, which just makes many of these situations worse.

What can you do when it seems the world is falling down around your shoulders? Stop. Take a deep breath, and then settle your mind on Jesus. Give Him the situation, the harried thoughts, the worries. God says that we can take anything to Him in prayer! He will provide whatever we need, even the peace that will get us through the most difficult circumstances.

Father God, we are thankful that we can take any worried
thought or situation to You in prayer. You tell us that You
will provide for us and will even give us Your peace! Help
us to trust You in this, Lord, to lay the situation at Your
feet and leave it there. Fill our minds and hearts with Your
peace and remind us of how much You love us. Amen!

Day 317
A PRINCESS MINDSET

For God is the King over all the earth.
Praise him with a psalm.
PSALM 47:7 NLT

You are a daughter of the King of kings, true royalty! Despite that fact, it's often difficult to see yourself that way, isn't it? When you're feeling bedraggled and tired, when you're facing mounting bills, when your enemies rise up against you, it's easier to feel like a little peasant girl.

It's time for a princess mindset! You've got to remember several things: First, the King welcomes you into His presence. In fact, He bids you to come as often as possible. Second, you're going to live forever with the King! You'll walk on streets of gold and live in a mansion. Third, the Prince of Peace lives in your heart. Accepting Jesus as Savior assures you of a personal, day-in, day-out conversation with the one who spun the heavens and the earth into existence.

You. Are. Royalty. Of course, that also means you have to live like a daughter of the King! You're representing Him, after all. So, chin up. Put all whining and complaining aside. People are watching you so that they can know how a daughter of the King lives. Lead by example, princess!

Father, You are the King of kings! How often I
forget that being Your child makes me a princess in
Your sight. I want to live in such a way that others
are drawn to my Daddy, God, by my actions.

Day 318

FINDING PEACE

And he will be called. . .Prince of Peace.
Isaiah 9:6 niv

We all long for a peaceful place. The desire for peace is etched into our genetic code. . .perhaps because we're made in God's image, and He is full of peace. When we think of peace, our minds fill with images of calm, quiet serenity. We picture a hilltop surrounded by lovely gardens, with birds singing and the gentle laughter of loved ones.

While it's good to seek out a peaceful, tranquil existence, that's not always possible. In this world, stress finds us. War happens. People can be mean and selfish. Diseases appear, accidents occur. So how can we have peace when the pressures and tensions of life seem to hunt us down?

It's possible to have peace amid chaos when we understand where peace is found. God's peace isn't confined to a specific location or a specific set of circumstances. His peace isn't something we have to maneuver and create. Jesus Christ is the Prince of Peace. Peace is His kingdom, and as long as He lives within us, that is where His peace dwells.

It's important to walk away from stress when we can. But when stress finds us, we can extinguish it—or at least diminish it greatly—by calling on the Prince of Peace within our hearts. When we respond with the calm, quiet assurance that comes from Christ alone, we will find peace.

Dear Father, thank You for sending the Prince of Peace.
Help me to call on Him when I need peace. Amen.

Day 319
PRAY INSTEAD OF
PLOTTING — OR FRETTING

*"Pray that the LORD your God will show
us what to do and where to go."*
JEREMIAH 42:3 NLT

Whether you're a mom, wife, employee, or friend, your list of to-dos never seems to get done. Meanwhile, the house is a wreck, the relatives are bickering, the bills keep coming—and amid the cacophony, God seems conspicuously absent.

However bleak your situation seems, God hasn't forgotten you. Philippians 4:6–7 (NIV) says, "Do not be anxious about anything, but in every situation, by prayer and petition, with thanksgiving, present your requests to God. And the peace of God, which transcends all understanding, will guard your hearts and your minds in Christ Jesus."

Jeremiah 42:3 echoes this statement. It urges believers to pray for guidance instead of setting out with a preconceived notion of how the day (or month or decade) will turn out.

When you begin to worry that you don't have what it takes to meet life's demands, remember that you don't have to—because God does. Author and speaker Rebekah Montgomery says, "If God asks you to build an ark, He'll give you the measurements. If He asks you to get out of the boat and walk on water, He'll show you the technique. If He asks you to pray, He'll teach you how. If He asks you to love your neighbor, He'll give you love."

*Jesus, thank You for Your presence and the peace You so freely give.
Help me to pray before I worry, categorize, or strategize. Amen.*

Day 320

THE SIMPLE THINGS

In him our hearts rejoice, for we trust in his holy name.
PSALM 33:21 NIV

Think about the simple pleasures in everyday life—that first sip of coffee in the morning, waking up to realize you still have a few more minutes to sleep, or putting on fresh, warm clothes right out of the dryer on a cold winter morning. Perhaps it's a walk along the beach or a hike up the mountains into the blue skies that gives you a simple peace.

God knows all the simple pleasures you enjoy—and He created them for your delight. When the simple things that can come only by His hand fill you with contentment, He is pleased. He takes pleasure in you. You are His delight. Giving you peace, comfort, and a sense of knowing that you belong to Him is a simple thing for Him.

Take a moment today and step away from the busyness of life. Take notice and fully experience some of those things you enjoy most. Then share that special joy with Him.

*Lord, thank You for the simple things that bring pleasure
to my day. I enjoy each gift You've given me. I invite
You to share those moments with me today. Amen.*

Day 321
JUNGLE OF LIFE

God's word is alive and working and is sharper than a double-edged sword. It cuts all the way into us, where the soul and the spirit are joined, to the center of our joints and bones. And it judges the thoughts and feelings in our hearts.
HEBREWS 4:12 NCV

Since the time Adam and Eve disobeyed God, the consequences of sin have often stood between us and God's best for our lives. Choosing a life of faith can feel like we are lost in a jungle, tangled in the underbrush. But God has given us a powerful tool that will cut through the debris of life in a fallen world.

When you take the Bible and live according to His plans, obeying Him, God's Word cuts like a machete through the entanglements of life. When you choose to use the sword of truth, it clears a path and can free you from the weights of the world that try to entrap and ensnare you.

No matter what the challenges of life are saying to you today, take His Word and speak His plans into your life. Choose His words of encouragement and peace instead of the negative things the circumstances are telling you.

God, I want to live in Your truth. I want to believe what You say about me in the Bible. Help me to speak Your words today instead of letting the problem speak to me. Help me believe. Amen.

Day 322
DON'T GIVE IN

But you'll welcome us with open arms when we run for
cover to you. Let the party last all night! Stand guard
over our celebration. You are famous, GOD, for welcoming
God-seekers, for decking us out in delight.
PSALM 5:11–12 MSG

From time to time, we can lose hope and become discouraged despite all the blessings surrounding us. When this happens, we need to remember Paul's words about the certainty of God's promises and realize that our God will never forsake us.

When we have those down-in-the-dumps days, we should encircle ourselves with encouragers, Christian friends who can hold up our arms, like Moses, when we're unable to continue the journey. We can reach for God's Word, which breathes life into our spirits. Moments of prayer will connect us to the life giver and refresh us.

Worry and discouragement are spiritual traps that sap our energy and cover us with a cloud of gloom. These evil twins can be dispelled by praise. Turn on the radio, hum an old hymn, or read a psalm aloud. We can choose to praise and look for joy in spite of our circumstances. David did. Paul and Silas did. We can too.

God has promised to give us peace and joy in spite of our trials and struggles. Let's reach out to Him and shed our veil of darkness for a mantle of praise.

Heavenly Father, I lift my eyes to the heavens and
ask for Your peace. Thank You for Your love and care.
Thank You for standing by my side. I praise Your name.

Day 323
LOOK TO THE PROMISE

Let us hold unswervingly to the hope we profess,
for he who promised is faithful.
HEBREWS 10:23 NIV

"I promise to pick up the dry cleaning." "The check is in the mail, I promise." How lightly we use the word *promise*. We toss it around with very little meaning attached. The definition of *promise* is a statement telling someone you will definitely do something, or that something will definitely happen in the future. The use of the word means you can hang your hat on it! This some*thing* is coming. Oh, how often we fail to carry through with our word. It's wonderful we can know for sure—definitely—that God's promise is eternal.

God's Word contains promises upon which we can and must depend. The Bible is a priceless gift, a tool God intends for us to use in our lives. Too often we look away from "The Manual."

Are you tired and discouraged? Fearful? Be comforted in the promises God has made to you through His Word. Experiencing worry or anxiety? Be courageous and call on God. He will protect you and then use you according to His purposes. Are you confused? Listen to the whisper of the Holy Spirit, for our God is not a God of confusion.

Talk to Him, listen to Him, and trust Him. Trust His promises. He is steadfast, and He will be by your side. Always.

Father, how we thank You for Your promises. You are steadfast,
loving, and caring. We cannot praise You enough. Amen.

Day 324
SING!

As for me, I will sing of Your strength. Yes, I will sing with joy of Your loving-kindness in the morning. For You have been a strong and safe place for me in times of trouble.
PSALM 59:16 NLV

Have you actually tried singing without caring who was listening? Or dancing like nobody's watching? Or laughing as loudly as you can without a care? When your heart wants to praise the Lord, openly and purely, do you allow it? Do you sing as the psalmist does?

Because God certainly sings for us. He blesses us with loving-kindness every morning. He is a source of strength for us as we go through our days. When we are overwhelmed, He's a place of comfort. When we're attacked, He's our place of safety. These are blessings to celebrate!

God wants us to sing to Him, to praise Him, in any way we can, not just seek Him out when we're in trouble or need His help. Today, acknowledge your blessings, the strength and comfort and safety God extends to you. Treasure them and Him in your heart and soul.

Find some time to celebrate all the things your Lord has gifted you. So when a season comes that reminds you of the not-so-good times of this life, you can still access that ever-present well of goodness.

I praise You, Lord, for everything You've done,
in all the ways You have worked in my life,
how You have blessed me. To You I sing! Amen.

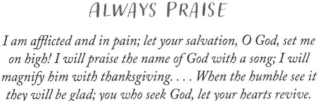

Day 325
ALWAYS PRAISE

I am afflicted and in pain; let your salvation, O God, set me on high! I will praise the name of God with a song; I will magnify him with thanksgiving. . . . When the humble see it they will be glad; you who seek God, let your hearts revive.
PSALM 69:29–30, 32 ESV

When you think about the life of a king, what comes to mind? Perhaps a luxurious palace, unimaginable wealth, a bevy of servants, an endless supply of food and drink. . .every whim fulfilled. Certainly, a life of ease.

However, this wasn't the case for King David. He lived a very troubled life. He was involved in adultery, deceit, and murder. His infant son died right after birth. David had many enemies. And the list of hardships goes on. Throughout the Psalms, David pleads with God, repeatedly asking for His help and deliverance. He knew God alone could ease his pain and suffering.

Rich or poor, king or servant, we all will experience troubles and trials throughout life. And while it's tempting to take on a woe-is-me attitude, we need only look to King David's example. For even when he faced adversity, David never failed to praise God. This kind of attitude pleases our heavenly Father! And if David, who faced every imaginable hardship in life, could do it, then we can too!

Father God, no matter what hardships I experience in life, let me always sing praises to You! Amen.

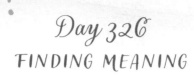

Day 326
FINDING MEANING

Yet when I surveyed all that my hands had done and what I had toiled to achieve, everything was meaningless, a chasing after the wind; nothing was gained under the sun.
ECCLESIASTES 2:11 NIV

Every person comes to this moment at some point. For some, it comes early—perhaps in adolescence. For others, it comes later in life, after retirement. It might even come at several points. It's the moment of meaning—the moment we stop and wonder what in the world we are doing on this earth, asking, *Does any of it matter?* It's a moment of awareness and accounting. It's a moment of honest reflection. And for some, it's a moment of utter despair.

The words of the writer of Ecclesiastes often sound to the modern reader like someone singing the blues. They are the words of Eeyore—nothing ever matters. Nothing ever happens. Nothing ever changes.

But if we look more closely at this little book in the Bible, we see a different message. We see that God "has made everything beautiful in its time. He has also set eternity in the human heart; yet no one can fathom what God has done from beginning to end" (Ecclesiastes 3:11 NIV). We ask these questions about meaning because God put the questions inside us. Because He wanted us, through the questioning, to find Him. To know that our meaning is found in Him.

*Lord, thank You for the longing
for purpose that leads me to You. Amen.*

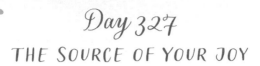

Day 327

THE SOURCE OF YOUR JOY

Rejoice in the Lord always. I will say it again: Rejoice!
PHILIPPIANS 4:4 NIV

Paul wrote these words from prison. Considering his circumstances, it doesn't seem like he had much reason to rejoice. Yet he knew what many of us forget: when we have the Lord on our side, we always have reason to rejoice.

He didn't say, "Rejoice in your circumstances." He told us to rejoice in the Lord. When we're feeling depressed, anxious, or lost in despair, we can think of our Lord. We can remind ourselves that we are so very loved. We are special to God. He adores us, and in His heart, each of us is irreplaceable.

Perhaps the reason we lose our joy sometimes is because we've let the wrong things be the source of our joy. If our joy is in our finances, our jobs, or our relationships, what happens when those things fall through? Our joy is lost.

But when God is the source of our joy, we will never lose that joy. Circumstances may frustrate us and break our hearts. But God is able to supply all our needs. He is able to restore broken relationships. He can give us a new job or help us to succeed at our current job. Through it all, despite it all, we can rejoice in knowing that we are God's and He loves us.

Dear Father, thank You for loving me.
Help me to make You the source of my joy. Amen.

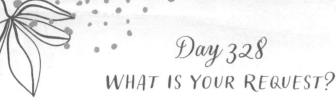

Day 328
WHAT IS YOUR REQUEST?

*And pray in the Spirit on all occasions with all
kinds of prayers and requests. With this in mind,
be alert and always keep on praying.*
EPHESIANS 6:18 NIV

What burdens your heart today? Is there a trial that engulfs you or someone you love? Present your request to your heavenly Father with the assurance that He will act on your behalf—either by changing your circumstances or by changing you. He is always concerned for you.

But be patient. What we may view as a nonanswer may simply be God saying, "Wait" or "I have something better for you." He *will* answer. Keep in mind that His ways are not our ways, nor are His thoughts our thoughts.

God knows what He's doing, even when He allows trials in our lives. We might think that saving a loved one from difficulty is a great idea—but God, in His wisdom, may decide that would be keeping them (or us) from an opportunity for spiritual growth. Since we don't know all God's plans, we must simply lay our requests before Him and trust Him to do what is right. He will never fail us!

*Father God, here are my needs. I lay them at Your feet,
walking away unburdened and assured that You
have it all under control. Thank You!*

Day 329
GOD ONLY KNOWS

*[Only] with [God] are [perfect] wisdom and might; He [alone]
has [true] counsel and understanding. Behold, He tears down,
and it cannot be built again. . . . He withholds the waters, and the
land dries up; again, He sends forth [rains], and they overwhelm
the land or transform it. With Him are might and wisdom;
the deceived and the deceiver are His [and in His power].*
JOB 12:13–16 AMPC

Some days you may have a million questions as to why God has
allowed certain things to happen. Why does He withhold the rains
then later pour them out in a flood that transforms the land? Why
does He allow good people to die too soon and the seemingly not-
so-good people to live into their nineties?

Instead of getting caught up in trying to figure out the whys of God,
trust that He knows best. Eckhart Tolle says, "Sometimes surrender
means giving up trying to understand and becoming comfortable
with not knowing."

God alone has perfect wisdom and might. He is in total control,
knows what He's doing, and has a plan for His people—including
you. So no matter what happens, relax. Everything in this world is
under God's power. You need not understand everything—but God
does. And that's all you need to know.

*Sometimes, Lord, I have trouble accepting certain things.
Help me to surrender to Your wisdom and might,
to acknowledge the idea that I don't have to understand
everything. But simply trust You for everything.*

Day 330
NOTHING TO FEAR

You may say to yourselves, "These nations are stronger than we are. How can we drive them out?" But do not be afraid of them; remember well what the LORD your God did to Pharaoh and to all Egypt. You saw with your own eyes the great trials, the signs and wonders, the mighty hand and outstretched arm, with which the LORD your God brought you out. The LORD your God will do the same to all the peoples you now fear.
DEUTERONOMY 7:17–19 NIV

If you have ever faced overwhelming odds, you have probably experienced fear. Today's scripture reminds you that when things seem hopeless, it's wise to remember that God does indeed answer prayers, just as He did when the oppressed Israelites called out to Him in Egypt. When Moses was finally able to lead the Israelites out of Egypt, things began to look bleak as Pharaoh was right on their heels. Yet God saved them by drowning the Egyptian army in the Red Sea.

When you hear words of fear echoing in your heart, remember that with God you're safe and secure. Just as He delivered His people from Egypt, He'll deliver you. Though sometimes you may feel like the underdog, with God on your side you'll always be triumphant.

Dear God, because You repeatedly perform miraculous deeds in delivering Your people, I know You will protect me from all that I fear and, no matter how bleak things may look, You will ultimately bring me to victory.

Day 331

DEEP WITHIN THE PIT

But I called on your name, LORD, from deep within the pit. You heard me when I cried, "Listen to my pleading! Hear my cry for help!" Yes, you came when I called; you told me, "Do not fear."

LAMENTATIONS 3:55–57 NLT

Maybe you've heard the old expression "He has to hit rock bottom before he'll come to God." It's true! Many people won't turn their eyes to Jesus until they're in such a deep, dark place that they have no other choice.

The book of Lamentations focuses on the people of God in deep torment, lamenting to the Lord about their troubles. Some situations were so painful, some pits were so deep, God's children may have felt they'd never escape them.

Perhaps you can relate to the people of God who'd hit rock bottom, as revealed in today's verses. Yet hope remains, for these verses also show that God hears our cries, no matter how low we've fallen. His response to us, even while we're sinking deep in our sin? "Do not fear."

Isn't that the most gracious thing you could say to a person who's buried in a pit, terrified she will stay there forever? God, the rescuer, comes to save even the ones most hopeless. What a wonderful Father!

Father, You've rescued me more times than I could count. How I praise You for snatching me out of the pit! Amen.

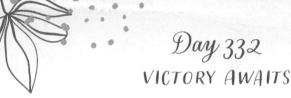

Day 332
VICTORY AWAITS

*"These will make war with the Lamb, and the Lamb will
overcome them, for He is Lord of lords and King of kings;
and those who are with Him are called, chosen, and faithful."*
REVELATION 17:14 NKJV

Amid stark apocalyptic imagery, Revelation provides this comfort: no
matter how long evil seems to prevail, Jesus will be victorious. And
just as He will win at Armageddon, He can gain the victory over the
things we struggle with in our lives.

But do we consistently bring our battles to Him? So often we
look to other places for comfort and help instead of Christ—friends,
favorite foods, vacations—all good and helpful things, but not sources
of lasting peace. On a similar note, the prophet Zechariah warned
the people that idols "comfort in vain," leaving the people wandering
like sheep without a shepherd (Zechariah 10:2 NKJV). Because earthly
comforts can only alleviate our problems temporarily, our focus needs
to be on Christ, our true and everlasting good.

The Word promises that Christ will give you the victory over the
sin that beats you down (1 Corinthians 15:57), that He works all
things together for good for those who love Him (Romans 8:28).
He, faithful and true, will lead you forward; you will hear His voice
as a shepherd calls his sheep (Zechariah 10:6). You have His promise.

*Jesus, when I'm tempted to look elsewhere for comfort,
please remind me and strengthen my heart with
the promise of Your Word and Your victory.*

Day 333
THE LORD WORKS IN INCREDIBLE WAYS

*When Elisha arrived, the child was indeed
dead, lying there on the prophet's bed.*
2 KINGS 4:32 NLT

Weren't some of God's Old Testament miracles just plain odd? A dinky jar of oil fills many jars (2 Kings 4:1–7). Poisoned stew is made edible with flour (2 Kings 4:38–41). Then there's the incident of the Shunammite's son.

Elisha had foretold the child's birth, but then the child died. So Elisha prayed to God. He stretched out over the child twice, pacing the room in between. After that the boy sneezed seven times and was alive and well. What was that all about?

The ways God works—either solo or through people—are sometimes surprising, not what *we* would expect or imagine. God simply isn't confined to convention. Still, how often do we feel unsettled looking at our situations because we are hoping for conventional solutions? We pray for God to intervene, but in the back of our minds we think there's no way things can change. Yet when Jesus told us that with faith we can say, "Mountain, move!" and it will move, He didn't spell out *how* the mountain would move (Matthew 17:20). We don't know how God will work either. And that should give us even more reason to hope.

*God, You can do anything—even in this "hopeless"
situation. I will trust You. And I will watch
for You to work in incredible ways.*

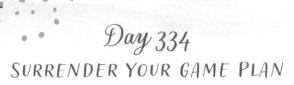

Day 334
SURRENDER YOUR GAME PLAN

*The Lord will fight for you, and you
shall hold your peace and remain at rest.*
EXODUS 14:14 AMPC

Letting God fight for us can be a tall order because we're capable women, ready and able to handle what comes our way. It may not be pretty, but we get the job done. We are moms and wives, company owners and shift managers, coaches and teachers, and everything in between. And when we're standing in God's strength and wisdom, we're a force to be reckoned with. Amen?

Yet there are times we're to let God fight for us. We're to take a step back and trust as He handles the situation. We're to wait on His timing and plan, even when it seems there's no movement whatsoever. And instead of jumping in and trying to make everything come together, we're to take a seat. We're to let God be God.

What makes that hard for you? Are you more comfortable in the driver's seat? Do you feel better when you're calling the shots? Is it easiest when you get to control all interactions and outcomes?

God is asking you to trust Him enough to surrender your game plan to His. And when you do, you'll find peace.

*Lord, I'll admit this is hard for me. I like being in control.
But I know that You are God and I am not. Will You
grow my faith so I can surrender to Your will and way?*

Day 335
OUR UNSTOPPABLE GOD

*And Jonathan said to his young armor-bearer, Come,
and let us go over to the garrison of these uncircumcised;
it may be that the Lord will work for us. For there is nothing
to prevent the Lord from saving by many or by few.*
1 SAMUEL 14:6 AMPC

We serve a mighty God who always wins. He has been, He is, and He will always be victorious because He is above all. God's plans are perfect, and His will is wonderful. There is nothing to prevent the Lord from doing what He sees fit to do.

Nothing.

Please let that truth comfort you. The Word clearly states over and over again that God is for you, that He loves you, and that His plans for you are good! That means that if you take a wrong turn in life or have a bad season of sinning, God's plans still win. If it's His will, *it will happen.*

Talk about taking away the pressure to perform or be perfect! Friend, your job is to keep taking the next right step, developing a relationship with Him, confessing and repenting your struggles, and trusting God's power over your circumstances. He's inviting you to live in a place of rest in Him.

Let God do the heavy lifting. Activate your faith in His abilities, because, unlike you, He is unstoppable.

*Lord, what a relief to know that Your will. . .
will be done. Thankfully, You're God and I am not.*

Day 336
DIVINE GPS

When my spirit grows faint within me,
it is you who watch over my way.
PSALM 142:3 NIV

Have you ever been lost on a country road and been unable to get a GPS signal? Soon a sense of desperation sets in. You begin to feel utterly alone and afraid. Nothing looks familiar as you drive aimlessly, trying to find your way. It is an unsettling feeling, to say the least.

These emotions are common to all, especially during difficult times. When living through times of fear and uncertainty, it's easy to become disheartened, feel alone, and feel unsettled. But when your spirit grows faint, do *not* lose hope! God is always there, watching over you, prepared to show you the path back to faith.

David was hiding out in a cave when he wrote this psalm. He was being persecuted and pursued. He feared for his life. Yet God inspired him to write these words, words that gave him comfort and hope and ultimately saved his life.

When you feel lost, helpless, and hopeless, lift your eyes to the mountains, to the source of your help, to "the LORD, the Maker of heaven and earth" (Psalm 121:2 NIV). Depend on God, using Him as your GPS as you go through this life.

Dear God, help me as I try to navigate my journey
through this life. Be with me always, guiding me
through in good times and bad. Sustain my spirit
in times of weakness and show me Your way.

Day 337
CONTINUAL REFUGE

Kiss the Son [pay homage to Him in purity]. . . .
O blessed (happy, fortunate, and to be envied) are all
those who seek refuge and put their trust in Him!
PSALM 2:12 AMPC

In the garden of Eden, Eve fell under the influence of the father of lies. Then Adam was persuaded to join her in his untruths. Next thing they knew, they realized they were naked and so hid from God.

Yet God, who knows all and sees all, quickly surmised what had happened. Of course, there were consequences to His children's actions. But He did not desert them in their time of need. Instead, He tenderly clothed them.

God is there for you in the same way. No matter what you do, where you are, or how you mess up, God will not desert you. Of course, when you err, there will be consequences. But keep in mind that God will always stick with you. When you seek out His refuge, He will open His arms to you and pull you close. When you need a shoulder to cry on, He will offer His. When you need direction, He will be there to listen to and counsel you. And when you are in danger, He will help you find a way out. For He never fails to bless those who trust in Him.

Help me to always remember, Lord, that You are
there for me—always have been, always will be.

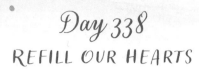

Day 338
REFILL OUR HEARTS

From the ends of the earth I call to you, I call as my
heart grows faint; lead me to the rock that is higher than I.
For you have been my refuge, a strong tower against the foe.
PSALM 61:2–3 NIV

"My heart grows faint." Darkness rises. A storm brews on the horizon. You're hurting. You're lost. You're lonely. Your heart, your soul, is tired.

Maybe you are in such a place. Once again, you're waiting for God to come through, to reach into your life and make you feel something other than exhaustion. Or maybe you have been through a season like this one, and while sunny days surround you now, you wait for the time when shadows may cover your life again. Either way, you dread tomorrow. You wonder, *What will it bring? Will I find my way through?*

We know life is hard. But we also know that God always offers us a refuge and a calm amid the pain. He gives us a place to recharge and refill our hearts with His presence and goodness. Our problems may not dissolve, but they will become bearable. With this new feeling in our hearts, we will be able to face the oncoming day in God's courage and strength.

My Comforter, I will find strength and encouragement
in Your everlasting and love-filled arms. Amen.

Day 339
SOFTEN MY HEART

Immediately he spoke to them and said, "Take courage! It is I. Don't be afraid." Then he climbed into the boat with them, and the wind died down. They were completely amazed, for they had not understood about the loaves; their hearts were hardened.

MARK 6:50–52 NIV

Can you believe the disciples in this passage? Right before they saw their companion and Savior, Jesus, walking on water, they saw Him feed five thousand people with only five loaves of bread and two fish. But because they did not understand it, "their hearts were hardened." And these were His closest friends!

We might like to say we would never be like them, but think on this: How many times have you seen loved ones and strangers turn from God because they did not understand His ways? How many times have you hardened your heart against Him because of a circumstance or a verse you couldn't put an explanation or reason to?

We crave stability and answers. We fear what we don't know. But Jesus tells us again and again, "Don't be afraid."

When your mind can't comprehend the fullness of God, may your heart soften instead of harden. Let your questions open you up to the love He provides and the peace He promises.

Lord, I may not have all the answers right now, but instead of turning from You in frustration, I open my arms to You for comfort, understanding, and amazement.

Day 340
EVEN IF. . .

Though the fig tree does not bud and there are no grapes on the
vines, though the olive crop fails and the fields produce no food,
though there are no sheep in the pen and no cattle in the stalls, yet
I will rejoice in the LORD, I will be joyful in God my Savior.
HABAKKUK 3:17–18 NIV

The fig tree mentioned in today's scripture produced fruit that was a food staple in ancient times. Grapes were picked from the vine and used to make wine. Sheep and cattle provided meat. With these things in scarce supply, it would have made sense if Habakkuk had written, "And so I will be unhappy." Rejoicing just doesn't make sense in this situation, does it?

What about you? Have you ever suffered a momentous loss? Have you invested time and labor into something important to you, only to have it all fall apart? Have you experienced a tremendous disappointment? How did you react to life's letdowns? Were you joyful? Or did you spiral into a dark, emotional abyss. . .angry, sad, hopeless? . . .

God's Word says, "Rejoice always, pray continually, give thanks in all circumstances; for this is God's will for you in Christ Jesus" (1 Thessalonians 5:16–18 NIV). No matter what life brings your way—good or bad—*rejoice*! Because you have Jesus!

Father, some days are just hard. It's comforting to know that
because of You, I can have joy despite my circumstances. Amen.

Day 341
ERASING YOUR FEARS

The LORD is my shepherd; I shall not want. He makes me lie down in green pastures. He leads me beside still waters. He restores my soul. He leads me in paths of righteousness for his name's sake. Even though I walk through the valley of the shadow of death, I will fear no evil, for you are with me; your rod and your staff, they comfort me.
PSALM 23:1–4 ESV

What makes you cringe in fear? Spiders? Snakes? Roller coasters? Tight spaces? Clowns? The dark? Evil? If you're being completely honest, you'll admit you're afraid of *something*. Each of us is afraid of one thing or another. That's the bad news. . . .

Now for the good news! No matter *what* you fear, and no matter *how big* your fear, it can be erased—because of Jesus! He will calm your deepest, darkest fears. And because of His loving sacrifice on the cross, even the fear of death can be overcome! What a beautiful promise His Word gives you: "For God so loved the world that he gave his one and only Son, that whoever believes in him shall not perish but have eternal life" (John 3:16 NIV).

Jesus died so that you might live and spend eternity in heaven! If you haven't already, say yes to His gift of fearless living today!

Lord Jesus, thank You for saving me!
Help me to overcome my fears!

Day 342

NEW EVERY MORNING

*This I recall to my mind, therefore I have hope. Through the
Lord's mercies we are not consumed, because His compassions
fail not. They are new every morning; great is Your faithfulness.*
LAMENTATIONS 3:21–23 NKJV

For many people, one of the most difficult times of the day is nighttime.
We fall into bed physically exhausted, grateful to finally be done with
the activity of the day. Suddenly our brains are awake and alert with
swirling thoughts. Thoughts of today lead to thoughts of yesterday
and ten years back. We think of things we should have said but didn't
and things we shouldn't have said but did. We rehearse bad decisions and mistakes and worry anxiously about the future. The thoughts
that keep us awake some nights can be daunting, to say the least. These
thoughts can consume us with worry, fear, and regret, robbing us of
peace and sleep. We feel hopeless and exhausted.

But God's Word says we don't have to be consumed by regrets from
the past or fears of the future. Every morning, with the rising of the
sun, comes a new measure of His mercy, compassion, and faithfulness.
So let your worrisome thoughts go and replace them with hope. His
mercy and compassion will never fail.

*Father, when I can't sleep, bring Your mercy and compassion to
my mind. Give me hope in Your faithfulness. Thank You for the
promise of the new morning, and help me to rest in You. Amen.*

Day 343
THE ONE CHOICE
THAT BRINGS PEACE

You will keep in perfect peace those whose minds
are steadfast, because they trust in you.
ISAIAH 26:3 NIV

For the woman who wants to experience the peace God promises, there are only two choices: trust or torment. We must ask ourselves, "Will I rely on God, choosing to believe He can be trusted with all I don't understand and the concerns that consume my thoughts, or will I choose not to believe and trust Him?" The first choice brings rest and peace. The latter only brings torment.

Isaiah 30:15 (NLT) says, "In quietness and confidence is your strength." The one who chooses belief and trust experiences a confidence and quietness of spirit. The one who chooses not to believe and not to trust her Lord experiences a lack of confidence, and chaos overtakes her spirit. "What will happen now?" "Oh no! Awful things are going to happen; I just know it!" In this, there is torment.

Belief and trust are chosen because life will always give you many reasons not to trust. It seems that every difficult experience invites us to experience unbelief, to focus on all that is going wrong and to look to the future in fear. It's not easy to make the choice to believe and trust, because it's willful. It's deliberate. And sometimes it's moment by moment.

Lord, please help me to choose trust each moment today
so I can live in the abundance of Your peace. Amen.

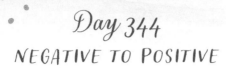

Day 344
NEGATIVE TO POSITIVE

*If I had not confessed the sin in my heart, the Lord
would not have listened. But God did listen! He paid
attention to my prayer. Praise God, who did not ignore
my prayer or withdraw his unfailing love from me.*
PSALM 66:18–20 NLT

Sometimes our thoughts lie. Our mind fills to overflowing with
negative messages:

I'm not good enough.
I'm boring.
I'm not talented.
I'm not smart.
God doesn't love me.
And He certainly doesn't care about anything I have to say.

Tune out those negative thoughts! Have a heart-to-heart with
God today. Ask Him to help drown out your negative thinking. Ask
Him to replace the lies with truths:

Because of God's love and grace, I am good enough.
God created me to be interesting, talented, and smart.
God loves me in a BIG way!
And He cares about every single thing I have to say!

No matter what your brain tries to tell you, God is faithful, and He
loves you more than you could ever imagine. Tell God exactly what you're
thinking and feeling. Confess the sin in your heart and keep your focus
wholly on Him. . .and He will be 100 percent tuned in to your prayers.

*Father, I praise You! Thank You for loving me perfectly.
Thank You for listening. You are everything I'll ever need
and more. Please take control of my thoughts. Help me to
let go of the negative and focus on the positive. Amen.*

Day 345
CHOOSE LIFE!

[If you obey the commandments of the Lord your God which] I command you today, to love the Lord your God, to walk in His ways, and to keep His commandments and His statutes and His ordinances. . .the Lord your God will bless you in the land into which you go to possess.
DEUTERONOMY 30:16 AMPC

We are bombarded every day with situations that require decisions. Some are simple: The red shoes or the black? Some require a bit more thought: The SUV or the minivan? And some are complex: Stay in your current job or change career paths? . . .

If you're a living, breathing human being, then you've probably made countless decisions throughout your life. How about making a life-altering decision right now: Will you choose the good life or a miserable life? Seems simple, doesn't it? Who would make the conscious choice to be miserable?

The good news is you really *do* have a choice. And blessings abound when you choose to love God, follow His path for your life, and obey His Word. How wonderful!

When you're having an awful day, reread these truths from Deuteronomy, and let them work their way from your head to your heart. Then choose life—choose the abundant blessings of Christ!

Heavenly Father, You are so good, so wonderful, so powerful. . .it's impossible to have a horrible, very bad day when You're the focus of my life! I choose life! I choose You! Amen.

Day 346
GOOD NEWS!

"But for you who fear my name, the Sun of Righteousness will rise with healing in his wings. And you will go free, leaping with joy like calves let out to pasture. On the day when I act, you will tread upon the wicked as if they were dust under your feet."
MALACHI 4:2–3 NLT

If it seems like you're constantly bombarded with bad news. . . If you ever find yourself in a difficult place. . . If your faith is faltering and your heart is hopeless. . . If you feel alone and abandoned. . . There's good news for you, dear one!

If you're a faithful follower of Jesus, you're on the receiving end of bountiful blessings. And they're yours for the taking. Part of those blessings include ultimate healing, joy, and freedom in Christ. How can you know this for certain? Because the promises of God's Word are unfaltering and trustworthy. If His Word says it, you can believe it! "GOD always does what he says, and is gracious in everything he does" (Psalm 145:13 MSG).

Today, thank God for making you one of His own. Praise Him for His saving grace. He is the one and only Redeemer!

Father God, because of Your steadfast love and grace, I am free. I have joy in my heart—even when life is hard. You give me hope, not just today, but for the future. I choose to follow You all the days of my life. Thank You! Amen.

Day 347
RESTORATION

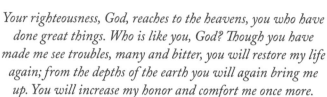

Your righteousness, God, reaches to the heavens, you who have done great things. Who is like you, God? Though you have made me see troubles, many and bitter, you will restore my life again; from the depths of the earth you will again bring me up. You will increase my honor and comfort me once more.
PSALM 71:19–21 NIV

Ever felt like the walls are closing in around you? No matter which way you look, you can't see a way out. You feel like you're beyond all hope. Your life is a wreck. And you're left wondering if it's beyond repair.

Although it doesn't seem possible, when you feel hopeless, you are presented with a wonderful opportunity. Because the very best way to grow your faith and increase your trust in God is through your trials. Whatever hardships you encounter in life, they all present you with delightful moments to recognize and embrace God's deliverance and grace. The God who heals (Jeremiah 17:14) offers complete restoration for your heart and soul.

The more your heart and mind are tuned to the heavenly Father's deliverance, the more you'll be able to release your bitter thoughts and burdens to Him. Just try it! You'll be so glad you did. Your thoughts and your soul will thank you! Ask the heavenly Father for His healing restoration today!

Father, restore my heart. Restore my hope. Thank You for taking my broken life, giving me healing, and covering me with Your grace. Amen.

Day 348
SOVEREIGN

"My soul is very sorrowful, even to death. Remain here and watch." And going a little farther, he fell on the ground and prayed that, if it were possible, the hour might pass from him. And he said, "Abba, Father, all things are possible for you. Remove this cup from me. Yet not what I will, but what you will."

MARK 14:34–36 ESV

What a heart-wrenching example of the fully human side of Jesus that He displays in this passage. Before His trial and crucifixion, Jesus shares with His Father the fear—the sorrow—in His heart for what is about to happen. He asks that circumstances change, for God to intervene. But He still ends His prayer with "Yet not what I will, but what you will." Jesus acknowledged that His Father not only knew what was to be but what was best.

When our hearts ache for change, for provision, but we see none in sight, we can still find peace that God is with us. That He feels our pain and anguish. That He has a plan moving forward from this moment that is perfectly aligned with His will, a plan that brings only goodness for His creation.

My heavenly Father, sovereign of all that was, is, and will be, even though You may not change my earthly circumstances, I will continue to trust and believe that You know what is best for me.

Day 349
LEAN ON ME

Lord, I seek refuge in You. . . . In Your justice, rescue and deliver me; listen closely to me and save me. Be a rock of refuge for me, where I can always go. Give the command to save me. . . . Deliver me, my God, from the power of the wicked. . . . For You are my hope, Lord God, my confidence from my youth. I have leaned on You from birth. . . . My praise is always about You.
Psalm 71:1–6 HCSB

We all need someone to lean on when life throws us a curveball. No matter how close we walk with God, He doesn't guarantee a trouble-free life (John 16:33). And when trouble comes, it's difficult to face the struggle alone.

When trouble comes in the form of a health scare. . .a financial crisis. . .a strained relationship. . .who is your go-to person? Our brains often train us to first approach a friend, family member, professional counselor, or other "expert" for help. But our first go-to should be the one who provides refuge, deliverance, and support through *all* life's trials. The heavenly Father is significant to our physical and mental well-being.

So when you need someone to lean on, recall this passage from the Psalms—and call out to the one who handles your heart with the very best care!

*God, when life is hard, remind me that
I can always lean on You! Amen.*

Day 350
TAKE HIM AT HIS WORD

As they were talking about these things, Jesus himself stood among them, and said to them, "Peace to you!" But they were startled and frightened and thought they saw a spirit. And he said to them, "Why are you troubled, and why do doubts arise in your hearts? See my hands and my feet, that it is I myself. Touch me, and see. For a spirit does not have flesh and bones as you see that I have." And when he had said this, he showed them his hands and his feet.
LUKE 24:36–40 ESV

When Jesus rose from the dead and appeared to the disciples, they experienced excitement, but with an unsettling mixture of doubt and even fear. Jesus compassionately confronted them on the issue. Then they went from doubt and fear to joy. And from hopelessness to the greatest hope humankind has ever known.

We can use this story to remind ourselves to ask questions about our own lives. What is illusion and what is real? Satan tells us all kinds of lies; but Jesus speaks the truth, and He means for us to have a thriving Christian life. A life of growth and maturity. A life that will encourage and inspire others. A life worth living!

Let's start taking Jesus at His word! In this moment, allow His peace to flood you from head to toe, from within and without.

Lord, help me move from doubt and fear to joy,
from hopelessness to hopefulness. Amen.

Day 351
IN THE WILDERNESS

*And after six days Jesus took with him Peter and
James and John, and led them up a high mountain by
themselves. And he was transfigured before them.*
MARK 9:2 ESV

If you've ever taken a hike in a deep forest or driven through the
mountains, you probably know there's a small chance of cell reception
once you're in the wilderness. You can lift that phone high above your
head or climb a tree, but you'll find no Wi-Fi routers or cell towers
out there.

Our Lord has a penchant for taking His followers into the wilderness. He brought the Israelites into the desert. Jesus led three
disciples up a mountain. Of course, there was always a reason. God
was fulfilling His promise to the Israelites of the Promised Land.
Jesus wanted three men to witness His transfiguration. Each time,
the God-followers were alone and isolated from the world but fully
present with the Lord.

Sometimes God disconnects us from the world so we can fully
connect with Him. He knows what's next in our life and where we've
been, so He knows when we need to fill up on Him. Just like the peace
you get after a day without your phone, you will find the calmness
Your Father gives when you spend alone time with Him.

*Dear God, instead of worrying about connecting with
the world, I will try my best to connect with You.*

Day 352
REMAIN FAITHFUL

"Wherever you go, I will go; wherever you live, I will live.
Your people will be my people, and your God will be my God."
RUTH 1:16 NLT

To whom have you been called to remain faithful?

For Ruth, it was her mother-in-law, Naomi. The custom of the day would have both of Naomi's daughters-in-law return to their birth families for support after their husbands died. Only Orpah followed through with this, whereas Ruth insisted on staying with Naomi, who was widowed herself.

Because of her faithfulness to Naomi, Ruth was blessed by the Lord. She was given special privileges in the fields belonging to Boaz. He later became her husband and the father of their son Obed, who became the grandfather of King David and ancestor of Jesus!

Perhaps you are in a marriage that is less than perfect. Or you may have a prodigal child or resident offspring who brings trouble and chaos into the home. Don't despair!

God is there to help you through the struggles. He honors loyalty. Stay true to your commitments. Outside of staying in a situation that is causing you real harm, stand firm. Just as God's people relied on Him in the desert and gathered only enough manna for one day at a time, trust in Him to provide.

Father, help me to remain faithful. I ask You to provide
peace and wisdom in my situation today. Amen.

Day 353
OUR TRUE COLORS

Consider it a sheer gift, friends, when tests and challenges come at you from all sides. You know that under pressure, your faith-life is forced into the open and shows its true colors. So don't try to get out of anything prematurely. Let it do its work so you become mature and well-developed, not deficient in any way.
JAMES 1:2–4 MSG

No one likes to be uncomfortable. Or to be tweaked or tested in their faith. We'd rather have an easy life with comfortable overstuffed furniture and a full pantry with lovely things to eat. And friends and family and coworkers with whom we get along fabulously. Or—well, you get the picture.

Yet sometimes life isn't all that comfortable. Sometimes it's messy. And when we are tested in this life, our true colors do show. And sometimes those colors are a dull, lifeless, cloudlike gray, not the way they were meant to be, such as the bright, brilliant, swirling colors of, say, a van Gogh painting!

When we are challenged and cornered by life, what colors do we show? Hopefully we will see our trials as a positive, as a gift to make us grow and bloom with new life.

Lord, please give me courage. Help me be grateful for the blessings as well as the challenges that come my way, seeing the latter as a sort of gift that will grow me into a mature and well-developed woman of faith! Amen.

Day 354
THE GREATEST

Great is our Lord and mighty in power;
his understanding has no limit.
PSALM 147:5 NIV

If ever a verse inspired confidence in God's infinite power, it's this one! It is inclusive and inviting. This passage lets you know that God is "our" God. He is *your* God. And He is strong. There is no foe He cannot vanquish, no problem He cannot solve, no challenge He cannot handle.

God's understanding is limitless, well beyond human comprehension. What does this mean for you? It means you can trust that His profound wisdom has your best interests at heart. He knows you intimately, inside and out. God will always be there to pick you up if you stumble. He will always be there to lift you up when you're struggling. With His divine arms wrapped around you, you will not fall. For in those arms, you are unshakable!

Woman of the Way, be secure in the fact that God knows what you need, even before you need it! That He knows all your concerns and your fears before they surface. That His compassion for you knows no limits. And most of all, that He loves you just as you are.

Dear God, how great You are! I am comforted to know
that Your power is endless, Your understanding unlimited.
You are there, ever present in my life. I pray I will
always feel Your loving arms around me, protecting me
and keeping me safe. With You, I can do anything!

Day 355
SPIRITUAL REALITY

For God did not give us a spirit of timidity (of cowardice,
of craven and cringing and fawning fear), but [He has
given us a spirit] of power and of love and of calm and
well-balanced mind and discipline and self-control.
2 TIMOTHY 1:7 AMPC

Our emotions come and go—but they do not always tell the truth about spiritual reality.

All of us experience feelings of depression and fear sometimes, but we need to remember that those emotions are not messages from God. Those feelings try to tell us we're not good enough, not strong enough, not smart enough; they say that the world is a frightening and hopeless place.

We can be gentle with those feelings, loving our own selves with God's unconditional love, but we need to remember that they are only feelings, not reality. And as we draw closer to God, He will replace those feelings with His Spirit of power, love, and wisdom. These are the qualities that give us the strength to choose the way we speak and act. And then, as our words and actions line up with God's love, we will find that our minds are calmer. Heart, mind, and action support one another in God's service.

I don't want my anxieties to rule my life anymore, God.
Fill me instead with Your Spirit. I know Your
love is stronger than all my fears.

Day 356
STEADY

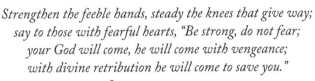

Strengthen the feeble hands, steady the knees that give way;
say to those with fearful hearts, "Be strong, do not fear;
your God will come, he will come with vengeance;
with divine retribution he will come to save you."
ISAIAH 35:3–4 NIV

These words of encouragement by Isaiah are as pertinent today as they were many years ago. If you are feeling weak in the knees or feeble or your heart is afraid, God has promised to come and save you. He'll protect you and strengthen you in your weakest hour. Just as in Isaiah's day, God is present in your life. He cares deeply for you. And He longs to deliver you.

No matter what you may be going through, God encourages you to continue on, to look to a future full of promise and hope. No matter what you have endured or what you fear you may encounter, don't ever lose hope.

God's promise that He'll come "with vengeance" to save you is your guarantee. And it has no expiration date! If you start to lose your balance, don't panic. He'll be there to catch you.

Remember, "GOD's loyal love couldn't have run out, his merciful love couldn't have dried up. They're created new every morning. How great your faithfulness! I'm sticking with GOD (I say it over and over)" (Lamentations 3:22–23 MSG).

Dear God, thank You for Your guarantee of protection.
You steady my knees, strengthen my hands, and
comfort my fearful heart. I'm sticking with You.

Day 357
THEREFORE GO

*"Now therefore go, and I will be with your mouth
and teach you what you shall speak." But he said,
"Oh, my Lord, please send someone else."*
EXODUS 4:12–13 ESV

Moses was shepherding sheep in the wilderness when he saw a burning bush and heard God's voice. The Lord told him about the trouble His people were in. That He'd heard their prayers. That He'd answer them by sending Moses to lead the Jews out of Egypt.

Moses kept imagining what would happen once he tried to fulfill a seemingly impossible calling. So he reminded the Lord whom He was enlisting. After all, he was a murderer, an outcast who spoke with a lisp. He was a nobody. Finally, Moses suggested God send someone else!

Like Moses, there are times when we too are plagued with distorted thoughts. When we too are presented with a challenge of faith and imagine what might happen if we step out of our comfort zone. And we come up with a mountain of excuses as to why we shouldn't go where we're called.

The thing is, we're neither fortune tellers nor mind readers. We're women of the Way. And if we keep our faith in God and our focus on Him, if we remind ourselves how He tends to do the impossible through mortal vessels, then we'll end up saying, "Lord, send me!" instead of asking Him to send someone else.

*Lord, help me to keep my mind on You,
to go wherever You call me to go.*

Day 358
NEVER LOST

*Jacob told everyone in his household, "Get rid of all your
pagan idols, purify yourselves, and put on clean clothing.
We are now going to Bethel, where I will build an altar
to the God who answered my prayers when I was in
distress. He has been with me wherever I have gone."*

Genesis 35:2–3 nlt

When you're feeling discouraged, when you need to get your heart and head back into God, retrace your steps. Go back to the place—physically, mentally, emotionally, or spiritually—where you first encountered God. A place where your spirit soared, where you had your first very real sense of God's presence.

Shake off all that has proved to be a false idol, a hindrance to the relationship between you and God. Physically dedicate a space in your home to God that would remind you of that first encounter with the Lord of all creation. Make it a place where you can and will spend time with Him—alone and uninterrupted.

Remember how God comforted you in the past, when He answered your prayers during troubled times, where He unstintingly gave you all the love, courage, and strength you needed, just when you needed it. Consider how He has been with you everywhere you have gone.

Woman of the Way, never forget that those who honor Him, those who walk His way, those who follow His light, will never get lost.

Lord, I'm back.

Day 359
HAPPY DAYS

When times are good, be happy; but when times are bad,
consider this: God has made the one as well as the other.
Therefore, no one can discover anything about their future.
ECCLESIASTES 7:14 NIV

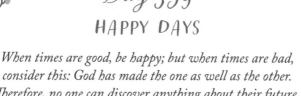

When things are going well, people don't need someone to remind them to be happy. No one ever asks, "Why me, Lord?" when things are on the upswing. No one ever questions good fortune! So it seems only natural that as soon as things go awry, prayers immediately go up asking, "Why me, Lord?"

The writer of Ecclesiastes says both good and bad exist in this world and God is bringer of both. The reason behind events, good or bad, is not for us to understand. Yet there exists a ray of hope. Because even though bad things may happen, "we know that in all things God works for the good of those who love him, who have been called according to his purpose" (Romans 8:28 NIV).

You've heard the saying "Behind every cloud is a silver lining." It's true, even if sometimes it's hard to identify the upside in a given situation. Just keep in mind that adversity and sadness most times leave us wiser. And the hardship you face may just enable you to help and comfort others.

Dear God, thank You for the wonderful times in my
life and the wisdom I've gleaned in the darker days.
Help me use my experiences to help others and to
gain a better perspective within and without.

Day 360
STEADFAST AND TRUE

*"I am God—yes, I Am. I haven't changed. And because I
haven't changed, you, the descendants of Jacob, haven't been
destroyed. You have a long history of ignoring my commands.
You haven't done a thing I've told you. Return to me so I
can return to you," says God-of-the-Angel-Armies.*
MALACHI 3:6–7 MSG

In our human relationships, it's virtually impossible to find a person who will never let us down. . .someone who follows through on every single promise. . .someone who always shows up. . .someone who loves us on our good days and our "difficult to love" days. No human being is perfect—including us. And imperfect people make for imperfect relationships.

In a world of all this imperfection, what a relief to know that we can have a beautifully secure relationship with the Father! He is steadfast and true to His Word. We never need to wonder where He stands or how He feels about us, because He is unchanging.

When you're feeling unsure, wrap your soul in these comforting scriptures:

- Hebrews 13:8
- James 1:17
- Numbers 23:19
- Isaiah 40:8
- Psalm 119:89
- Psalm 33:11

Praise the unchangeable God! The one who is faithful and true. His mercies are everlasting!

*Great is Your faithfulness, Lord. And I am forever grateful
that I can know You—and that Your love and expectations for
me never change. Your constant presence and unconditional
love are sources of peace, comfort, and joy. Amen.*

Day 361
ANOINTED, SUSTAINED

"I have found David my servant; with my sacred oil I have anointed him. My hand will sustain him; surely my arm will strengthen him."
PSALM 89:20–21 NIV

God has promised to sustain you, no matter what valleys you walk through. Even if you're in the deepest pit, His hand is right there, ready to lift you up and give you the necessary strength. Yet what does this promise mean, specifically? Will He deliver you from your situation? Maybe not. But He promises to give you the physical and emotional strength to bear up under any burden.

To be anointed by God means you're covered. His protective hand will shield you, lead you, guide you, sustain you. When He has anointed you for a task, you have nothing to be afraid of. No enemy can penetrate the anointing.

What are you waiting for? If God has called and anointed you for the task ahead, then run toward the goal, your willing heart leading the way.

Father, I read about so many men and women in the Bible who were anointed for specific tasks. I wonder what it would feel like to have Your anointing. Then I'm reminded that You have anointed me as well. You've called me to reach my community, my circle, for You. Thank You for preparing me for the task at hand, Lord, for sustaining and strengthening me. Amen.

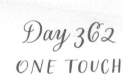

Day 362
ONE TOUCH

There was a woman who had had a discharge of blood for twelve years, and though she had spent all her living on physicians, she could not be healed. . . . She came up behind him and touched the fringe of his garment, and immediately her discharge of blood ceased. And Jesus said, "Who was it that touched me?" . . . She came trembling, and. . .declared in the presence of all the people why she had touched him, and how she had been immediately healed. And he said to her, "Daughter, your faith has made you well; go in peace."
LUKE 8:43–45, 47–48 ESV

What a difficult life this woman had experienced! Twelve *long* years. Twelve years of being untouchable—not a hug or shoulder squeeze from family, friends. . .not one touch from *anyone*. She had spent everything she had on doctors who couldn't heal her. Certainly, *before* her encounter with Jesus, she was poor, discouraged, lonely, depressed, hopeless. Surely her faith had taken a beating. By all accounts, she didn't have much to live for. But. . .

But *then*. In a single moment, she gained *everything*. One touch. One moment of pure, unfettered faith, followed by these words: "Daughter, your faith has made you well."

Have you allowed your circumstances and negative thoughts to limit your faith? Believe. Reach out and touch Jesus today!

Father, strengthen my faith. When my faith is big, my actions are sure to follow! Amen.

Day 363
NEVER SHRINK

*"I found he had done nothing deserving of death,
but because he made his appeal to the Emperor
I decided to send him to Rome."*
ACTS 25:25 NIV

Paul had done nothing wrong. Much like his Savior before him, he was an innocent man whom many feared and hated because he spoke truth.

You may be wrongly accused at different times in your life. You may be misunderstood or may even experience persecution. If these things come to you because of your faith, rest assured that your judge and King will take care of it for you.

From the beginning of time, innocent men and women of faith have been mistreated for standing up for what is right. The Bible assures God-followers that this will only get worse. In the last days, God's people will be persecuted.

Even though you are living in difficult times, you need not sink down in despair. For Jesus is your Redeemer, your Savior. He provides the way for you to stand completely guiltless and stain-free before God. And until that day, He is about the business of watching over His own.

Stand up. Never shrink in the face of persecution for being a follower of the Master. It will all be worth it in the end.

*Father, give me strength to stand for You even
if I am misunderstood or falsely accused. Amen.*

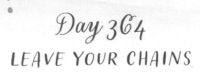

Day 364

LEAVE YOUR CHAINS

So Moses spoke thus to the children of Israel; but they did not heed Moses, because of anguish of spirit and cruel bondage.
EXODUS 6:9 NKJV

His message was nothing but good news. The God of their fathers had heard their groaning! He was coming! He would rescue them and redeem them. They would be His people, and He would be their God.

But when Moses delivered this good news, the people couldn't hear it. They were so sunk down into pain and despair, so weighed down by their chains, they couldn't even imagine being anywhere else—much less having the God of heaven care about them.

The dying to self and loss of life that Jesus speaks of in Matthew 16:24–25 is not just aimed at those who are on top of the world and full of themselves. It's aimed at the lowest of the low as well. No matter where we are in our lives, we all have to be willing to set aside our cares, set aside the view that fills our sight, set aside the soundtracks that play over and over in our ears, and listen to the message of the Lord. We are sometimes like prisoners who have been given keys but won't leave our cells because we have grown so accustomed to our chains.

Leave your chains. Go out to what God has ready for you.

Lord, help me to accept my freedom in You. Amen.

Day 365
POLAR OPPOSITES

To every thing there is a season, and a time
to every purpose under the heaven.
ECCLESIASTES 3:1 KJV

Ecclesiastes 3:1 introduces an often-repeated passage of scripture. The lyrical chain of verses depicts the dual sides of life—the positive and negative that define our days. Perhaps you've witnessed, or even experienced, some of these opposites: "A time to give birth and a time to die. . .a time to weep and a time to laugh; a time to mourn and a time to dance. . .a time to search and a time to count as lost. . .a time to love and a time to hate; a time for war and a time for peace" (Ecclesiastes 3:2, 4, 6, 8 HCSB).

Perhaps you tend to zoom in on the negative. You read Solomon's words, "What do people really get for all their hard work? I have seen the burden God has placed on us all" (Ecclesiastes 3:9–10 NLT), and your heart adds, *Ain't it the truth!*

Yes, it's the truth, but don't call it quits there. We may not be able to escape the bad, yet we *can* cling to the good. We can hold on to the assurance that "God has made everything beautiful for its own time" (Ecclesiastes 3:11 NLT). *And* we can hold on to the God-given promise of a perfect time to come: "He has planted eternity in the human heart" (Ecclesiastes 3:11 NLT).

God, help me hold tightly to the good. Amen.

SPECIAL THANKS TO THESE CONTRIBUTING AUTHORS

Terry Alburger

Emily Biggers

Joanna Bloss

Dena Dyer

Betty Ost-Everley

Nancy Farrier

Carol Lynn Fitzpatrick

Renae Brumbaugh Green

Shanna Gregor

Linda Hang

Marcia Hornok

Eileen Key

Ardythe Kolb

Tina Kraus

Shelley Lee

Marian Leslie

Donna K. Maltese

Kimm Reid-Matchett

Sabrina McDonald

Becky McGlone

Kelly McIntosh

Nicole O'Dell

MariLee Parrish

Valorie Quesenberry

Shana Schutte

Carey Scott

Karen Dahl Silver

Leah Slawson

Janice Thompson

Stacey Thureen

Annie Tipton

Amy Trent

Marjorie Vawter

Ellie Zumbach

SCRIPTURE INDEX

OLD TESTAMENT

PROVERBS

NEW TESTAMENT

MORE INSPIRATION FOR YOUR LOVELY HEART

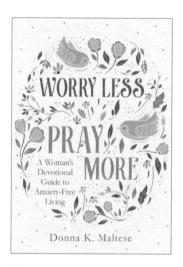

Worry Less, Pray More

This purposeful devotional guide features 180 readings and prayers designed to help alleviate your worries as you learn to live in the peace of the Almighty God, who offers calm for your anxiety-filled soul. *Worry Less, Pray More* reinforces the truth that, with God, you can live anxiety-free every single day—whether you worry about your work, relationships, bills, the turmoil of the world, or something more.

Paperback / 978-1-68322-861-5